LOOK GREAT, NOT DONE!

THE ART & SCIENCE OF AGEING WELL — HOW AESTHETIC TREATMENTS CAN WORK FOR YOU

Dr Stefanie Williams
MD, Dermatologist

DISCLAIMER

The recommendations outlined in this book are personal opinions of the author. None of the information included here or on any of our websites should be construed as an attempt to offer medical advice. It is meant to be of a general educational nature and is not a substitute for the advice of your own practitioner.

We cannot take any responsibility for the consequences of attempts to adopt any of the recommendations presented in this book or on any featured website. We will not be liable for any damages arising from the use of this book or any website that we refer to.

No warranty is made that any of this information is accurate or up-to-date. Although the author has made every effort to ensure that the information in this book was correct at the time of writing, we do not assume and hereby disclaim any liability caused by errors or omissions, whether such errors or omissions result from negligence, accident or any other cause. All warranties are disclaimed, express and implied.

Evidence is naturally constantly evolving, especially in this area, so before you set out to follow any of our recommendations, please do your own research and, most importantly, speak to your practitioner. Please note that the treatments described in this book are for adults and, for various reasons, not designed for children.

Mention of specific companies, organizations or authorities in this book or on our website does not imply endorsement by the author, nor does mention of specific companies, organizations or authorities imply that they endorse this book or its author.

© 2017 Dr Stefanie Williams

This book may be purchased for business or promotional use, or for special sales. For information, please write to: admin@eudelo.com.

ISBN-13: 978-0-9926362-3-4

www.Eudelo.com & www.EudeloBoutique.com

TO MY BEAUTIFUL MOTHER

CONTENTS

Please connect on social media:

Twitter: @EudeloClinic and @DrStefanieW
Facebook: @Eudelo
Instagram: @Eudelo and @DrStefanieW

I'M ON A MISSION

I won't beat around the bush. I'm jumping straight in, here.

Too many cosmetic treatments leave faces looking overdone and unnatural – and I'm on a mission to change that.

I hate seeing 'overdone' celebrities in the press and indeed, on the street. Frankly, as both a practitioner and a patient, they make me shiver. Not only do they look weird, they also give cosmetic procedures a bad name. That's why I've written this book – to challenge that outdated mind-set.

My mission is to enable you to benefit properly from the positive help aesthetic treatments offer without that fear of looking 'done'.

I'll tell you about a paradigm shift that's happening in aesthetic medicine; I can barely put into words how excited I am to share this news with you! And I'll tell you about my personal story and how I became involved in the world of aesthetic dermatology.

But first, let's talk about another bugbear of mine – that much-abused term, 'ageing gracefully'. What does it actually mean?

•

HOW DO YOU PLAN TO AGE GRACEFULLY?

In my opinion, 'ageing gracefully' is one of the most misconstrued phrases in our time; when I hear it, I invariably feel worried. Often, what people mean by 'ageing gracefully' involves a prejudice against procedures such as BTX ('botox') and fillers. The assumption is that should you 'cave in' and accept the help of aesthetic procedures, you will inevitably end up looking obviously, pitifully 'done' – the polar opposite of naturally graceful. Aesthetic procedures are often seen as shameful, and those who determine to 'age gracefully' are proud to remain 'undone'.

In my personal and professional opinion as a dermatologist, this is a highly outdated way of looking at skin ageing. However, I'll say now that I can't blame those who hold this view. In fact, I routinely see both women and men in my clinic who ask me to tailor a good skincare regime for them, but who categorically state they're not interested in any procedures. Now, I completely understand where they're coming from. Looking at celebrities in magazines and on TV - and, forgive me, some of my own colleagues at aesthetic congresses - is enough to scare you off cosmetic procedures for life. But let's look at this in a more rational, objective light.

Here's some empowering news. Today, it's 100% possible to take charge of how well your skin ages without ending up with one of those disastrous faces we sometimes see in the press. Today's non-surgical aesthetic treatments are able to slow down the ageing process dramatically, while remaining so subtle that no-one would ever know you've accepted a helping hand. If – and it's a big if – you get it right.

> Today's non-surgical aesthetic treatments are able to slow down the ageing process dramatically - without looking obvious or unnatural.

How to get it right is what this book is all about. And honestly, it's not rocket science. Getting it right is easy if you follow the simple principles outlined in this book. I'm passionate about achieving the kind of results from procedures that will leave you feeling not merely comfortable, but with a renewed confidence in your own skin. And I'm delighted to share the essential principles that I've discovered over the years, so that whether you see us here at EUDELO or visit another clinic there's a single, important priority. You're in charge!

So, let me ask you a question. What's graceful about adopting a defeatist stance along the lines of "it's out of my control", or "there's not a lot I can do"? Once you're in charge, then ageing gracefully will completely change direction. For me, ageing gracefully means taking charge of how well your skin will age by utilizing the latest advances and resources of modern aesthetic medicine to intelligent and full advantage. Ageing gracefully means feeling great about myself and how I look. Ageing gracefully means ageing on *my* terms.

> For me, 'ageing gracefully' means utilizing the latest advances in aesthetic medicine intelligently, so that you feel and look *your* best, whatever your age.

•

MY PERSONAL STORY

You might wonder how aesthetic medicine became my passion. By training, I'm a qualified specialist dermatologist. To become a dermatologist takes more than ten years of seriously gruelling training. First, you have to study medicine, which takes five years of full-time university. I went to medical school in Germany. Then came another five years of post-graduate training in general dermatology to become a fully qualified specialist dermatologist.

For quite a few years, I treated everything from acne to skin cancer. And I really enjoyed my job, first in Germany, then in the UK where I moved with my British husband Jason over twelve years ago now. Working in two very different European countries made me appreciate the differences in the diagnosis and treatment of skin diseases and allowed me to learn and exploit the best of both worlds.

When I first came to the UK, I worked as a locum consultant dermatologist in the National Health Service (NHS). I can only compare working in the NHS to firefighting: patients here in the UK need a referral from their General Practitioner (GP) to see a hospital dermatologist, so only the most 'deserving' cases are referred. Anything deemed not sufficiently severe to warrant a referral will be treated in general practice, mostly by non skin-specialist GPs.

As for those lucky enough to get to see a dermatologist, I personally found it challenging to look after them as well as I would have liked. Time and resources never seemed sufficient to provide a superior service. Not that the NHS provides a bad service – everyone working within the system does so with great enthusiasm and expertise, given ever-increasing pressures of funding and resources.

The UK simply does not have sufficient dermatologists given its population. The Royal College of Physicians (RCP) recommends one full-time consultant dermatologist per 62,500 head of population. However, no region in Britain currently has enough dermatologists to meet this, in my opinion, modest basic requirement. Even more importantly, I feel that this target is set way too low and would still not allow optimal care of skin concerns. Consider this: each year 54% of the UK population is affected by some type of skin disease, with a reported 23% - 33% suffering from a condition that would benefit from dermatology care at any given time. So there is a huge demand for dermatologists in the UK, which is clearly not being met. In Germany, each dermatologist has to look after less than 14,000 people, meaning that German dermatologists outnumber their UK colleagues more than 4.5 times! I'm a perfectionist used to the level of care in German dermatology - which if you ask my mother, is *still* not good enough...

I found it increasingly frustrating to have to provide what I felt was less than optimal service in the NHS, compared to that which I would far rather have offered my patients. And I was tired of the constant firefighting.

Around that time I had my third baby, my daughter Kaia (now 11 years old) after my two sons Elias (now 15) and Cyrus (14). This made me re-evaluate my situation and I decided to start offering private dermatology services, at the level I would like to be treated at, were I the patient myself. Initially I ran my (very) part-time private practice alongside my work with the

NHS. But as I began to get glowing reviews and my patient list grew and grew, I gradually extended my private service to meet the ever-increasing demand.

Nevertheless, initially I only saw medical dermatology patients in my private clinic. In those days I called the clinic *European Dermatology London* as a nod to my German roots. We've now shortened it to EUDELO as this was what most people called it anyway. (Much less of a mouthful). But in contrast to my NHS work, my private work was more about fine-tuning rather than mere damage limitation. I was able to see patients – many of them with acne and rosacea – who felt abandoned or let down by the public health system which refused to deem their condition severe enough to warrant ongoing, in-depth care. They often told me they felt the NHS didn't really care about their skin issues – not surprising given the chronic lack of resources.

Now, I feel passionately that everyone deserves to be happy in their own skin. No one should feel bad about their skin's condition even if others may not see it as particularly serious. Believe me, I can empathise fully here, as I suffer from a combination of adult acne and rosacea myself.

My new private patients were incredibly grateful for the opportunity to see a specialist dermatologist about problems that had been eroding their self-esteem, confidence and quality of life for years - day in, day out. As for me, I discovered I absolutely loved helping them. In the process, I also discovered a special talent for fine-tuning. I had found my true calling. But something else happened with the birth of my third child.

Anyone who has had three kids in relatively quick succession (there's less than 18 months between my first and second son) will know how seriously stressful, not to mention sleep-deprived, that period of your life can be. My first son, Elias, was very easy-going and slept through the night at just five weeks, bless him! So when he was nine months old, we decided to have another baby. After all, Elias had made it all so blissfully easy, I couldn't understand why other mothers kept complaining how tiring babies were! Then my second son, Cyrus, was born.

From the moment he arrived, Cyrus cried and screamed at the top of his little lungs non-stop for six or seven hours every night, no matter what we did. That in combination with an active year-and-a-half-old toddler and a demanding day job really took its toll. My daughter Kaia was born less than three years after Cyrus and is headstrong to say the least. She never seems to need much sleep – never did…

Let's be clear, I am utterly grateful for each and every one of my three amazing children and my love for them is, well… limitless. The reason I'm telling you all this is that the level of sleep-deprivation and stress I underwent (not to mention all the comfort food and overeating…), led to my face ageing by decades in those brief early years. I was in my mid-thirties and had begun to feel really depressed about how much my face and my body had changed so quickly. One of my worst features I felt were my dark under-eye hollows (so-called tear troughs). You see even as a child and teenager I suffered from deep hollows under my eyes, even after a good night's sleep – a hereditary trait. From my thirties onwards, these dark shadows seemed to progressively worsen. I constantly looked so sad and exhausted that I lost count of the times well-meaning people asked me if I was OK. "You look so tired," they'd say.

Of course, it didn't help that years and years of chronic hay fever as a child and relentlessly rubbing my constantly swollen, inflamed eyelids had eventually weakened the skin. (I remember my mum even taking me to hospital once when both my eyes had completely closed up. Were there no antihistamines then, I wonder?) The result was prematurely reduced skin elasticity in both of my lower eyelids.

So I started looking for help. I figured that being a dermatologist and knowing what amazing medical advancements were taking place, there must surely be something that could be done. And there was.

After some research, I decided to see a colleague for treatment of my under-eye hollows – and that changed everything. My colleague lifted my depressed under-eyes with a hyaluronic acid filler (completely painless after intense cooling) which not only softened my deep tear troughs and hushed my dark circles, but also enabled my face to reflect how I felt inside – happy and well, not sad and tired. At the same time I also started researching how to change my way of eating, to improve not only my general health, but also support skin

> For those of you who want to see how terrible I looked and felt around that time (I am not exaggerating…), I have put together a collage of 12 (never before shown!) photographs of myself on www.Eudelo.com/Photographs From age 3 to age 46, they show my very personal skin journey. Tell me what you think on social media (@DrStefanieW). My personal favourite photo is the one aged 17, you will know why when you see it. Go on, have a look!

wellbeing. The results were truly life changing and I later wrote a book on this topic, it's called *Future Proof Your Skin. Slow down the ageing process by changing the way you eat.*

My under-eye procedure was a total revelation. Even my husband Jason, who at the time was anti-cosmetic procedures, admitted the transformation was astonishing. Now he's a complete convert and even took over the management of our clinic after he witnessed first-hand what a difference - emotionally as well as physically - cosmetic treatments can make when done well.

Since then, I've had various aesthetic treatments with great success, not only to improve my skin's appearance, but more importantly as preventative measures, too. All was well until recently, when life served me a curve ball (as it does when you least expect it), which may affect which cosmetic procedures I can and can't have in the future. I'll tell you more about that later, but first let's get back to how I started my career in cosmetic dermatology.

The first cosmetic treatment I had under my eyes all those years ago convinced me that this was something I wanted to learn to do myself and offer to my own patients. Often what I saw in clinic was that once I'd cleared up a medical condition such as acne or rosacea, my patients' priorities switched to wanting to make their skin look better overall. Of course, as a dermatologist – the most expert individual to deal with skin-related issues – I was in the perfect position to help.

So began my quest to master the art of non-surgical cosmetic treatments. After countless courses and more than ten years of continual professional development in aesthetic medicine, today I am an acknowledged opinion leader in this field. I have lectured and trained colleagues in aesthetic medicine worldwide and am also featured regularly in the media as an expert in cosmetic medicine. I don't do half measures!

> With cosmetic procedures, we're not trying to turn everyone into an army of super-models. That's not the point. Simply accentuating your good features and tweaking the not so good ones can mean a major change in self-esteem. It's these 'tweakments' that make all the difference.

Now, a confession. I have to admit that for a dermatologist, I wasn't always particularly careful with what I did to my skin. My skincare routine was very basic in the past. I didn't really protect my skin from the environment and I dare say that for a few years prior to having children, I even resorted to sun beds when I felt I needed some 'healthy colour.' I didn't really think or care much about the damage I did with my negligence, let alone that I increased my risk of skin cancer. When you're young, you think you're invincible. That's all changed now and educating my patients about prevention is a priority.

•

BEAUTY IS HOW YOU FEEL INSIDE

Those are Sophia Loren's words – and there's wisdom in them. How you feel inside has a major influence on how you feel about the way you look and there's no lack of scientific research to confirm this. If we're happy, we tend to feel much more attractive than when we're sad or depressed. When we're low, everything feels bleak and we tend to be hypercritical about our appearance too.

We all know the saying 'you're only as old as you feel'. As our understanding of the ageing process and what constitutes true beauty has evolved, we appreciate more and more that looking good at any age always includes inner health and vitality. One of my most passionately held convictions is that in order to get the very best results from that aesthetic 'helping hand' on the outside, I must also empower my patients with all the knowledge they need to lead a lifestyle that will help them to age well from the inside out, too.

I have spent years researching ageing and how it manifests itself, both from a cellular level right up to the visible signs we see on our skin. By studying the science of ageing in detail and applying these principles in my daily practice, I have developed a healthy ageing lifestyle protocol called *FuturApproved*®, which encourages my patients to look their very best on the outside while ageing well from within. To learn more, I strongly recommend you read my first book, *Future Proof Your Skin. Slow down the biological clock by changing the way you eat*, if you haven't already done so.

Combining a *FuturApproved*® lifestyle with the helping hand of aesthetic procedures is, in my opinion, the gold standard of 'ageing gracefully'!

> A *FuturApproved*® lifestyle enables you to look your very best on the outside, while ageing well from within.

•

ANTI-AGEING IS OUT

'Anti-ageing' is a term we hear all too often on TV or see in adverts and beauty articles in magazines, but for me 'anti-ageing' is way past its sell-by date. Ageing is a natural process that happens to us all. So let's be real about this. How can we be 'anti' something that's inevitable? This outdated concept creates unwarranted fear and distress around the ageing process. It's vital then, that we update our perception and start to think about ageing in a healthy light, so that we remain comfortable and confident, as we grow older instead of struggling to fight a battle we can never win.

> Looking better or more attractive doesn't necessarily mean looking younger!

When it comes to skin, the overreaching concept of the 'ageing well' paradigm is focusing on skin health and wellbeing. Aiming to maintain a beautifully glowing, smooth, blemish-free, evenly coloured and resilient skin with strong facial contours is as important as limiting wrinkles. My clinical practice has taught me that looking better doesn't necessarily mean looking younger. This of course, is a radical departure from the traditional view of aesthetic medicine and procedures that are carried out with the sole aim of looking younger.

Taking charge of your skin isn't only for 40-plus men and women who already see signs of ageing in their faces. It's arguably even more relevant if you're 30-something and able to *prevent* visible signs of ageing before they escalate. Prevention is a really smart strategy. In fact I envy you if you're reading this book in your 20s or 30s: you're more fortunate than you know to have the opportunity of a lifetime quite literally in your hands.

In fact, I can't stress enough how important it is to begin a preventative skin care programme early. If you start too late, then it might be… well, too late for the best results at least. If you want to look the best you can whatever your age, I strongly advise you to start right now. Follow the system I've outlined in this book and take the steps you need to at every age.

•

AGE TRANSCENDING BEAUTY

The term 'ageless' is another one of those misused epithets that drives me utterly crazy. I sincerely hope we can all agree that we don't want to look ageless - nor can we. That would be freakishly unnatural. Besides, we've all seen those women (and a good few men) whose preternaturally smooth faces look oddly frozen in time, but nevertheless fail to escape the decade they're in. 'Ageless' should never be the aim of a procedure. Neither should 'ten years younger', come to that.

Here's a thought. According to the Office of National Statistics, 40 is now the average age in the UK. Over a third of the population (23.6 million) are over 50 and there are 15 million people over 60, a figure predicted to rise above 20 million by 2030. With such excellent company, what's the point of being in denial about our age?

Especially since older faces can genuinely possess a beauty that transcends their years. Think of Helen Mirren, now in her seventies and, I believe, looking her age (air-brushing apart).

But she also looks really well – beautiful, in fact. And that's precisely what we should aim for with aesthetic treatments.

I'm here to reassure you that age is no barrier to looking and feeling great. We should never feel embarrassed about getting older, but celebrate each passing year in style. We should congratulate ourselves for all we have achieved and experienced in our lifetime. And we should celebrate all those amazing and inspirational older men and women who live life to the full, take pride in how they look – and genuinely look amazing.

> Age is no barrier to looking and feeling great. We don't want to look ageless, but to celebrate a beauty that transcends age. Aesthetic treatment can help us achieve that.

I am 46 years old. I've never hidden my age – why would I? Today someone actually asked me how much longer I plan to work in the aesthetic industry! Clearly, the implication is that at some stage, I'll be too long in the tooth to provide 'anti-ageing' treatments credibly. But to answer that leading, but I'm sure well-meaning question, let me be clear. Beauty has nothing to do with age (nor has the quality of my work come to that!). If we look after ourselves and care for our skin, we can and will always look our best, whatever our age. I am planning to work in the aesthetic industry until I retire – if I ever do.

I love my work, not only because I'm actually really good at it, but because I also love making a difference to people's lives. I test the majority of the treatments I offer to patients on myself and I like the fact that I can showcase that I'm proud to look my age, while also looking well cared-for. And here's another thing. With each year that passes, I'll be able to empathise with my patients whatever their age and understand their concerns first hand. No pressure to hide or retire like a 25-year-old gymnast. Agreed?

•

A SHIFT IN ATTITUDE

Society has changed too – our ageing population has meant it's had to keep up. Men and women in their 60s now often don't feel as close to retirement as their parents' generation did. They likely still enjoy a successful career or may even consider starting a new study course. Their social life is active and they may even have just started dating again. It seems 60 really is the new 40.

Today we stay active and feel younger for much longer, but this can sometimes conflict with what we see in the mirror. And this is true whatever age we are. Whether we're 30 or 60, we simply want to feel good about ourselves and look our very best. We want our outside image to mirror our inner ambitions, simple as that.

So here's the good news. How well we age is to a major extent our choice. Whatever our age or skin concern we can – and should – take positive action. I founded *EUDELO Dermatology & Skin Wellbeing* with the philosophy of providing natural-looking results through using safe and well-researched treatments that can transform skin and make you look as good as you feel. My approach combines diet and lifestyle changes with different levels

> How well you age is to a large extent your choice. Yes, you can take control!

of non-surgical intervention to suit each individual. And this personalised programme is key.

•

THE PROBLEM WITH THE AESTHETIC INDUSTRY

Due to significant improvements, refinements and innovations over recent years, non-surgical cosmetic interventions are becoming increasingly popular. Yet astoundingly given the wealth of new treatments and products out there, there is no proper regulation of providers. I will talk more about this later. Making sure you're as educated as you can be about these procedures is therefore essential if you want to make the right choices. But it's not easy.

Despite considerable growth in the market, the fact that 83% of consumers are aware of cosmetic injectables and just over 30% are potentially interested in having them done, it's surprising that only 2.7% (5.2 million) have actually gone ahead and had treatment (Allergan 2013). So why is that?

Horror stories in the press about procedures going wrong, fear around certain treatments, concerns about looking unnatural and/or cost factors may all play a part. But when carried out by an appropriately trained professional in a safe environment, non-surgical treatments can be life transforming.

Nevertheless, the term 'cosmetic cowboy' is one we hear only too often. As the popularity of aesthetic treatments has grown, so have the numbers of unscrupulous clinics and practitioners trying to make a quick buck by offering treatments without the necessary background training, skills or expertise to perform them safely. The lack of proper regulation in the aesthetic industry has led to numerous negative headlines in the press about 'Botched Botox', 'Bat Faces,' 'Trout Pouts' and 'Pillow Faces' to name but a few. Of course, all of this detracts from practitioners like myself and many of my peers, for whom high ethical standards, patient safety and natural results are paramount.

Following the widely-publicised PIP breast implant scandal in 2012, which exposed poor practice in an industry that was almost entirely unregulated, the government called for a review to be carried out by NHS England's Medical Director, Sir Bruce Keogh. The *Review of the Regulation of Cosmetic Interventions*, widely referred to as 'The Keogh Review', recognised the need for universal high standards of care, an informed and empowered public and accessible redress and resolution in cases where things go wrong. Unfortunately, little has been done as yet to ignite real change and so it's still down to ethical clinics such as EUDELO to set their own standards of good practice.

A number of voluntary registers have been set up in a bid to give clinics a sort of kite mark (similar to a gas safety mark), but as there are various competing schemes around - none of which are compulsory or seen as having 'real teeth' - few clinics are signing up. Of course, those who operate outside the standards of good practice are hardly likely to put themselves in the spotlight voluntarily. All of which has left the treatment-seeking public in a difficult and often confusing position.

As a medical clinic, EUDELO is registered with the Care Quality Commission (CQC), the healthcare watchdog all medical clinics must register with by law, and which inspects us regularly. Personally, at the time of writing, I would be in favour of bringing all *aesthetic* clinics under the current 'gold standard' umbrella of CQC regulation too, but this discussion will no doubt run…

What all this boils down to then, is that it's never been so crucially important for people considering aesthetic interventions to arm themselves with the appropriate knowledge to make an informed choice about what treatments they have, how they're done and most importantly – who will do them.

I have to say very clearly here, that as I see it, the problem with 'cosmetic cowboys' isn't entirely down to the lack of regulation. At least as much responsibility lies with the patients to choose wisely as to who they will see and avoid the temptation of low-price procedures. Nobody forces anyone to have their BTX ('botox') done at the local hairdresser's or go to a 'botox party'. It's beyond me why anyone in their right mind would consider either of these a safe environment for a medical procedure to take place. It really is your choice, your duty to yourself to assume responsibility for your decisions. I understand it's tempting to go for some £99 internet 'botox deal', or whatever. But then you have to live with the potential consequences – simple as that. Personally, I would want to visit the best and not the cheapest for my aesthetic procedures.

THE EUDELO SYSTEM

To help you to make the right choices for your skin, I have evolved a unique system, the *EUDELO system*. It's based on three crucial principles, which I will explain in much more detail later:

1.) The *3-Key Principle*
2.) The *Foundation Principle*
3.) The *Staircase Principle*

Having seen first-hand the effects of badly done faces – a syndrome that seems to be escalating – I'm adamant that the time has come to end this disfiguring trend. I don't want you to end up being a victim of a botched or badly done procedure and neither do I welcome the negative reputation the aesthetic industry is starting to attract. Frankly that wouldn't help anyone.

So I have condensed all my knowledge and years of experience heading up my multi-award winning EUDELO clinic into developing my game-changing system. Here at *EUDELO Dermatology & Skin Wellbeing*, we're constantly striving to provide aesthetic medicine to the highest standard possible and I initially established the *EUDELO system* to provide a consistent, trustworthy level of care in our own clinic. The aim was to ensure every EUDELO practitioner treats patients not only in the safest way possible, but also to guarantee the natural-looking results that each individual patient aspires to.

However, having refined the *EUDELO system* over many years of clinical practice combining the knowledge and experience I've gleaned from attending international conferences, lecturing on a wide range of aesthetic topics as well as discussions with colleagues, I decided to set my system down in writing. So now, you can use the *EUDELO system* to plan your own aesthetic journey and finally take charge of your skin and its wellbeing. I can't tell you how excited I am to be with you on your journey.

> The dermatologist-developed *EUDELO system* strives to treat patients in the safest way possible while guaranteeing natural-looking, aspirational results.

This book is designed to help you navigate the myths and misinformation surrounding non-surgical interventions, so that you feel empowered to make informed choices should you consider treatment. From skincare and lasers to BTX, fillers and fat-busting injections, I will give you the hard facts behind the buzzwords and cut through the marketing spiel to reveal the truth about aesthetic procedures and why ageing well should happen from the inside out. And of course, preventative aesthetic dermatology is the perfect complement to healthy ageing overall. So let's begin!

THE SCIENCE OF
SKIN AGEING

•

WHAT HAPPENS WHEN
SKIN AGES?

Until now, you might not have thought of ageing as a science. But ageing isn't just about how we look. The science of ageing is rooted in many different and diverse areas of medicine from oncology and neurology to trichology and gynaecology. In this book, we'll examine how ageing affects the skin. Research continues to shed light on what happens and why, and as a dermatologist, this is an area I'm particularly passionate about. I firmly believe that understanding the causes of premature skin ageing can not only help us to prevent further damage, but also to address and correct existing problems so that we can actually *age better*.

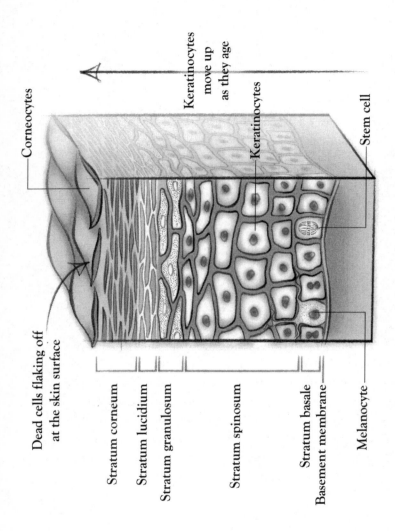

Fig. 1: Anatomy of the epidermis, the outer layer of our skin.

ANATOMY OF THE SKIN

The skin is our body's largest organ and serves as a crucial protective barrier against infection, disease and a hostile environment. Without your skin, you wouldn't be able to survive. The skin is primarily made up of three different layers, which, from the surface inwards, are known as the epidermis, dermis and subcutaneous fat layer.

Epidermis   The epidermis is the top, outer layer of the skin which itself comprises five layers. These are (from lowest to highest) the stratum basale; stratum spinosum; stratum granulosum; stratum lucidium; and stratum corneum.

The stratum basale is the single-cell thick basal layer of the epidermis that is separated from the collagen-rich dermis beneath by the basement membrane. In this basal layer, plump new cells are formed from epidermal stem cells. During the next four weeks, the cuboid-formed basal layer cells move upwards towards the skin's surface in a complex maturation process. During this journey, they become progressively flatter until they transform into nucleus-free cells.

The main type of cell in the epidermis is known as a keratinocyte (keratin is the major protein in our skin, nails and hair) while the basal layer of the epidermis also contains melanocytes, cells that produce the brown melanin pigment in our skin. The epidermis does not contain blood vessels.

The stratum corneum – the outer, horny layer – does not contain living cells but is vital for our skin's protective barrier function and so its overall health. For many years the importance of the stratum corneum was underestimated and we have only recently started to understand its true significance (Lee et al. 2016). There are now international congresses entirely devoted to this ultra-thin layer – the ultimate barrier between our environment and ourselves.

The stratum corneum is made of dead, flat cells called corneocytes. This horny layer is often compared to a brick wall with the corneocyte 'bricks' held together by a special lipid 'cement' in between. If the skin's barrier function is damaged or impaired, one of the consequences is excessive water loss from the skin (TEWL, transepidermal water loss), which then becomes dry and possibly even inflamed. This is the case in eczema for example, but also happens (to a lesser degree) as we age.

Keratinocytes take about four weeks to travel from the basal layer of the epidermis to the horny, surface layer before they shed off. So under optimal conditions, our epidermis renews itself about once a month, however, as we age this turnaround time slows down, contributing to dull, lacklustre skin.

Dermis   The dermis is the skin's 'backbone' and is made up of two layers: the upper, papillary dermis and the lower, reticular dermis (McLafferty et al. 2012). The dermis contains collagen and elastin – two crucial, structural fibres produced by important cells called fibroblasts. The fibroblasts also produce hyaluronic acid (HA) and other vital components of the ground substance – the gel-like matter between cells and fibres. The dermis is very important to our skin's structure and firmness and many of the tell-tale processes of skin ageing take place here.

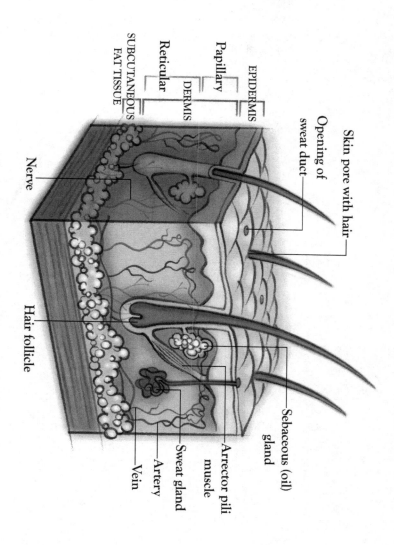

SUBCUTANEOUS
FAT TISSUE

Reticular

DERMIS

Papillary

EPIDERMIS

Opening of
sweat duct

Skin pore with hair

Nerve

Hair follicle

Sebaceous (oil)
gland

Arrector pili
muscle

Sweat gland

Artery

Vein

Fig. 2: The three layers of our skin – epidermis, dermis and subcutis

> Many of the typical signs of ageing such as wrinkles and slackness have their origin in the dermis, the collagen-containing middle layer of our skin.

The dermis contains a variety of other specialist cells and structures including hair follicles, sebaceous (oil) glands and eccrine (sweat) glands. Blood vessels to feed the skin, and nerves responsible for feeling sensations also run through this layer.

Subcutaneous tissue

Literally the layer underlying the skin, the subcutaneous layer mainly consists of fat with some fibrous tissue in between the fat lobules (Driskell et al 2014). Larger blood vessels and nerves are also found here. The thickness of this subcutaneous fat layer can vary from less than a millimetre (in certain areas of the face, for example) to, in some people, several inches on the body, for example on the thighs and abdomen.

THE PROCESSES OF SKIN AGEING

As we get older, the thickness and function of all three skin layers decreases. At a cellular level, other key skin ageing processes include (Rittié et al. 2015):

• **Fibroblasts** become less active and collagen biosynthesis decreases, resulting in reduced skin firmness
• **Levels of hyaluronic acid** also deplete, leaving the skin looking less plump and hydrated

- **The epidermal barrier function** becomes less effective, leading to increased water loss from the skin
- **Sebaceous and sweat gland activity** slows down, also causing the skin to become drier with increasing age, and less able to regulate temperature
- **Certain facial fat pads and other tissues** lose volume. Our cheeks and lips, for example, seem to 'lose weight' with age
- **Bone resorption** shrinks the underlying supporting structure of the skin. Our entire face essentially 'deflates' with age
- **Wound healing capabilities** are reduced – this is even more pronounced in smokers
- **Sun damage-related** irregular, mottled pigmentation becomes more pronounced

All of the above processes are a natural part of skin ageing. They can, however, be accelerated. As our understanding of skin ageing has increased, we have come to appreciate that a variety of factors are involved. Genetics certainly influence how our biological clock ticks and different skin types age in different ways. However, environmental factors such as sun exposure and pollution are major contributors to premature ageing, as are lifestyle factors including stress, smoking, excess alcohol consumption, drug use and a poor diet.

BIOLOGICAL CLOCK VERSUS LIFESTYLE

The ageing process is complex, but can be simplified into two main causes (Khavkin et al. 2011, Makrantonaki at al. 2015, Rittié et al. 2015, Tobin 2017). Although there are inevitable overlaps, we can broadly distinguish between:

Chronological, or intrinsic ageing. This is our natural ageing process or 'biological clock', governed by internal influences such as genetics and hormones.

Premature, or extrinsic ageing. An accelerated ageing process triggered by environmental influences, such as excessive sun exposure and urban pollution. Lifestyle choices including a high sugar diet, lack of sleep and high stress levels are also contributing to premature ageing.

•

LINES AND WRINKLES

There are many contributing factors to how well we age at a cellular level. Yet the main outward concerns – those most visible on the skin's surface, which drive people to seek non-surgical aesthetic interventions – remain lines and wrinkles. Millions of pounds are spent each year on trying to prevent or eradicate lines and wrinkles. As we age, the loss of collagen and elastin from our skin leads to reduced firmness and elasticity. This, combined with the effects of gravity, causes our skin to sag and wrinkle. Some wrinkles appear as small, fine lines while others form deep ridges, folds or furrows.

Let's take a closer look at the different types of lines and wrinkles, which determine which kind of treatment you may wish to consider. You see, while some types of lines respond amazingly well to certain interventions, others may be wholly unsuitable for that particular treatment, so it's important to distinguish the 'who's who' in the wrinkle world.

But first, what do we actually mean by 'lines and wrinkles'? After all, the two are routinely lumped together and used synonymously. There are various definitions of their distinctions floating around. But generally, when we talk about lines we mean 'fine lines' which are essentially an early, more superficial form of wrinkle formation. The medical term for wrinkles is *rhytides* – but let's not drown in semantics...

Basically, lines and wrinkles fall into two distinct categories (Anson at al. 2016). *Dynamic lines* (or mimic lines) are caused by facial movements repeated over many years and are driven by the action of mimic muscles under the skin. In their initial stages, dynamic lines may only be visible when you move your face and soften out fully when the muscles relax again. Examples of dynamic lines are frown lines between our eyebrows (glabella lines); worry lines on the forehead; and crow's feet at the corners of the eyes.

In contrast to dynamic lines, *static lines* are caused by age-related loss of elasticity and firmness in the skin and are visible even when our face isn't moving and all our muscles remain relaxed.

Often, what started as a dynamic line will eventually become static, in that they're visible even when you relax your face. I like to call these *'secondary static'* lines (in contrast to *'primary static'* lines that are independent of muscle movements). Any dynamic line can become static and deeper crow's feet, frown lines, worry lines and smoker's 'pucker' lines around the mouth etched into the skin after years of over-movement fall into this category. It's at this point that treatment options change fundamentally.

I'll go into the different treatment options in a later chapter, but for now, it's important to understand that for an aesthetic treatment to be truly successful, we need to address the underlying cause of each individual line rather than simply 'papering over the cracks.' One treatment definitely does not fit all!

> It's important to distinguish between *dynamic* and *static* lines in order to decide the correct type of aesthetic treatment for either.
>
> My strong advice is to get your dynamic lines treated *before* they turn into secondary static lines when they will still be much easier to correct.

You can test yourself if a dynamic line has turned 'secondary static' by trying to stretch it out between two fingers. If your frown lines, say, completely smooth out when the skin is stretched, they they're still fully dynamic. If on the other hand, stretching your skin doesn't make them fully disappear, they have partly turned into secondary static lines.

There is another type of wrinkle, called a gravitational fold. Nose-to-mouth furrows (nasolabial folds) are a prime example. This deeper furrow is formed through a combination of two causal factors – a loss of facial volume and gravity. With age, our faces lose fat and the fat pads in our cheeks tend to go first. This loss

Dynamic (mimic) lines are caused by repeated over-movement of underlying muscles. Frown lines between the eyebrows, worry lines on the forehead and crow's feet are all examples.

Static lines are independent of muscular movement. They can develop on their own (primary static lines) or from long-established dynamic lines (secondary static lines).

Gravitational folds such as nasolabial folds are deeper furrows caused by a combination of loss of volume (often mid face) plus gravity.

of mid face volume with flattening of our cheeks leads to an envelope of loose skin which gravity pulls downwards – hence the folds (and the jowls…). (General loss of skin elasticity is a contributing factor too, of course).

To treat gravitational folds, we often need a combination approach, which takes into account the underlying cause. That can mean treating a separate area to the perceived problem. For example, deep nose-to-mouth lines – a common concern for both men and women in clinic – might need a two-pronged approach. Firstly, we put some 'scaffolding' and plumpness back into the cheeks; then we fill the line itself, if in fact we still need to after we've re-contoured the cheeks.

> Gravitational nose-to-mouth furrows often need re-contouring of the cheeks as a primary measure, rather than just filling the fold and risking unnatural results.

"But I don't want to end up with a *pillow face*", I hear you gasp. Honestly, don't worry. I can tell you that anyone walking around with a pillow face has quite simply been overdone. What I'm talking about here is putting back the lovely plumpness you had when you were younger – and you didn't have a pillow face then, did you? Trust me – the dose makes the poison…

LINE CHECK: DOES YOUR FACE REVEAL ANY OF THESE?

• **Nasolabial folds** are the lines that run from the nose to the corners of the mouth. They are typical examples of gravitational folds and are caused by loss of volume (flattening fat pads) in our cheeks, plus gravity, which results in the overlying skin envelope becoming too big and sagging.

• **Glabella lines** are the lines above the bridge of the nose between the eyebrows. Also known as 'frown lines' or 'elevens' (because they are often two running parallel), they are typical examples of dynamic lines caused by frowning, squinting in bright sunlight and/or concentration staring at a computer or mobile phone screen.

• **Bunny lines** are a group of 'whiskery' dynamic lines on the sides of the nose, often visible when you smile.

• **Forehead lines** as they sound, are horizontal lines on the forehead also known as 'worry lines'. These dynamic lines are caused by repeated contraction of the frontalis muscle, which raises the eyebrows in a surprised or worried expression, say.

- **Comma lines** are fine lines just above the outer half of the eyebrows, often forming a single line on each side, parallel to the eyebrow. They are another example of dynamic lines, caused by the frontalis muscle.
- **Periorbital lines** are 'crow's feet' which appear around the eyes, radiating from the outer corners. Because our eye area creases when we smile or laugh, these dynamic lines are also known as 'smile lines'.
- **Perioral lines** are the fine, vertical lines that appear above the top, and sometimes below the lower, lip. They are also known as 'lipstick bleed lines' as lipstick tends to 'bleed' into them. As they are associated with lip pursing, they are more prevalent in smokers and so are often called 'smoker's lines'. Sadly, non-smokers can have these too.
- **Marionette lines** are folds running from the mouth corners towards the chin. They are caused by a combination of factors, including loss of facial volume and over-engaging the depressor angularis oris (DAO) muscle, which runs from the corner of the mouth to the jawline and pulls down the mouth corners. (The DAO tends to get stronger as we age). Majonette lines give your mouth a down turned, sad look.

Majonette lines aren't really wrinkles, but sagging of the corners of the mouth. Sometimes these are called 'oral commissures', although this is actually the name of the anatomical region rather than the lines.

• **Accordion lines** (sometimes also called 'smile lines' or 'laugh lines') are curved vertical lines on the lower cheeks that appear next to the corners of the mouth when you smile. In more advanced stages of facial ageing, these can connect with crow's feet, turning the entire cheek into a sea of lines.

•

FACIAL VOLUME AND CONTOUR

While lines and wrinkles are still the most common reason for men and women to seek aesthetic treatment, there are other age-related changes taking place in our face that are often ignored. Arguably, it's much more important to address these 'silent' changes so that your face remains youthfully attractive. Loss of facial volume and contour is a key case in point.

When we're young, a female face tends to be shaped like a heart, or inverted triangle with the base parallel to our cheekbones and the point at our chin – the youth triangle. As we age and facial fat is redistributed, this triangle is reversed. We lose volume in our mid-face (for example loss of fat in our cheeks) leading to sagging and heaviness in our lower face and jowls (Ramanadham at al. 2015, Rohrich at al. 2007 & 2008).

Volume loss is one of the main factors of visible facial ageing. However, compared to lines and wrinkles, still comparatively few people seek aesthetic interventions for this, which is, in my opinion a huge oversight. When we're young, the fat pads in our cheeks are full and high and hold up our skin nicely.

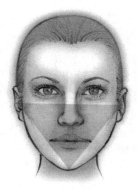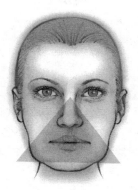

Fig. 3: Youthful facial triangle, versus bottom-heavy reversed triangle of the ageing face

However, as we age gravity and the loss of underlying structures that support the skin cause our cheeks to slide further down the face (Rohrich at al. 2008). The cheeks look flatter and you may be left looking tired, gaunt and hollow in the mid-face.

At the same time, fat tissue is redistributed 'south' making our jowls more pronounced.

As I've already mentioned, loss of volume in our cheeks is also one of the main causes for the formation of nose-to-mouth lines. Many people become fixated on their nasolabial folds, but I would like to stress that it's entirely natural to have some sort of depression here. Imagine

In youth, the fat pads in our cheeks are full and high. But as we age, these fat pads deflate and our supporting facial bones also lose bulk. Loss of volume in our mid-face causes skin and remaining fat to slip downwards. Your cheeks appear flatter, you look more drawn and jowls are forming.

if your skin was completely and utterly smooth without any dip here. You'd look more like a fish than a human, wouldn't you? (last time I checked aesthetic medicine was not about species reassignment...) It's only when this natural fold becomes deeply unattractive (or a line starts edging into the skin sharply) that it warrants correction.

We now understand that by replacing lost cheek volume we can often soften the appearance of exaggerated nasolabial folds. In many cases, this might be all we need to do. In others, we may need to fill the nasolabial fold gently and directly in a second step – for this should never be done in isolation, since unnatural-looking results could well happen.

Frankly, there's no point in trying to erase your nasolabial folds completely. The temptation may be great, but it's important to leave a slight depression to keep your face looking natural. Even children have soft folds here.

Fig. 4: Nose-to-mouth lines are not always an ageing feature, as my daughter (aged nine at the time) shows.

The type of soft, natural fold I'm talking about is of course, different from the sharp, superficial line some people have etched into their skin, which can't easily be stretched out between two fingers. This is an advanced warning of declining skin quality and should be treated as early as possible.

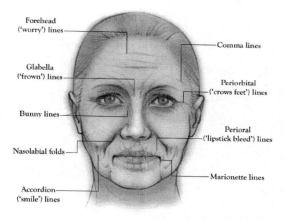

Fig. 5: The ageing face with a mix of loss of volume and contour, and development of lines and wrinkles.

Isolated filling of nasolabial folds is a hugely overdone procedure in this country. This often happens because for in-experienced practitioners nasolabial folds seem an easy target

It's important not to become fixated on your nasolabial folds. A soft depression running from the nose to the mouth corners is normal. Trying to correct it fully would look utterly unnatural. A superficial, sharply etched in nose-to-mouth line however, should be treated early, before it becomes irreversible.

to get started with (far from it!), as most filler courses sadly teach this technique first.

Back to changes in facial volume and contour, lower face sagging with jowl formation and loss of youthful jawline contours is also linked to cheek volume deflation, as mentioned. However, loss of volume in the temple area can also contribute to facial sagging and even the appearance of nasolabial folds! You see, the real problem might not be where you think it is: detailed facial analysis is crucial prior to any aesthetic treatment.

> Age-related deflation of the cheeks and temple area will contribute to sagging in the lower face. Jowls and loss of youthful jawline contours are a consequence.

Sadly, something else that happens when we age is deflation of our lips (Penna et al. 2015). Often this happens so slowly that we hardly notice the change in lip shape over the years until the 'lipstick bleed' lines appear. Women in particular complain about these pesky pucker lines feathering around, and often into, the lips. However, trying to correct them in isolation without addressing the underlying loss of lip volume would only give unnatural-looking results. The effective approach is to gently plump up the lips first, then work on the lines themselves as a second step, if needed.

The idea of adding volume to the lips, of course, generates huge anxiety, since no one wants to look as if they've had their lips 'done.' (At least, none of our Eudelo patients do, as thankfully we seem to attract clients who want to look great, not artificial). But really, the fear is unfounded. Once again, it's all in the dose, so if you see an obvious 'trout pout', those lips have simply been overdone.

Lips deflate with age, leading to 'lipstick bleed' lines on and around the lips. The correct way to treat them is to gently re-plump the lips first, rather than chase the lines in isolation. This approach gives the most natural results – think gently turning back time, not trout pout!

A dead giveaway of a bad job is also that unattractive sharp edge between the red of the lips and surrounding skin that's all too often seen after lip filler treatments. At EUDELO, we prefer to gently and softly re-plump the body of the lip to replace what's been lost, rather than over-fill with a stiff product that makes the border between lip and skin look ledge-like.

Another thing that contributes to 'lipstick bleed' lines is the very gradual resorption of bone from the jaw, which everyone experiences with age (Wong et al. 2015). Like skin, bone is a highly dynamic organ that's constantly changing and renewing itself. In young bones, resorption and formation (both of which happen without you realising) is in equal proportions, meaning that your net bone mass doesn't change significantly. However, shockingly bone mass peaks around 30 years of age (Sasson et al. 2013, Shaw et al. 2012). After that, bone resorption gradually begins to exceed new bone formation leading to a slow decrease in total bone volume that the menopause accelerates. Natural age-related bone loss is a physiological phenomenon that affects us all (osteoporosis on the other hand, is a more marked deterioration in bone mass and micro-architecture, with an increased risk of fractures).

Fig.6: Bone changes during the facial ageing process, starting already mid-life.

Another consequence of age-related jaw bone loss is teeth crowding. If you notice this is happening to you (some teeth beginning to turn diagonal, or protrude like fangs, say) it might be worth chatting to an orthodontist about adult braces. Don't panic – there are far less obtrusive options than the good old silver 'train tracks' available these days. As I write this, I'm wearing fixed braces hidden *behind* my own teeth (so-called lingual braces). Not exactly pure joy, but completely tolerable and very well worth it.

Summing up, facial ageing is a complex biological issue associated with various processes. Changes in all three skin layers; loss of facial volume; decline and redistribution of fat tissue; loss of skeletal support; changes in muscular action (such as overbearing of facial muscles that pull down); and gravity impact are all factors which lead to the face sagging and changing its shape and contour.

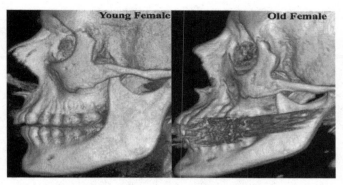

Fig. 7: CT images showing the skull of a young woman compared to an older woman: age-related facial bone loss is clearly visible – look at the weaker cheek bone for example (images kindly supplied by Howard N. Langstein & Robert B. Shaw, University of Rochester Medical Center. US).

THE FALLACY OF FACIAL EXERCISES

It's a popular idea that facial exercises can prevent or reverse the signs of facial ageing such as sagging. Sadly, this is a myth. Loss of mid-face volume with sagging is mainly caused by fat tissue deflating and underlying bone structure resorbing – not loss of muscle bulk. So far from helping, facial exercises may even hinder your attempts to slow ageing. Remember, many lines and wrinkles form as a result of facial expression – think smile and frown lines.

For any truly successful rejuvenation programme, the issue of age-related facial volume and contour change has to be addressed. The good news is that there are some great options available these days – without a single scalpel in sight. But more about these later.

•

SKIN SURFACE CHANGES

Alongside wrinkles and facial volume changes, the third major sign of skin ageing involves changes in the skin surface. These include signs such as visible sun damage, irregular pigmentation, general loss of elasticity with fine crinkling of the skin and enlarged pores.

Yes, you heard it. Gradually enlarging pores can be a visible sign of skin ageing. While your large pores may be due to a genetic predisposition (for example, oily skin with a tendency for acne breakouts), pore size also tends to get bigger with age, in the same way that acne scars may also become more obvious. The reason is that our collagen and elastin quotas decline with age and with that, our skin becomes less firm and elastic. Pores and depressed acne scars then 'relax' and slacken.

Having said that, the most often complained about skin surface change is irregular pigmentation. Interestingly, scientific studies have revealed that we can quite accurately guess someone's age just by looking at a localised, cropped image of their skin surface. The less even the skin tone, the older the subject is judged to be (Fink et al. 2012b). That's a scientific fact. So, what is irregular pigmentation and how many types are there?

Abnormally strong skin pigmentation (*hyper*-pigmentation as opposed to *hypo*-pigmentation, or too little pigment) occurs through over-production of melanin, the pigment that gives skin, hair and eyes their colour. The greatest cause of mottled hyperpigmentation is sun damage. This is because the melanin in our skin absorbs the sun's rays in an attempt to protect cells from over-exposure and damage. The more sun exposure you subject your skin to, the more melanin it produces. And, as you know well, it turns darker – or tans (unless you are a so-called skin phototype 1 - more about that later).

TYPES OF PIGMENTATION: IS IT FRECKLES OR SUN DAMAGE?

• **Age spots / sun spots / liver spots.** Medically called solar lentigines (singular, lentigo) these are pigmentations caused by both genetic predisposition and sun exposure – hence their popular name, 'sun spots'. They often appear on the backs of the hands and face, but never on sun-protected areas, like the buttocks, say. More common in older people and related to ageing, they're also known as 'age spots'. Their 'liver spot' moniker comes from their red to dark brown colouring – not liver problems which were once thought to cause them. Although solar lentigines do not have the ability to turn cancerous, they can be a dreaded sign of sun damage (Bastiaens et al. 2004). Those with significant cumulative sun damage may have thousands of lentigines in skin areas such as the arms, shoulders, upper back and/or chest. When these become partly confluent, it leads to the mottled, irregular pigmentation characteristic of chronic sun damage.

• **Freckles.** Ephelides are harmless pigmentations that are inherited rather than a sign of sun damage (Bastiaens et al. 2004). However, freckly people can be more susceptible to other forms of sun-induced pigmentation such as UV damage-related lentigines. Freckles are more common in children and those with red hair and pale skin. They tend to be more symmetrically round compared to lentigines, and fluctuate throughout the seasons, becoming more visible in summer and fading in winter.

• **Melasma.** Also known as chloasma, these larger dark patches of pigmentation are sharply demarcated and bizarrely configured. Melasma often also shows a typical confetti-like sparing (Wu et al. 2016). Melasma may appear as mask-like patches on the cheeks, temples, above the upper lip and/or forehead, also called 'pregnancy mask' as they often occur with hormonal changes at this time (Handel et al. 2014). Other hormonal changes such as when taking the contraceptive pill can also make the skin more susceptible to melasma. It is more common in people who tan easily or have Mediterranean-type olive complexions

• **Post-inflammatory hyperpigmentation (PIH).** Stubborn brown patches triggered by inflammation. PIH is much more common in darker-skinned individuals and may occur after acne, eczema, trauma or any other type of inflammation in the skin. The melanin pigment in PIH may be located in the epidermis (easier to treat) or may drop down into the papillary dermis ('pigment incontinence').

In the skincare section, you will find out what types of ingredients to look out for when trying to soften irregular pigmentation. An even complexion makes skin appear much more attractive. However, sometimes patients ask me to lighten their skin tone overall. I never advise that. I believe wholeheartedly that we should love and accept our skin's natural colour. Whether porcelain, golden-brown or dark chocolate, each skin colour has its own unique beauty. How attractive our complexions are depends on so much more than mere colour. So why not love the shade we are naturally? The point is to keep our skin tone beautifully even, not try to change it.

•

PREVENTION IS BETTER THAN CURE

This adage is particularly apposite when it comes to facial ageing. It's far better – and easier – to take preventative measures early on than it is to undergo corrective procedures. This does of course include sun avoidance and protection. And, if you're committed to keeping your skin in the very best shape possible, your regime should also include regular in-clinic aesthetic treatments designed to help your skin regenerate optimally.

Don't wait until significant signs of ageing are already visible, then go for drastic interventions. It's much, much better to start *before* the tell-tale signs show and have regular upkeep 'tweakments' to maintain the positive effects.

I like to view aesthetic interventions as a gradual, continuous process of small improvements and preventative measures that allow you to choose the way your face ages, rather than hoping for a one-off 'miracle cure' when you enter a midlife crisis. That way, your face will always look naturally beautiful - not 'done.' Never be fooled by TV makeover shows boasting '10 years younger' results by giving some candidate every procedure under the sun over the course of a week or so.

THE ART & SCIENCE OF FACIAL ANALYSIS

•

THE EUDELO 3-KEY PRINCIPLE

The *3-Key Principle* is the first of the three vital principles of the *EUDELO system* and is absolutely crucial to genuinely balanced aesthetics and the natural results all patients should expect.

In the past, aesthetic interventions were mainly focused on 'chasing the line' – erasing wrinkles without taking into consideration other factors that contribute to facial ageing. This out-dated strictly two-dimensional approach is sadly still used by the vast majority of practitioners today, and in my view is one of the causes of unnatural results that make you look as if you've had 'work done'. You know when you look at someone and something's not quite right? Maybe the skin is too smooth for an obviously older woman. Something doesn't quite fit – she looks odd, somehow. Our brain intuits those disparities instantly without us even consciously realising.

You may register that she doesn't have wrinkles, yet wouldn't want to look 'artificial' like her. That's when you might come to the conclusion that 'ageing gracefully' is the better pathway. Think again. You're only thinking that because this person's practitioner has failed to respect the *3-Key Principle*. The main factors that give us clues about how old someone might be haven't been addressed and that person just looks weird. No lines, but obviously not young. Spookily ageless. Not a good look. If, however, she had been treated according to the *3-Key Principle*, you wouldn't even have looked twice. Nothing to make your brain trip. You would simply have thought she was an attractive woman.

The first of our three *EUDELO system* principles, the *3-Key Principle*, states that for a truly successful aesthetic intervention, we must not only concern ourselves with lines and wrinkles, as was traditionally the case, but analyse and treat *all* three key areas of facial ageing. The three keys to a believable outcome are: i) Skin Quality & Skin Health, ii) Facial Volume & Contour and iii) Lines, Wrinkles & Furrows. There's no point in being wrinkle-free if your skin is in bad condition; if your cheeks look gaunt; and your jawline sags. See the picture?

Let's talk about our three keys in a little more detail.

Key 1:	The first key of facial analysis and treatment
Skin Quality &	aims to improve the quality of your skin and
Skin Health	optimise its health. This key is crucial. Think
	skin surface texture, including enlarged
	pores, fine crinkling, loss of elasticity, acne

scarring, dull appearance and irregular pigmentation. Now imagine healthy, radiant, firm skin, clear from spots, pimples, flaking and other blemishes. That's what this key is all about.

Optimising this is far more important than you might think (Samson et al. 2010). It has been shown in studies that irregular pigmentation for example not only makes others see you as older and less attractive, but astonishingly less healthy, too (Fink et al. 2012a, Matts et al. 2007). And this is cross-cultural, as a recent study revealed. In this study men and women of two traditional societies, the Maasai (Tanzania) and the Tsimane' (Bolivia), unfamiliar with fair coloured skin, judged images of British women's facial skin. In both groups, images with more even skin colour were judged to be younger and healthier than corresponding images with a more uneven skin tone (Fink et al. 2017).

In addition to skin colouring, the skin surface topography, a central *skin quality* parameter, has also been shown to strongly affect age perception (Samson et al. 2011). The importance of skin health and skin quality simply cannot be overestimated. And it doesn't stop with age, attractiveness and health perception. Another study revealed that people with skin surface issues, in this case acne scarring, were sadly less likely to be considered as confident, happy and successful than those with clear, smooth skin (Dréno et al. 2016). All this demonstrates the major difference that treating and optimizing skin surface and texture can make.

Key 2:
Facial Volume
& Contour
_____

Aesthetic treatments used to be all about chasing lines and wrinkles, but for the past few years, the focus has started to shift to re-contouring the face and replacing lost volume (Baumann et al. 2015, Few at al. 2015, Kestemont et al. 2012, Moradi et al 2015). There's no doubt that sculpted cheekbones, naturally plump 'apple' cheeks and a firm jawline contribute to a younger-looking, more attractive profile. However, facial contouring does much more than simply making you look better. It also builds a vital 'scaffolding' to help prevent facial deflation and sagging.

So if you've lost facial volume (as we all do with age) or your features weren't well defined in the first place (like my own recessed chin for example), non-surgical contouring and volumising treatments can help considerably. But do make sure you don't end up with a dreaded 'pillow face'. I hate that look as much as you do – and it's totally avoidable.

Key 3:
Lines, Wrinkles &
Furrows (Folds)

The most notorious of the three key aims of facial aesthetics is, of course, smoothing lines and wrinkles. But being so well known doesn't make it the most important. I see softening lines and wrinkles as the icing on the cake, but we have to get our house in order first.

Out of our three keys, this one is arguably the least important one, albeit a very popular one with patients. You might remember the different types of wrinkles we discussed earlier – dynamic and static lines for example. Different lines need different therapeutic approaches, but all can be eased nicely.

Based on a *3-Key Principle* analysis, your practitioner will develop a bespoke aesthetic treatment plan, which will very likely involve different modalities. Think of it this way: if you go to the gym, you'd never stick to just one exercise machine. Your personal trainer would design a tailored exercise plan involving different machines to strengthen your different muscle groups. And so it should be with your skin. In order

THE 3-KEY PRINCIPLE OF
FACIAL ANALYSIS AND TREATMENT

These are the three key areas of facial ageing that must *all* be taken into consideration for a balanced, natural looking outcome of aesthetic treatment.

1: Skin Quality & Skin Health
2: Facial Volume & Contour
3: Lines, Wrinkles & Furrows

to boost your skin's fitness and wellbeing – and maintain these results long term – we routinely use different techniques.

These days, we are lucky to have various great treatment modalities at our disposal, which address the different aspects of the three key areas of facial ageing. I am looking forward to telling you about some of my favourite ones later. It's really amazing what can be done today.

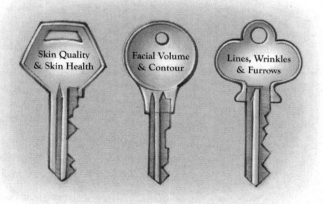

Fig. 8: The 3-Key Principle of facial analysis and aesthetic treatment.

I believe there's also a fourth dimension to assessing the face as a whole and achieving genuinely balanced, natural looking results. It's only when you examine the *moving* face that you can analyse the problem fully. So, as well as fixing lines and wrinkles, loss of volume and contours and skin quality and health, movement patterns should be taken into consideration. If you team those three key areas with an analysis of the face both at rest *and* in motion, you have a true 4-D approach to facial assessment.

•

WHAT TO EXPECT ON YOUR FIRST DAY

I strongly recommend you have a complete facial assessment and analysis with your practitioner prior to deciding on any aesthetic treatments, even if that full assessment costs more money. That's because if you're considering a procedure's helping hand and want to look great, not 'done', the most important thing to do is a *3-Key Principle* analysis. This facial assessment should also be repeated as and when needed during the course of your treatment as your face changes over time.

So you get a good idea of what should ideally happen at your full assessment appointment, let me talk you through the one we offer at EUDELO. Of course, if you merely want to see someone for a complementary, exploratory chat first, that might be an excellent starting point, but a full analysis with an aesthetic doctor or nurse is the gold standard. And don't expect this to be free of charge – you generally get what you pay for.

At your full assessment appointment at EUDELO, we first chat about your concerns and aspirations for your skin and appearance. The consultation should also include taking your medical history before your skin is examined.

> The first appointment – your skin analysis – is of the utmost importance for the planning of your subsequent treatments and should never be rushed. Don't be pushed to have a procedure on that first crucial day.

I'm a huge believer in putting my patients onto a medical couch properly and examining the skin both with the naked eye and a large, illuminated magnifying lamp. I simply don't believe I can get the same insights about a patient's skin from across a desk.

This initial consultation is also extremely important in order to make sure the patient has realistic expectations as to what's achievable – or not. The patient might also be over-concerned about something that might not, in fact, warrant treatment. A colleague told me about his 'dinner party rule', which is an excellent model to use during difficult consultations. If the person opposite you at a dinner party can't see the imperfection that troubles you, then it probably isn't worth treating. Looking at the situation this way is also useful when assessing whether or not the patient's in the right mind-set to undergo treatment.

While wishing to improve or enhance your looks is perfectly natural, we need to make sure patients aren't suffering from

STORIES FROM THE CLINIC

It's hard to say no to procedures that patients really want, but may not be suitable for. This is why an unrushed first consultation is so important. I've been in a few heated discussions with disappointed patients myself, who I turned down because I simply felt they didn't need the procedure, or the results would look overdone. Admittedly, this is a tricky situation, but I simply have to stand by my principles.

Body Dysmorphic Disorder, BDD, which is not uncommon in aesthetic practice (Veale et al. 2016). BDD is an anxiety disorder where the patient has an excessive preoccupation with perceived defects or flaws in their appearance that in reality are nowhere near as bad as they think. They will spend a lot of time worrying about that perceived flaw, which might even impact their everyday life. They might for example be convinced that a hardly visible scar is a major defect, and may stop going out with friends as they feel people are staring at them. Many BDD sufferers end up undergoing numerous cosmetic procedures they may not even need – and are still unhappy with the way they look. Sadly, these patients need psychological, not aesthetic treatment.

But let's come back to the close-up examination. This is crucially important for checking chronic sun damage and ruling out common skin issues such as adult acne and/or rosacea, which may need prescription treatment before going ahead with aesthetic procedures.

Remember, skin conditions like these need proper medical

STORIES FROM THE CLINIC

A patient came to see me because she was extremely distressed about dark circles under her eyes. She even wore sunglasses in the waiting room to hide them when she came to see me. Now, no one at conversational distance would have even noticed them. They were actually quite faint, especially in contrast to her very severe melasma patches that really jumped out at first sight. This goes to show that what we think is our face's worst feature might not be a problem, objectively. That's why it's important to listen to your practitioner as an objective observer.

treatment, not salon or spa masks or over-the-counter remedies. I've seen numerous patients in clinic with acne and rosacea who for years, had been treated in beauty salons. By the time they came to see me, they had become increasingly frustrated and in some cases, scarred. The good news? Just three months into my prescription treatment, their condition turned around completely. I can remember one patient shedding tears of joy.

Make sure your practitioner is experienced in treating other potential skin issues such as chronic sun damage, adult acne and/or rosacea with prescription treatment if needed. Never attempt to get medical skin issues such as breakouts treated in beauty salons, but see a dermatologist for proper treatment.

If there are any lesions on your skin (such as moles, sun spots or overgrowing oil glands) your practitioner should examine them under a dermatoscope – a special magnifying lamp with cross-polarised light. A dermatoscope is the dermatologist's favourite tool, as it makes features visible that the naked eye can't see, for example the pigment net structure of a mole or the shape of tiny blood vessels in the skin. That way they can judge whether it's a healthy mole or not, distinguish between an overgrowing oil gland and a basal cell skin cancer and various other things.

However, in addition to examining the skin close up, it's also important to sit the patient up, step back and study the face from around a metre's distance to gain an overall impression of the entire face. The overview is as critical as the detail. This is the 'first impression' everyday people will have of your face – their unconscious assessment of how attractive you are that takes only milliseconds. It's important for the practitioner to take this overview with the patient sitting up or standing, so that the effects of gravity can be taken into account. This upright 'gravity-included' view can reveal very different insights compared to the 'laid-back' examination on the couch.

The naked, unmade-up face should also be photographed upright with a digital camera against a neutral background with consistent lighting. Standardised views may include frontal; left and right profile; left and right semi-profile; and slightly from above, with the head tilting down towards the chest. Various facial expressions such as smiling, frowning and raising the eyebrows are also invaluable for both the patient and practitioner to examine together.

If your practitioner merely chucks a mirror into your hand

and airily points out a few imperfections – that's not a good sign. You can never see yourself objectively in the mirror because we a) automatically auto-edit what we see and b) we instantly hone in on those pesky little details that have bugged us for years. Apart from being able to see the bigger picture, a standardized 'before' photo-record will also allow you to appreciate the results of your procedure objectively. I'm not saying we can never look at our face dispassionately, just that photos allow us to stand back and observe whatever your practitioner points out more objectively.

Although not every clinic has this technical ability, your first appointment should ideally include a digital skin surface scan and skin physiology analysis. A typical skin surface scan measures parameters such as cumulative sun damage (invisible to the naked eye), pore size, redness (caused by tiny broken blood vessels, for example), skin texture and visible pigmentation. Depending on which device your clinic uses, your results might be compared to a worldwide database (anonymously, of course) which ranks you within your peer group – that's people of the same age, gender and skin type. This way we can find out whether your skin's results are average for your age, or better or worse. You may even be able to find out exactly what percentage of your peer group's skin is better or worse than yours in each of the measured parameters.

> Make sure your aesthetic practitioner takes a series of standardised photographs covering different angles and facial expressions – and talks you through them, rather than just pointing out things in a mirror.

The next step might be an *in vivo* analysis of different skin physiology parameters. Clever non-invasive measurement devices can objectively quantify parameters such as hydration, invisible water loss from the skin surface (ever wondered why your skin's dry even though you drink plenty of water?), oil production, skin elasticity and surface pH (Luebberding et al. 2014). Your practitioner should explain the outcome of these tests in detail and print a summary report for you to take home, too. These measurements help us determine your skin's weaknesses and strengths and how best to support them. The results will also help us to put together your optimal skincare regime, which you should receive in writing.

YOUR FEATURES ANALYSED

A full facial aesthetic assessment and analysis should ideally include the following:
- **'First impression'** overview of the face
- **Evaluation of facial features** while sitting or standing
- **Examination of the skin surface** with a magnifying lamp while you're lying down
- **Examination of any skin lesions** such as moles using a dermatoscope (magnifying lamp with cross-polarised light) held directly onto the lesions
- **Clinical photographs** in different standardised positions with consistent lighting, including a variety of facial expressions
- **Digital skin surface scan** to assess invisible sun damage, pore size, redness, skin texture and pigmentation

> • **Skin physiology analysis** of hydration, water evaporation from the skin surface, oil production, surface pH, skin elasticity etc.

Another interesting test is to find out how your skin performs on a genetic level. This might not be part of a routine assessment as it's a highly advanced test, but it should be available as an add-on. At EUDELO, we work with a specialist lab abroad to offer genetic profiling for important skin-related genes.

I had my own DNA analysis done and I can tell you it wasn't all great news! While my free radical protection coding was fine, the test revealed that I have a genetic tendency for collagen breakdown – a shock if you're aiming for smooth skin low on wrinkles – and it didn't stop there. It turns out that my genes aren't great at fighting inflammation, sun damage *and* glycation (a process that cross-links and weakens collagen – more about this later). Thanks Mum and Dad…

The really good news, though, is that despite not being blessed with the best age-fighting genes, my skin currently actually looks younger than my age (long may it last…). That's all down to good skincare, regular regenerative treatments and a skin-friendly lifestyle. That shows how much you can do, even if you're not genetically lucky.

This book is all about teaching you how to make use of the amazing tools in our aesthetic armamentarium – without ending up looking as if you'd dabbled a little too often.

•

WHO IS GETTING
UNDER YOUR SKIN?

Before I launch into treatment planning and the treatments we use to address the three key aspects of facial skin ageing, I'd like to stress how important it is to choose the right clinic to achieve the best – and safest – results.

There are various medical practitioners, including doctors, dentists and nurses with various backgrounds, offering cosmetic treatments. While many are extremely experienced and technically excellent, there is one group of physicians I want to talk about in more detail, as they are very close to my heart. Dermatologists!

I am a dermatologist myself. I went to university in Germany for five years to complete a general medical degree, then began my post-graduate specialist training in dermatology. After a further five intense years, I was awarded the title of dermatologist on passing the rigorous German specialisation exam. So it takes a whopping 10 years or more of training to become a fully qualified dermatologist. In addition to that, a cosmetic (or aesthetic) dermatologist must undertake a multitude of sub-speciality courses and training in the aesthetics field.

So cosmetic dermatologists know a thing or two about skin and are the experts on skin-related issues. They are in a unique position to combine expertise in cosmetic treatments with an in-depth knowledge of skin biology and skin diseases. In short, they know exactly what they're doing.

Personally, I have more than 20 years of training and experience under my belt, but most importantly, it mustn't stop here. The learning and training has to be on-going to keep me in touch with the latest developments. To qualify and then rest on your laurels thinking you know it all, is one of the most dangerous attitudes an aesthetic practitioner can have. And sadly, it's seen more often than not.

Another great thing about choosing a dermatologist-led clinic for your aesthetic treatments is that whether your skin concerns are medical or aesthetic, you'll visit the same, one-stop address for them all. We see an overlap of medical and aesthetic issues in our clinic all the time – think breakouts plus frown lines, hair loss plus jowls. Hardly anyone comes with just one concern.

So seeing a dermatologist has a host of advantages; but if you can't, at least make sure you see a medical professional who can prescribe as well as treat your skin aesthetically. The advantage is that we might have to prescribe you medication linked to your aesthetic treatment – tablets to prevent cold sores, say, when you're having your lips treated or preventative antibiotics to support certain procedures. Or you might wish to start using the gold standard collagen-boosting, sun damage-repairing ingredient tretinoin – the prescription-only cream most discerning dermatologists use on their own skin. And did you know that botulinum toxin injections such as Botox® and Bocouture® are prescription-only? Non-prescribing cosmetic practitioners either won't be able to offer you the full spectrum of possible options, or there's the risk they're getting some products illegally.

One of the things I love about having completed my dermatology training in Germany is that in Continental Europe, aesthetic dermatology has become much more integrated into general dermatology than in the UK, thus ensuring the highest and safest possible standards. I'm confident I bring a sound dermatologist's approach to our clinic, so my patients can be sure everything we do is dermatologist approved.

WHO'S GETTING UNDER YOUR SKIN?

• **What is a dermatologist?** Dermatologists are fully qualified doctors. First, they study at medical school to get a general medical degree; then undergo several years of post-graduate specialist training to become a dermatologist. Most UK dermatologists are listed on the GMC's specialist register (www.gmc-uk.org). However, if they trained abroad, they might not. The majority of UK dermatologists concentrate on treating medical skin concerns, however, there are some dermatologists who sub-specialise further to offer cosmetic dermatology in addition to medical dermatology.

• **What is a cosmetic dermatologist?** Not every dermatologist is experienced in cosmetic dermatology / aesthetic medicine – or even interested in it. However, cosmetic dermatologists have completed additional training in aesthetic procedures such as line-smoothing injections and may also have a special interest in cosmeceutical skincare. So for a truly holistic approach to your skin issues, you may want to look for a dermatologist with special interest in aesthetic medicine, i.e. a cosmetic / aesthetic dermatologist. A good starting point is to check the 'Find a practitioner' section on the *British Cosmetic Dermatology Group* website (www.bcdg.info).

• **What is a GP with special interest in dermatology?**
There are also GPs with special interest in
dermatology (GPSI). That means they have
completed a shorter diploma course in dermatology,
but are not fully qualified dermatologists.

• **What is a skin specialist?** The term 'skin specialist'
is confusingly vague and doesn't really mean
anything. It's often used by both medical and
non-medical practitioners. Frankly anyone can
use this term, so if you hear it, it's wise to ask for
further details.

THE ART & SCIENCE OF TREATMENT PLANNING

Now we can come back to planning your treatment. We've already outlined the *3-Key Principle* of facial analysis and I highly recommend basing your treatment plan on this template. Remember, the best results are achieved via a holistic approach that combines different treatment methods that address the whole of the face and *all* three key aspects of facial ageing: i) Skin Quality & Skin Health, ii) Facial Volume & Contour and iii) Lines, Wrinkles & Furrows. When this is done successfully by an experienced practitioner, you can get fantastic results without surgery – results that look so natural, they won't make your brain trip or give the impression that 'something's weird'.

Whatever you do, the signature look to aim for should always be natural, balanced and harmonious. You want people to comment on how well you look, or ask if you've been on holiday rather than scrutinising your face for tell-tale signs. Every day we meet people who look great for

> As a rule of thumb, if you can tell that someone's had 'work done' – it's been overdone or done badly.

their age and are evidently 'happy in their own skin'. Chances are, many of them have had aesthetic treatments. You'd never guess because it's all been done well.

As Eleanor Roosevelt said perceptively: "Beautiful young people are accidents of nature, but beautiful old people are works of art." For me, this includes the helping hand of aesthetic medicine.

> In your 20s, nature determines how you look. From your 30s onwards, it's up to you!

Before we speak about the second principle of the *EUDELO system*, let me stress that looking after other exposed skin areas such as the hands, neck and chest is equally important as caring for your face (Jakubietz et al. 2008). It's all too easy to forget these zones, yet they contribute to an overall impression of youthful good looks.

> Just treating the face and ignoring other exposed zones such as neck, chest and hands leads to incongruent results. A congruent, or harmonious first impression is extremely important to a credible rejuvenation overall.

Now let's move on to the next principle of the *EUDELO system*, the *Foundation Principle*.

•

THE EUDELO FOUNDATION PRINCIPLE

A rare historic treasure hidden down a narrow street in London's Farringdon illustrates *The Foundation Principle* of the *EUDELO system* perfectly. The house at 41/42 Cloth Fair is one of the oldest still standing in London. According to historic records, this house was built between 1597 and 1614 and survived the Great Fire of London in 1666 and two world wars as well as consideration for demolition in 1929. Happily, in 1995, it was acquired by new owners and underwent extensive renovation. And, as a testament to the quality of that restoration, it proudly displays the 2000 City Heritage Award.

Now, I'm no expert in the construction of venerable buildings, but one thing I'm certain of is that in order for this structure to remain standing after four centuries, its foundation must be sound. Because if you want to build something that will stand the test of time, a weak foundation simply won't hold up. It may look fine for a while, but over the years your building will begin to shift, cracks will appear and eventually it may even collapse. By now, you'll doubtless see where I'm coming from and how firm foundations in the construction industry are analogous to the *Foundation Principle* of looking after your skin.

There's a crucial reality about skin health and wellbeing that most men and women – and, shockingly, a great many of my colleagues – are overlooking. But there are consequences. Just like great buildings, great looking skin also needs a strong, enduring foundation if it is to withstand the test of time and the elements of nature.

By foundation, I mean the subsurface layer of our skin known as the dermis. Comprised largely of collagen and elastin proteins, the dermis provides structure and support to the skin's upper layers. Healthy young skin naturally produces collagen and elastin fibres as well as sufficient quantities and quality of the gelatinous substance in between. These structures are regenerated regularly, maintaining and supporting this foundation nicely. But only for a while…

Because as you age, this natural process slows down. Exacerbated by other destructive elements of our daily life – such as sun, pollution, sub-optimal diet and stress – your skin's foundation begins to lose some of its integrity, as evidenced by fine lines and wrinkles and further signs of premature skin ageing.

We see this in clinic every day. In fact, one of the most common concerns I hear from my patients is that the overall quality and elasticity of their skin is just not what it used to be and they're starting to look older than they feel. Their skin looks a little crepey, fine lines are showing and their jawline is starting to sag. The other thing that happens when our skin elasticity declines is that enlarged pores and acne scarring may become more obvious, as mentioned before.

For all these reasons, it's important to get into the habit of doing something that helps you keep control of how well your skin ages. Something that supports a strong foundation so that you feel confident and happy, loving the skin you're in long-term.

What keeps me up at night? It concerns me to know that many of my fellow professionals are only interested in instant corrective anti-ageing interventions. You know the ones – freezing lines here, pumping up furrows there. That's all they do; omitting to educate their patients on the importance of working on skin quality in order to prevent the gradual decline on a much more foundational level.

And while corrective procedures are of course a vital part

of aesthetic medicine, I really am disturbed by the lack of enthusiasm some colleagues show for true skin regeneration and the maintenance of a radiant complexion at any age.

Regenerative aesthetic dermatology is an innovative concept in skin health that uses advanced, yet natural 'bio-stimulatory' treatments to encourage tissue repair, renewal and regeneration at the cellular foundation level. Years of experience have convinced me that there really is no point in painting over the cracks, temporarily fixing the skin's surface merely to hide a degrading foundation beneath.

> Whether you're 25 or 55, if you genuinely want to look as good as you feel long-term, you should include regular regenerative treatments in your regime. A monthly schedule is ideal to support optimal skin renewal. This is what we call the *Foundation Principle*.

The hidden problem

Think of it like this. Having purely *corrective* aesthetic procedures such as freezing, filling and augmenting treatments without maintaining a youthful level of skin regeneration is like building a house on sand. Superficially, your skin might look great for years and no one would be any the wiser that deep down, it's getting progressively weaker. Until of course, the cracks begin to show.

With an overall decline of skin quality, firmness and elasticity, your face will age faster than needs be. Eventually the 'cracks' will show and become difficult to correct. Your skin just won't look good for your age any longer. The compliments will start to go quiet and your confidence in your skin won't be what it was.

Fig. 9: A house without a foundation. Eventually subsidence will set in and cracks will show!

Building a strong foundation

Regenerative procedures help the skin help itself. They improve overall skin quality and slow down the ageing process on a cellular level. They make skin cells act younger so that your skin remains stronger, healthier and more beautiful overall – no matter what your age. Glowing, healthy skin is like a strong house with a firm foundation.

Fig. 10: The EUDELO Foundation Principle – symbolised by a firm foundation to keep your 'house' strong over the long term.

In short, the *Foundation Principle* states that if you are truly committed to long-term skin health and beauty, you should have regular regenerative bio-stimulatory treatments, ideally every month. And the good news is that should you want a bit more of a helping hand, regenerative procedures work in perfect synergy with corrective treatments. This step-wise approach is integral to the *EUDELO system* and the basis of our third principle, the *Staircase Principle*.

•

THE EUDELO STAIRCASE PRINCIPLE

The *Staircase Principle* is an ascension model that shows how the different steps of looking after your skin relate to each other. As the numerous non-surgical procedures available these days can be confusing and you might not know where to start, I have organised everything in an easy-to-understand way to help you to prioritise. Remember, it's your personal commitment to keep your skin in optimal shape that will determine which step you want to move up to. Whatever you decide to do, you should always begin at the bottom of the staircase and resist temptation to jump a step.

I'll go into each individual step of the *EUDELO staircase* later, but let me give you a heads up. The first step on our staircase is a genuinely skin-friendly lifestyle (think good diet, no smoking, no excessive sun exposure, enough sleep – you get the gist). I call this lifestyle *FuturApproved®*. This is an issue close to my heart, as our lifestyle must be the first thing to change if we decide to take better care of our skin. I have written two entire books on this topic in the past, which show my commitment to a holistic approach.

My first book, *'Future Proof Your Skin. Slow down the biological clock by changing the way you eat'* and my mindfulness kit, *'Future Proof Your Skin (And Live Longer!) With Stress Management'* are both available on Amazon and are well worth getting, since I'll only be able to outline some general principles in the book you're reading right now. Also have a look at www.FuturApproved.com to find out more.

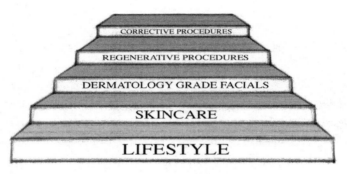

Fig. 11: The EUDELO Staircase Principle.

The next step on your commitment staircase is to use good cosmeceutical skincare at home on a daily basis. An expert should put together a tailored skincare regime for you: please don't try to do this on your own as there's so much misinformation out there that it's impossible for the layperson to distinguish between superior skincare and slick marketing. Visit www.EudeloBoutique.com to book a complimentary Skype consultation with one of our experts, if you are unable to come to clinic. I've trained them personally to design your tailored skincare regime, so why not do it now?

Naturally, you'll be continuing your good work by leading a *FuturApproved*® lifestyle which, by the way, has the happy side-effect of supporting your overall health and lifespan, too.

You'd never think "now I'm using good skincare I can go back to smoking two packs a day", now would you? 'Course not. When you ascend the commitment staircase, you take each step with you as you go.

If you want to achieve even more for your skin (you're a high achiever, after all!) the next logical step is to have a regular non-invasive regenerative treatment. These *dermatology grade facials* are very different from salon and spa facials which aim to pamper, relax and hydrate, but don't achieve anywhere near the same long-lasting results on your skin's biology and physiology – I will speak about this in more detail later. Non-invasive regenerative treatments are gentle and don't involve downtime. Typically, you'll have one once a month.

Non-invasive regenerative treatments should be done *in addition* to your daily skincare at home, while leading your skin- and longevity-friendly lifestyle. Remember commitment means never skipping a step. What use would regular regenerative treatments be if you smoked like a chimney, chomped gummy chews all day, hit the sun bed several times a week and used nothing but petroleum jelly on your skin? That would be a total waste of time, effort and money and a sure route to sub-optimal results. In fact we might just refuse to treat you until you sorted out your lifestyle.

If you step up higher still on our imaginary commitment staircase, the next level involves *minimal-invasive* regenerative procedures. These are stronger types of regenerative treatments and slightly more involving than *dermatology grade facials*. Note how these are still positioned *underneath* corrective treatments in our diagram. That's because regenerative procedures form a mandatory *foundation* for corrective treatments.

Should you decide to opt for corrective procedures (which considering they're non-surgical can give mind-blowing results!) in my opinion you must still support your skin with on-going regenerative procedures to keep its foundation strong. I can't stress enough how important this principle is! Because in addition to a *FuturApproved*® lifestyle and superior skincare, regular regenerative treatments underpin any serious corrective work. Remember – you can't construct a stately building without building a strong foundation.

THE EUDELO 5-STEP STAIRCASE PRINCIPLE

Each of these five steps of caring for your skin non-surgically should relate to each other. Start at the bottom – and never jump a step.

1: **Lifestyle changes** – i.e. leading a skin- and longevity-friendly, *FuturApproved*® lifestyle

2: **Cosmeceutial skincare** – i.e. using a superior, evidence-based skincare regime twice daily at home

3: **Dermatology grade facials** – to gently support skin regeneration non-invasively, once per month

4: **Regenerative procedures** – e.g. medical needling, carboxy facials, platelet rich plasma therapy, mesotherapy and laser facials for a more intense regeneration boost

5: **Corrective procedures** – e.g. line-smoothing and contouring injections for an immediate, non-surgical 'wow' effect

---

Beyond the non-surgical *EUDELO staircase* there is of course, the option of surgical intervention. However, the primary focus of this book is on non-surgical treatments.

I will explain all five steps of the *EUDELO staircase* in much more detail later. But first, a few words about the concept of skin wellbeing and skin fitness in relation to regenerative treatments, because it is so very important.

SKIN WELLBEING &
SKIN FITNESS

You don't expect to reach peak physical fitness after a single trip to the gym, do you? It's much the same with regenerative treatments. Initially, your skin will just look and feel fresh and radiant. But with an on-going commitment to your monthly treatment protocol (and daily home skincare plan...), you'll take charge of how well your skin ages, strengthening your skin's foundation layer and maintaining your radiantly smooth skin for years to come.

We accept without question that for optimal long-term health, we should exercise at least two or three times a week. A gym membership helps you to prioritise your physical fitness regimen and provides a structure to your workout routine that makes it easier to stay in shape. For the most part, you don't even have to think about it. So long as you show up regularly and plug into the gym's resources, you'll get fitter, look more toned and stay healthier. Other than feeling better, the immediate benefit might be subtle, as the best results are cumulative and achieved over time.

Just as regularly following a bespoke fitness plan designed

by an expert is the best way to stay physically fit and well, healthy and injury-free, in my professional opinion it's the best way to get your skin into top shape, too. You can't just give your skin a random 'workout' once in a while and expect great results. If you're aiming to keep your skin happy and healthy, you're in it for the long term.

I'm always amazed, though, how many people come to see us in clinic and ask: "What's THE best treatment to make my skin look 10 years younger?" or something along those lines. Would they ask a personal trainer which exercise machine to use, so they walk out an hour later with a figure to die for? No single machine – whether in a gym or clinic – can deliver it all, especially in a single session. All muscle groups in your body need the challenge of varied, balanced, *regular* workouts. And essentially it's the same for your skin; regular visits to your aesthetic medicine clinic and a variety of regenerative treatments and procedures will give the best, long-term results. If you wish, corrective procedures are the cherry on the top. And

> I'm fascinated that while people understand the role gym membership plays in physical fitness and wellbeing, they don't get it that the same regular commitment applies to skin wellbeing and skin fitness.

like your gym membership, some sort of skin regeneration plan commits you to following a prescribed regime tailored to your skin's specific profile and desired outcomes.

And the 'membership fee'? That's the investment you make in your skin's future and healthy good looks for years to come. Think of it as an investment in *yourself* for a change, rather than a designer handbag or yet another pair of shoes destined for the back of the wardrobe when fashion passes them by. As one of my patients put it rather pithily, "nothing looks and feels as good as wearing great skin".

Because consistency is so important to skin regeneration, at EUDELO I have pioneered a membership programme called *The Skin Care Elite*. You might have seen it mentioned in Tatler magazine. This is a new concept in skin care: it combines the philosophy of regenerative aesthetic dermatology and a structured treatment protocol with a clear plan of action and peace of mind. Instead of random, one-off treatments, a club structure commits you to follow an optimal monthly schedule of natural regenerative treatments and procedures, tailored to your skin's needs. But even if you don't live in London, I'm confident that the principles I outline in this book will help you to put together an effective plan of regenerative treatments with a reputable clinic near you.

> Remember - Good skin never goes out of fashion!

I always tell my patients that *'joining EUDELO'* – or any other good skin clinic's regeneration program – comes with a 'personal skin trainer', but without the sweat.

The concept of a no-hassle 'skin gym' membership actually grew out of my professional experience with regenerative aesthetic dermatology. As I've already explained, regenerative dermatology gently helps the skin to help itself by means of bio-stimulatory protocols that slow down skin ageing naturally, improve overall skin quality and help it to look radiantly healthy at every stage of your life. I based our club protocols on my professional expertise and personal experience, compiling the same treatment regimes I myself used personally. I am of course now an avid EUDELO *Skin Care Elite* member myself.

THE EUDELO STEPS
EXPLAINED

We all age differently and step through the clinic doorway at various stages of our lives. There are many motivations for seeking help from a cosmetic dermatologist like myself. Some people may have noticed the first signs of ageing; others may have a particular skin problem or issue; and yet more may feel that what they see in the mirror doesn't reflect the way they feel inside. Whether you're 30 or 60, have looked after your skin well and aim to continue, or are just starting off on your skin care journey, we need to determine your objectives and find the right programme for you. Everyone is different – and so is everyone's degree of commitment.

Some people we see in clinic just want help with their skincare regime and maybe a few supportive *dermatology grade facials*, while others are happy to take advantage of whatever we offer non-surgically to keep their skin looking its very best. At the end of the day, the choice is yours. Only you can decide how far you you're willing to commit and that's why I've written this book. Opting for the helping hand of aesthetic medicine can be game-changing; so rather than basing your decisions on hearsay, this book is here to give you all the information necessary to make informed choices not only for now, but for the future of your skin.

Of course, skin grows and changes and it's also likely your objectives might change over time. But whatever your commitment, this guide will help you to make the wisest choices.

I urge you to read all of the chapters on the different cosmetic treatments – don't skim or skip those you *think* aren't for you. You need *all* the information before you make an informed decision.

This brings me back to something I alluded to earlier. Remember when I mentioned that life served me a curve ball recently? What actually happened is that I developed a reaction to a hyaluronic acid dermal filler under my eyes. A hypersensitivity reaction like mine is very rare, so it's ironic that it happened to me, a cosmetic dermatologist! With prescription treatment, my reaction settled within a couple of months, but as I write this, I don't know yet whether I'll ever be able to have fillers again as there's a potential I may react again. On the other hand, it could turn out that I only react to certain HA filler brands but can tolerate others. Time will tell.

It would, of course, be extremely disappointing for me if I had to avoid all filler treatments in future. However, the beauty of the *EUDELO system* is that it also caters for patients who can't or simply don't want to have corrective procedures. The *EUDELO system* aims to help you towards the best version of yourself, whatever your preference or profile.

I discourage everyone from aspiring to look like other people - we should only compare ourselves to ourselves and the *EUDELO system* is dedicated to improving our *individual* skin's appearance.

I developed the *EUDELO Skin Enhancement Staircase* as a clear way of outlining the five levels of non-surgical cosmetic interventions available to us today. Not every patient will need, or want to progress through all the steps – and that's perfectly okay. Whatever your objectives and level of commitment, the *EUDELO system* has a clear solution for every skin at every age, no matter how far you wish to take it. Each step allows us to lay a foundation and build upon it as we progress – they all support and strengthen each other.

> Everyone's different and most of us don't look like supermodels – nor should we aspire to. We simply want to tweak what we have to be the best we can.

Progressing up the staircase step by step is vital – no skipping. Going straight to corrective procedures without addressing skin regeneration quite frankly won't work in the long-term. Remember the house without its foundation? You may have noticed the 'sudden collapse syndrome' in some celebrities. They may have looked youthfully fabulous for years – then crash! There's an image in the media where they suddenly look far older – not younger - than their age and really odd with it. I'm sure you know exactly what I mean. Could this be because of enthusiastic corrective procedures without regular regenerative treatments to support them? Don't make the same mistake. Put skin regeneration first, then build correction on top of that firm foundation. This principle is crucial – and if there's only one thing you take away from this book, I hope this is it.

Now, let's dig into the five EUDELO steps in more detail.

•

LIFESTYLE CHANGE — AN INSIDE JOB

There's an excellent reason that a skin- and longevity-friendly lifestyle is the first step on the *EUDELO staircase*. We simply cannot hope to change our skin on the outside without first changing what's happening at a cellular level, inside. The stresses of modern day living – busy lives, pollution, sun exposure, poor diet, excess alcohol, lack of sleep and smoking – all contribute to premature skin ageing as they affect the way our body, and so our skin, is functioning.

> Lifestyle choices have a huge impact on how long we're likely to live and how good our skin will look along the way.

Scientific evidence confirms the connection between inner health and outer youthful looks and studies have proven that our perceived age is a good estimate of our general health (Noordam et al. 2013). Studies have also shown that the younger we look, the more likely we are to live a long life (Gunn et al. 2013). However, things we do or are unwittingly exposed to on a daily basis may speed up the ageing process and even diminish the chance of reaching our full age potential. These lifestyle factors can cause a cascade of events internally which has a knock-on effect on our external looks. Key internal ageing processes that can be dramatically influenced by daily lifestyle choices include:

- Oxidative stress
- Glycation
- Inflammation
- Telomere shortening
- DNA mutations
- Hormonal changes

Let's take a look at these factors in detail.

Oxidative stress
___

First introduced around 1991, this is a relatively new concept in biology. Essentially, oxidative stress is caused when our body creates too many free radicals. These reactive oxygen species (ROS) and reactive nitrogen species (RNS) are unstable molecules that steal electrons from other molecules including proteins, lipids and even DNA – the molecule that encodes our genetic information. Some degree of free radical production in the human body is inevitable (and even needed for proper cellular functioning) – every single one of our cells generates them as by-products of routine metabolism that take place every second of every day. Usually these free radicals are neutralised by antioxidants – and our skin contains an entire network of these (Masaki et al. 2010, Rinnerthaler et al. 2015). Enzymatic antioxidants (bigger molecules) including superoxide dismutase (SOD), catalase and glutathione peroxidase; and smaller, non-enzymatic molecules such as vitamins A, C and E, glutathione, uric acid and ubiquinol all work to keep free radicals in check. However, our modern lifestyles increase free radical generation significantly and our antioxidant pool can't cope with the increased demand (Krutmann et al. 2017).

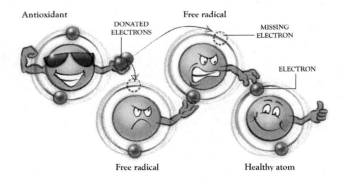

Fig. 12: Free radicals are highly reactive molecules with an unpaired electron. They 'steal' electrons from neighbouring molecules, which starts a harmful chain reaction. Antioxidants donate one of their electrons to stop the damaging chain reaction.

Oxidative stress is today understood to be one of the key mechanisms in ageing, not only in our skin, but all the major systems in our body (Nikolakis et al. 2013, Rinnerthaler et al. 2015). A number of lifestyle factors contribute to oxidative stress including alcohol, smoking, certain medications, physical and emotional trauma, air pollutants, toxins and radiation.

> Both internal and external stressors can increase free radical levels in our skin ('oxidative stress'), accelerating the ageing process.

This is potentially extremely dangerous, since free radicals can react indiscriminately with neighbouring molecules. This process, known as 'electron stealing' leads to oxidation and extensive cellular damage. One of the main pillars in combating premature ageing is to reduce free radical production and increase antioxidant levels in the body and skin.

Glycation   Glycation is also a very important mechanism of ageing (Nguyen et al. 2015, Pageon et al. 2014). During this process, sugar molecules, such as glucose and fructose, attach themselves to other molecules including collagen in our skin, to form tissue-damaging cross-links called advanced glycation end products (AGEs).

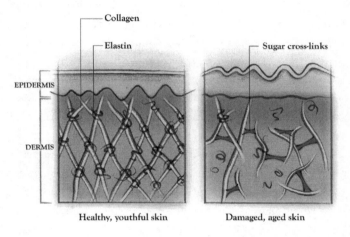

Healthy, youthful skin   Damaged, aged skin

Fig. 13: Sugar cross-links are an important mechanism of action in skin ageing.

These cross-links make collagen stiffer and more brittle, preventing it from performing its optimal function as a major supporting skin structure. Glycation also causes other destructive reactions, including free radical formation, oxidative stress and inflammation, which all accelerate ageing. Each of these changes creates an environment that encourages collagen degradation and compromises the integrity and regeneration of our skin. Excess glycation also makes the skin appear more sallow (Ohshima at al. 2009).

> Sugar molecules can cross-link collagen and accelerate the skin's ageing process.

Some degree of glycation occurs all the time, which is inevitable. But glycation is greatly increased when we consume a diet high in sugar. We can significantly reduce the rate of glycation by reducing the amount of sugary foods we eat on a daily basis.

It's worth noting that studies have shown that fructose (which is not only present in large amounts in sugary soft drinks, but also plentiful in the seemingly saintly agave syrup!) is even more active in regenerating AGEs than glucose and thus conventional cane sugar (Schalkwijk et al. 2004), which contains 50% fructose and 50% glucose. Interestingly, glycation in our skin is also increased after excessive sun exposure (Crisan et al. 2013).

And don't forget that starch is actually one long string of sugar molecules. As soon as you eat starchy carbohydrates, your digestive enzymes break down those strings into sugar molecules that raise your blood sugar level.

Fig. 14: Starch is a long string of sugar molecules. As soon as you eat starch, your digestive enzymes cut the starch molecule into sugar molecules.

Studies have confirmed accelerated skin ageing in people with high blood sugar levels (Park et al. 2011); and not surprisingly, this accelerated ageing was found to be in direct proportion to the duration of hyperglycaemia (raised blood sugar level). Hyperglycaemia has also been shown to reduce growth factor release including human growth hormone (HGH), which has skin-rejuvenating properties. Yet another scientific study confirmed that higher blood sugar levels correlate with a higher perceived age (van Drielen et al. 2015). In other words, people with higher blood sugar tend to look older (Noordam et al. 2013).

It's also known that familial longevity is associated with better blood sugar control (Rozing et al. 2010). So controlling your blood sugar levels not only makes you look younger on the outside, but actually rejuvenates your insides and makes you live longer, too.

Inflammation   In the times before antibiotics, acute inflammation with redness, heat and swelling was a vital process in infection fighting and healing. However, long-term, low-level inflammation – also referred to as chronic micro-inflammation – can take its toll on both our skin and general health (Zhuang et al. 2014).

The more chronic inflammation in our body, the higher the rate of collagen and elastin degradation in our skin – and here's why. As we age, our skin is unable to produce important proteins such as collagen and elastin as well as it used to. To make matters worse, it also degrades

> Chronic micro-inflammation is known to contribute to premature skin and general ageing.

them quicker via a group of enzymes called matrix-metallo-proteinases (MMPs). Inflammation induces more of these MMPs in our skin.

Bad diet and stress are two key lifestyle factors that are known to contribute to chronic inflammation. Oxidative stress, high blood sugar and insulin (an important sugar-regulating hormone) levels will all contribute to invisible, low-level inflammation which can be present in the body for decades without obvious symptoms, silently and systematically accelerating the ageing process.

Telomere shortening
Like the little cap on shoelaces, telomeres sit on the end of our chromosomes protecting them and so the integrity of our genetic material. Each time a cell divides, its chromosomes shorten a little. The telomeres take the brunt, shielding the vital genetic information between them. Yet at some point, the telomeres get used up.

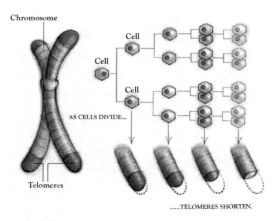

Fig. 15: Telomere shortening occurs with every cell division.

Skin cells have been described as particularly susceptible to accelerated telomere shortening because of their high proliferation rate and exposure to DNA-damage from influences such as oxidative stress (Buckingham et al. 2011; Boukamp et al. 2005). Shorter telomeres have even been linked to a shortened life span (Wentzensen et al. 2011; Shen et al. 2007).

Although telomeres shorten with every cell division, we know today that this happens at different rates and our lifestyle plays a role in this, too. Chronic stress and raised stress hormone levels have for example been linked to accelerated telomere shortening, as have other lifestyle influences such as high blood sugar levels, obesity and inflammation (Epel et al. 2006, Rizvi et al. 2014, Shammas 2011). On the other hand, positive lifestyle interventions can, amazingly, improve telomere length, making the length of our telomeres important data when assessing our real – as opposed to chronological – cell age.

> Both internal and external stressors have been linked to the accelerated shortening of telomeres – the protective caps on all our chromosomes, which is highly relevant for skin ageing.

DNA mutations

The DNA sequences in our genes are inherited. However, with time mutations in our DNA may occur. A chance event or environmental factors including sun exposure can do the damage and more and more of this DNA damage accumulates as we age.

> Sun exposure and environmental pollution can cause DNA mutations in our skin cells.

Some DNA mutations may be 'silent' and never cause problems; others may even be beneficial. But some DNA mutations can be highly dangerous and lead to impaired cell function, illness or cancer.

Hormones These are our body's chemical messengers which travel in our blood and influence many different internal processes including ageing (Zouboulis et al. 2012). Two of the hormones that play a significant role in ageing are cortisol and insulin (van Drielen et al. 2015). Cortisol is an extremely important stress hormone. Normally, cortisol levels are high when we get up in the morning, then decline and level off in the afternoon. However, chronic stress can lead to elevated levels of cortisol throughout the day, which in turn contributes to collagen destruction in the skin.

Insulin is one of our sugar-regulating hormones, which is secreted by the pancreas' beta cells and performs the vital function of clearing excess sugar from the bloodstream. Excess insulin release contributes to free radical generation, oxidative stress, inflammation and a marked acceleration in skin ageing.

After a meal high in sugary or starchy carbohydrates, especially the processed type, our blood sugar level rockets, triggering an insulin spike that makes our blood sugar plummet a couple of hours later, leaving us craving for yet more carbs. Giving in to this renewed hunger creates

> Hormones such as cortisol and insulin are known to accelerate the skin's ageing process.

a vicious cycle, which ultimately leads to rollercoaster-like fluctuating blood sugar (glucose) levels throughout the day. The repeated ups and downs of glucose and insulin are highly stressful for our body. It responds by releasing pro-ageing stress hormones such as cortisol, which further encourages collagen breakdown.

Eventually, these continuous waves of sugar intake, blood sugar spikes and insulin hikes will make our cells less responsive to insulin thereby creating 'insulin resistance', where even higher levels of insulin are needed to do the same job. Good insulin sensitivity however, is important for optimum ageing. Superior insulin sensitivity has been linked to longevity in families (Wijsman et al. 2011) – so thank your lucky genes.

But let's not be complacent. A typical Western diet is often highly insulinemic – it triggers lots of insulin spikes and our low-fat, high sugar, starch-crunching habits can greatly accelerate the skin's ageing process in the Western World. In order to age well, one of the most important lifestyle moves we can make to fight ageing at a cellular level is to moderate our insulin secretion by avoiding high blood sugar levels.

Age accelerators –
the nasty nine

Now we've analysed the molecular mechanisms of ageing, let's look at the practical ways we can change our everyday lives to limit the damage. Remember, lifestyle changes are the first important step on our *EUDELO staircase* – a step no one committed to maintaining great-looking skin should skip.

I can spontaneously think of no less than nine major lifestyle factors, which can greatly accelerate skin ageing. Think of them as skin-damaging S-factors.

> ### THE 9 SKIN DAMAGING S-FACTORS
>
> 1: Smoking – including e-cigarettes (vaping)
> 2: Sugar – in both foods and drinks
> 3: Starch – a low-fat, high starch diet (especially processed carbs)
> 4: Shots – high alcohol consumption
> 5: Sipping – not drinking enough water throughout the day
> 6: Sun – including UV and infrared light
> 7: Smog – urban pollution
> 8: Stress – chronic stress
> 9: Sleep debt – less than seven to nine hours each night

The good news is that the harm of these skin-ageing hazards can be reduced with lifestyle measures. Here's the plan.

Give up smoking – now!

It's a well-known fact that smoking seriously damages health. It is also incredibly harmful to skin and is one of the major contributing factors to premature skin ageing (Krutmann et al. 2017). The effects of smoking are highly visible and often obvious: not only does it lead to 'lipstick bleed lines' around the mouth (not surprisingly known as 'smoker's lines') but leaves skin overall looking more lined, sallow and dull. Not a good look at all.

We always perform digital facial scans in all our full aesthetic assessments. This measures different parameters of skin quality

– and I have to say that the worst results always seem to be from smokers.

Cigarette smoke contains countless skin-damaging components many of which are similar to urban pollution. And, thanks to their nicotine content, don't believe 'cleaner' electronic cigarettes (e-cigarettes) are completely safe either. Nicotine causes vasoconstriction, a narrowing of blood vessels that can severely limit oxygen and nutrient supply to our skin. A new study showed that e-cigarettes can starve your skin of oxygen as much as tobacco cigarettes (Rau et al. 2017)! Smoking can also increase your risk of certain skin conditions, such as psoriasis (Armstrong et al. 2014).

> Smoking contributes to more rapid, visible skin ageing including lipstick bleed lines around the mouth and a sallow, dull and more wrinkled skin overall.

Adopt a FuturApproved® way of eating

As we've already seen, dietary change is one of the critical parts of a skin-friendly lifestyle adjustment. I have spent a lot of time extensively researching the scientific literature on how to slow ageing at a cellular level and, having devised a comprehensive system based on my research, I began to make lifestyle changes of my own some years back. The difference in the way I both look and feel have been dramatic. My skin glows healthily, I lost weight and I have so much more energy than before. I have since shared this *FuturApproved®* way of eating with countless of my patients and have written in detail about it in my book, *Future Proof Your Skin. Slow down your biological clock by changing the way you eat*. The Daily Mail newspaper ran a full-page feature on it at the time.

> *FuturApproved*® eating helps to maintain optimal health and slow down the ageing process, inside and out.

The basis of my *FuturApproved*® eating plan is not only about keeping your skin looking healthy and beautiful, but also about supporting general health and trying to extend your lifespan by staying youthful within. The fundamental principle is to nurture optimal health. It is also a great eating strategy for those with inflammatory skin conditions such as acne and rosacea.

Eating the *FuturApproved*® way turns the old, outdated food pyramid on its head. Here's how.

• GET YOUR CARBS FROM VEG

Instead of grain-based foods, vegetables form the large base of our new, *FuturApproved*® healthy-eating pyramid. There is a plethora of scientific evidence that supports the benefits of eating lots of fibrous vegetables. High-fibre vegetables are by far the most nutritious form of carbohydrates – you can't have too many of these 'good carbs'. Non-starchy vegetables are not only more nutritious than grain-based carbohydrates, they also won't mess with your blood sugar levels, while still providing you with all the 'cleansing' fibre you need. I like to think of vegetables as 'living carbs', compared to 'dead carbs' from beige, industrial, grain-based foods such as bread. Personally, I avoid all grains and grain-based products, even if whole-grain. So no bread, no pasta, no breakfast cereal etc.

Good dietary habits are also a major determinant of our body's antioxidant status and oxidative stress level. We can raise our internal antioxidant levels significantly by eating antioxidant-rich foods such as vegetables. A higher intake of green and yellow vegetables for example has been linked to decreased skin wrinkling (Nagata et al. 2010). There are also studies, which show that high vegetable consumption is associated with longer telomores and therefore a younger biological age (Marcon et al. 2012, Fossel et al. 2011, Tiainen et al. 2012, Xu et al. 2009). Broccoli, tomatoes, cabbage, kale and sea vegetables have all been named as particularly telomere friendly.

And here is some good news – certain types of antioxidant rich dark chocolate can also provide antioxidant benefits for our skin, as we were able to show in a clinical study (Williams et al. 2009b), so a couple of pieces of high quality dark chocolate are a sensible indulgence in my opinion. But coming back to vegetables…

Eating a wide variety of veg also supports our gut micro-biome – the army of friendly bacteria in our gut. Did you know our gut bacteria outnumber the human cells in our entire body? So we better look after them. The gut microbiome has been referred to as our second genome, as it's so integral to optimum health and longevity. Of course our skin also has its own microbiome, but there are substantial interactions between the gut microbiome and our skin, too (Maguire et al. 2017, Reid et al. 2017).

I recommend *at least* seven portions of fresh (or frozen) vegetables per day, one of which may be fruit. Low-sugar fruit such as berries is ideal. Make sure to fill your plate to a minimum of two thirds or three quarters with vegetables. This is easy if you replace traditional starchy side dishes with vegetable based substitutes – think cauliflower mash, aubergine chips and courgette spaghetti. The wider the variety and the

> Eat your carbs
> in their most
> nutritious form –
> vegetables! Include
> a wide variety and
> always make them
> the largest portion
> on your plate.

more colourful the better, as this will greatly enhance the diversity of your gut microbiome – so eat the rainbow! And yes … life without sandwiches is perfectly possible – I have done it for years.

Adding herbs and spices to your vegetables not only enhances flavour but health benefits, too. Certain spices such as turmeric have strong antioxidant and anti-inflammatory benefits and many herbs nourish your gut microbiome.

• DON'T BE FOOLED BY THE FAT MYTH

Over the past 30 years, we've all been brainwashed into thinking of fat as the enemy. Yet our body and skin need fat to thrive. Lipids form the main component of every single cell membrane, helping to maintain cell structure and function. A low-fat diet is therefore not supportive to general health and will also encourage your skin to age prematurely. Just say no to low-fat diets!

But we want 'good fats' – NOT processed vegetable oils. My extensive research of the scientific literature leads me to sternly advise against consumption of omega-6 rich processed oils, such as polyunsaturated vegetable and seed oils including sunflower, safflower, rapeseed, grapeseed, cottonseed, canola, corn and soya oils. This may sound controversial, but in my opinion, the highly-praised vegetable and seed oils are one of the worst types of fat you could punish your body with. They are chemically altered, highly processed and inherently unstable – so liberate yourself from the brainwashing.

Another reason for avoiding omega-6 rich polyunsaturated oils is that our diet is already heavily omega-6 dominant. Ideally, we want to aim for an omega-6/omega 3 ratio of 1:1 (2:1 at a push), but in our typical Western diet, 15:1 is more the norm. I don't want to imply that omega-6 fatty acids are all bad, but they must balance with omaga-3 to avoid turning potentially pro-inflammatory. If you are interested in more details (with lots of scientific references!), check out my book *Future Proof Your Skin. Slow down your biological clock by changing the way you eat.*

There is only one type of fat that's worse – and that's trans fat, which, incidentally, is often derived from polyunsaturated fats. As it's well known now that trans fats are nutritional hell, food manufacturers often substitute them with 'interesterified' fats. Sadly, the unnatural, highly industrialised process of interesterifying fat molecules raises similar health concerns to trans fats

> Avoid processed omega-6 rich polyunsaturated vegetable oils as they are inherently unstable and may be pro-inflammatory.

and I'm convinced that science will eventually confirm that they may actually be no better. Studies already show that interesterified fat raises both blood glucose levels and the ratio of bad to good cholesterol (Sundram et al. 2007). So make sure you avoid not only trans fats, hydrogenated and partially hydrogenated fat, but also the interesterified types common in today's processed foods. This also includes margarines (hydrogenation turns fluid oils into spreadable form) - organic butter is much better in my opinion.

Omega-3 fatty acids such as eicosapentaenoic acid (EPA) and docosahexanoic acid (DHA) on the other hand are highly beneficial to our general health and skin. Anti-inflammatory and antioxidant, they have also been shown to help protect telomere length. EPA and DHA can be found in oily fish, krill and certain marine algae. Both EPA and DHA are much more bioavailable than the alpha-linolenic acid (ALA) form of omega-3 we get from plants such as flaxseed. A study showed that regular consumption of fish might even be protective against melanoma skin cancer (Fortes et al. 2008).

However, we should remember that omega-3 fatty acids are naturally unstable due to their 'super-unsaturated' chemical structure. They need to be treated with utmost care – EPA and DHA capsules often turn rancid before you even take them, so my recommendation is to try and get most of your omega-3 fatty acids from natural food such as oily fish rather than processed capsules.

Monounsaturated fats such as olive, avocado and macadamia nut oils are also highly recommended, especially for dressing cold dishes.

Saturated fats are fine too in my professional opinion, so long as your gut is healthy, but good quality is key. The latest meta-analyses (the highest grade of scientific evidence!) confirm that a connection between saturated fat and heart disease is unlikely after all (de Souza et al. 2015, Hamley 2017, Siri-Tarino et al. 2010) – the original scaremongering studies were flawed in many ways, if you look into it. So I much prefer high quality saturated fats to chemically processed, omega-6 rich, polyunsaturated vegetable oils. As well as being vital for optimal hormone production, saturated fats are highly stable when heated and so make a good choice for cooking.

Good saturated fats include organic extra-virgin coconut oil, organic butter or ghee and animal fat from organic pasture-fed stock. Apart from coconut oil, goose and duck fats are two of my favourites as they contain a mix of saturated and monounsaturated fats – and of course, taste amazing.

So, here's the bottom line. Chuck out all your vegetable and seed oils as the historic recommendation to substitute them in place of saturated fats seems to me and my critical-thinking colleagues, to be based on flawed science. If you're interested enough to find out more, Tina Teicholz' *The Big Fat Surprise* is an excellent read.

So what are the benefits of eating good fats for our skin? There are many, but studies confirm that higher intakes of total fat – monounsaturated and saturated – are associated with increased skin elasticity (Nagata et al. 2010). Eating more saturated fat is also associated with a lower wrinkling score according to this study (Nagata et al. 2010).

There's another good reason to avoid falling into the low-fat trap. When the food industry creates a low-fat food product, the fat removed must be replaced with something and in the vast majority of cases, refined carbohydrates are added. Many supposedly 'healthy' low-fat products are in fact, stuffed with processed carbohydrates which spike blood sugar and insulin levels, increase glycation and oxidative stress and contribute to chronic inflammation. All of this adversely affects skin health, whereas healthy fats support optimal skin function.

> Don't fall into the fat trap! A low-fat diet ages your skin prematurely and is not supportive of good health. Include good fats in your daily diet, such as coconut oil, olive oil, avocados, nuts and oily fish. High quality saturated fats are a good option for cooking.

• EAT COMPLETE PROTEIN

Protein provides amino acids, crucial building blocks for muscle, hair, skin and connective tissue. Some amino acids are 'essential' – the body can't produce them by itself – and we need to ensure our supply by eating sources of complete protein. As our body has little capacity to store protein, we should feed it sufficient amounts on a daily basis.

The best sources of *complete* protein are fish, meat and eggs. It's beyond the scope of this book to explain why, from a medical perspective, a vegan diet isn't ideal for human health, but I understand that there might be other reasons, such as ethical motives, to choose a vegan diet. Should you wish to find out more, I can recommend Liz Wolfe's very well referenced book, *Eat the Yolks*.

> For optimal skin health, I recommend eating *complete* protein daily. Great sources are organic meat, wild fish and pastured eggs.

Fish of course, is highly beneficial not only for its protein quota, but because of its anti-inflammatory omega-3 fatty acids, too. High quality, unprocessed, pastured, organic meat is also a great source of skin-friendly complete protein. To get all the benefits try to eat more of 'the whole animal', not just muscle meat. What I mean is don't leave out the organ meat – such as liver and kidneys – and make collagen-rich broth from the bones. Much more than super-trending quinoa, eggs are on my 'super food' list, too. Don't even think about leaving the yolk – some of the best nutrients such as choline, which also supports optimal collagen and elastin formation, are in there. And remember – we left the low-fat diet con behind us!

Whereas we should feed our body daily protein, we shouldn't

overdo it in exchange for vegetables. In my diet book, I go into much more detail about exactly how much protein to eat, but a good rule of thumb is to fill your plate with three quarters of vegetables and one quarter with a mix of protein and good fat. That will supply your body with sufficient protein without going overboard.

Make sure you choose the highest quality protein, which means wild fish (not farmed, even if it's organic), organic pasture-fed animal meat and free-range eggs from foraging hens. Organically produced, pastured meat contains fewer undesirable 'additives' such as antibiotics and hormones and has a better nutrient profile, for example a more beneficial omega 3/6 fatty acid ratio (Kamihiro at al. 2015).

• MONITOR YOUR HYDRATION

Amazingly, given the volume of advice we read, there's no scientific proof of the exact amount of water we need each day (Valtin 2002). We do know there are many health benefits that come with drinking plenty of water – not least for your skin. A clinical study we did some years ago confirmed that drinking habits can have a significant impact on skin physiology and that the exact effects within the skin differ depending on the nature of the water ingested (Williams et al. 2007). Skin is largely made up of water and proper hydration is an important element in skin health as well as cell function throughout the body, so it's vital to stay well hydrated.

However, don't obsess over the 8-glass rule. The exact amount of water you need depends on various factors, including your activity level and the season and climate. (Imagine the difference in volume you'd need if you lived in Africa, compared to chilly Northern Europe). You'll also absorb significant amounts of water from food, such as fluid-rich vegetables – especially if you're following the *FuturApproved®* way of eating. And this is a great type of water – you could call it 'living water', compared to the plain old stuff from the tap.

Much as water benefits skin, the idea that increasing your intake is a 'cure' for dry skin is a myth as the ability of your skin to hold water depends primarily on the barrier function of the horny layer. Yes, skin is largely made up of water – our body is composed of 70% in total, 20% of which is located in the skin. Of that 20%, the water content of the living epidermis is 70% compared to 15-30% in the stratum corneum (Guzman-Alonso et al. 2016). We know that when the water content of this horny layer falls below 10-15%, our skin feels dry and can even look more wrinkled. However, dry skin is usually caused by a damaged skin barrier allowing too much moisture to evaporate from the epidermis. Drink as much water as you like, but unless you fix this moisture loss by improving your skin's barrier function, your skin will still feel dry.

With regards to *what* to drink, you won't be surprised to hear that filtered water's better than plain tap. Personally, I distil my water at home to remove gut flora-disruptive chloride completely along with possible fluoride and other contaminants. Anti-oxidant rich green, white and herbal teas are also great choices. Avoid excessive coffee consumption, as caffeine can bring up the level of your stress hormone cortisol, but an occasional coffee is a sensible indulgence in my opinion (one of my personal favourites is a café latte with unsweetened almond milk).

Avoid fizzy drinks, colas and sodas whether sugary

or low calorie/diet versions. Artificial sweeteners such as aspartame, suclalose and cyclamate are highly chemically processed substances that have been connected to a variety of health issues. Also steer clear of fruit juices and commercial smoothies, as these are glorified sugar waters. Homemade organic vegetable smoothies are fine, so long as you include very little fruit, if any!

Excessive alcohol can also impact the ageing process negatively. As well as causing dehydration, oxidative stress and immune dysfunction, too much alcohol can also disturb your gut flora and contribute to wrinkles and accelerated ageing (Boule et al. 2017, Nielsen et al. 1997). In my opinion a moderate amount, such as the occasional glass of resveratrol-containing red wine, is a sensible treat. But binge-drinking and routine imbibing should certainly be avoided. Alcoholic drinks often also contain a lot of sugar, which as we know, has a negative impact on skin and overall health.

> Drink plenty of filtered water and herbal teas throughout the day. Antioxidant green and white tea is also very skin-friendly. Avoid fruit juices and commercial smoothies – they're just glorified sugar water.

• FOLLOW THE WRAPPER RULE

Having discussed what's good to eat more of and what's best to eat less of, I'll finish with arguably *the* most important principle - say no to industrially processed and refined food! As a rule of thumb, if it comes in a wrapper or is pre-packed, think again.

Most pre-packed, processed food in supermarkets contains a plethora of unwelcome ingredients such as sugar, soy

> Eating whole, unprocessed food is one of the most important dietary changes you can make for the health of your skin.

protein, processed starches and/or unstable polyunsaturated oils. Opting for natural, unprocessed whole foods puts you in control of your diet. By simply sticking to natural whole foods and cutting out anything manipulated by the manufacturer, you will have automatically adopted the single most important dietary change recommended to future proof your skin. So always ask yourself, "am I eating real food or fake food?" But remember – natural sugar is still sugar!

• SUCCESSFUL AGEING ROCKET FUEL

I'm also very keen on intermittent fasting to support skin health and longevity, as it promotes healthy autophagy (a vital cellular process that helps tidy up and recycle faulty cell components) and various other cellular functions (Mattson et al. 2016). Scientific studies have shown that intermittent fasting can improve insulin sensitivity and blood sugar control, decrease oxidative stress and improve immune function (Azevedo et al. 2013, Cheng et al. 2014). A study even demonstrated that promoting autophagy has the potential to extend lifespan by as much as 50% (Vellai 2009).

> Intermittent fasting is rocket fuel for successful ageing and long-term skin wellbeing.

Intermittent fasting involves 16-24 hours of drinking water and herbal tea only – no food. Don't worry, once your metabolism has adapted to the *FuturApproved*® way of eating, it's easy to do and I recommend fasting once or twice a week for health reasons.

If you don't want to fast that long, make sure you naturally fast for at least 12 hours each night to allow your body to go into full regeneration mode. This means you shouldn't eat anything for a full 12 hours between dinner and breakfast (that also includes drinks, apart from water!) and your last meal should be at least three hours before bedtime.

THE DELICIOUS DOZEN

FuturApproved® food rules for skin wellbeing and longevity:

1: **Eat heaps of fibrous, non-starchy vegetables.** Add herbs and spices for flavour and health.

2: **Say no to low-fat diets!** Include plenty of healthy fats, such as olive and coconut oils, avocados, oily fish and nuts. High quality saturated fats in moderation are fine, too. Avoid polyunsaturated, omega-6 rich vegetable and seed oils.

3: **Eat high quality, non-processed protein daily** – wild fish, organic pasture raised meat and eggs are all good options of complete protein.

4: **Eat moderate amounts of low-sugar fruit** such as berries.

5: **Include moderate amounts of root vegetables** – sweet potatoes are great, but limit white potatoes.

6: **Reduce or avoid grain-based foods** – bread, pasta, biscuits, cakes and breakfast cereals, as well as rice should be limited. Instead, opt to eat carbohydrates in their most nutritious form – vegetables!

7: **Reduce or avoid or drinking sugar and artificial sweeteners**. No flavoured fizzy drinks, colas and sodas, both full-sugar and low-cal / diet versions.

8: **Drink plenty of filtered water** and white, green and herbal teas.

9: **Avoid fruit juices,** dried fruit and commercial smoothies, as they are high in sugar. Make your own pure organic vegetable smoothies instead.

10: **Limit alcohol intake**. An occasional glass of red wine is a good choice.

11: **You may eat moderate amounts of fermented A2 dairy products, but go for full-fat versions** – e.g. organic, full-fat, live sheep or goat yoghurt, kefir and cheese. Swap soy and dairy milk for nut milk such as unsweetened almond, coconut or hazelnut milk.

12: **Most importantly – stick to whole foods** as nature intended. Shun all 'fake' processed foods – skin's archenemies.

Never forget that the current Western low-fat obsession with its over-reliance on starchy, grain-based and sugary foods won't do your skin any favours. Neither will replacing saturated fat with supposedly 'healthier' vegetable oils. With the *FuturApproved*® way of eating, we're able to reduce oxidative stress, inflammation, glycation and telomere shortening while encouraging a more youth-promoting hormonal balance.

Dodge excess Sun damage is by far one of the biggest
sun exposure causes of premature skin ageing – not
much else ages your skin so rapidly and
visibly (Krutman et al. 2017). Mottled
pigmentation caused by chronic sun damage is a major skin
concern we see in our clinic every day. Even more importantly,
excessive sun exposure increases the risk of skin cancer.

If you want to keep your skin looking youthfully beautiful,
there's no way round wearing a broad-spectrum, high SPF sun
protection moisturiser every single day, year-round – and I'll
come back to that, later. But preventing premature skin ageing
doesn't end with SPFs. You need to change your approach and
actively practice sun avoidance to keep your skin in best shape.

You see, sun damage is a cumulative process. Right from
childhood, our skin clocks up all those hours of sun exposure.
No, skin does not forget. What are the most dangerous rays
in the sun spectrum? Very simply put, UVA rays cause our
skin to age prematurely; while UVB rays are the ones that
cause sunburn. Remember the maxim: 'A is for ageing, B is for
burning'. However, both these rays are involved in skin cancer
generation, too.

UVA rays penetrate deeper
into the skin than UVB and
can even penetrate windows
and clouds, so don't think you
are safe behind glass or on a
hazy day. There's yet another
type of irradiation emitted by
the sun that also contributes
to premature skin ageing –
infrared-A irradiation (IRA),

Excessive sun exposure
is one of the single most
damaging ways to age your
skin prematurely. If you
really want to preserve your
skin's long-term health
and beauty, there is no way
round sun avoidance and
sun protection.

which is the sun's intense heat (Krutman et al. 2017). IRA penetrates even deeper into our skin than UVA and no sun protection filter is able to shield our skin from the damage it causes. Once again, this is where sun-avoidance comes in, along with topical application of antioxidants, which I'll tell you about later.

UVA levels fluctuate less than UVB throughout the seasons and the course of the day – you will be exposed to significant amounts of UVA even early in the morning and in winter.

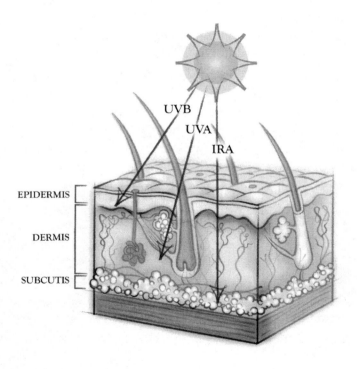

Fig. 16: Ultraviolet A and B (UVA / UVB) and infrared-A (IRA) irradiation penetration depths into the skin.

And, unlike for UVB rays, there are no acute warning signs such as sunburn, that you have over-exposed your skin. UVA causes silent damage, which remains invisible until many years later. This is why it's important to wear sun protection all year round, every single day.

WHAT'S ALL THIS ABOUT VITAMIN D?

There's been a lot in the press about vitamin D deficiency and how extreme sun protection may encourage it. The sun stimulates our skin to synthesise vitamin D naturally and good vitamin D levels are important for both physical and psychological health. So should we risk our wellbeing to save our skin? My best advice is to have a blood test to check your vitamin D level. A simple over-the-counter vitamin D3 supplement can remedy any deficiency while you don't have to compromise on sun protection for your skin's health and beauty.

Make anti-pollution measures

We know only too well the damage sun can do, but what about other environmental factors? In my opinion, until recently pollution has been vastly underestimated as an environmental aggressor. It can severely impact on health, causing a wide range of problems from decreased life expectancy to premature skin ageing and irregular pigmentation (Correia et al. 2013, Dziubanek et al. 2017, Puri et al. 2017, Vierkötter et al. 2010). Pollution's most significant mechanisms of action include generating free radicals, depleting antioxidant defences and inflammation (Magnani et al. 2016). Pollution has even been linked to an increased risk of skin diseases such as eczema, rashes, hives and infectious skin diseases (Kim et al. 2016).

The skin is the body's first line of defence and it is under increasing stress on a daily basis as a result of exposure to hazardous free radicals from urban pollution. And, as global environmental pollutants reach unprecedented levels, the potential for skin damage escalates. The UK is one of five countries repeatedly breaking the European commission's pollution targets and London, Glasgow, Birmingham and Leeds are among 16 UK areas where European air quality thresholds are repeatedly being breached. In January 2017 London had breached its legal pollution limits for the *entire year* in just five days! In fact, London has broken its pollution limits for six years in a row, and remains the worst offender in Europe, which is really bad news for our skin.

Pollutants fall into different categories, most of which increase oxidative stress in our skin. Urban pollution and sun exposure work in synergy to overwhelm skin's internal defences, triggering a cascade of damage deep within skin, which causes a wide range of deleterious effects.

> Pollution works hand in hand with sun exposure to overwhelm our skin's defences, accelerate skin ageing and increase the risk of skin health issues.

Ideally, we should reduce our skin's exposure to air pollution as much as possible. Practically though, that's not always possible, making it even more important to remove pollution residues from skin meticulously each evening - don't even think about going to bed without cleansing! Unfortunately, manual cleansing has been found to be inefficient at removing pollutants from skin fully: pollutants can be very sticky and are even able to enter our pores. So whenever your skin has undergone high levels of exposure (after a day in the city, say) you may wish to use an electronic facial cleansing brush in the evening. Some brands such as Clarisonic and Philips have conducted impressive scientific studies to prove they remove pollutants more efficiently than manual cleansing alone. There is also an electronic cleansing brush by Philips that has a built-in anti-pollution charcoal sponge in the centre to help trap pollution chemicals. For an even deeper cleanse and protection, some clinics like EUDELO offer *dermatology grade anti-pollution facials* that use high-tech suction cleansing devices coupled with infusion of antioxidant serums. Daily application of high grade antioxidants at home will also help to protect your skin from the harmful effects of urban pollution.

Combat stress Stress is a combination of physiological reactions that respond to certain stimuli, whether external or internal. For our primal ancestors, a short, sharp burst of stress hormone release triggered the impetus to escape danger – the famous 'fight or flight' reaction.

The release of stress hormones enables the body to become super-alert: blood sugar levels surge to provide instant energy, heart and breathing rates accelerate, blood pressure rises, pain sensation is reduced and blood clotting increases ahead of potential wounding. At the same time, parasympathetic functions such as digestion and libido are dialled down as they're not needed right now. (Priorities, guys…). So overall, you have perfectly orchestrated physical conditions for standing your ground or legging it, fast.

In a natural world, intense physical activity such as fighting or fleeing would burn off the sugar energy provided and all other changes would quickly revert to normal, no harm done. But in our modern society, we're exposed to a fairly constant, albeit mostly low level of stress for which there is usually no physical outlet.

This chronic low-level stress has worse long-term consequences than occasional stronger, but shorter bursts. Chronic stress will age our skin prematurely and can even shorten our life (Epel et al. 2014, Romana-Souza et al. 2015). One way it does this is by elevating the level of cortisol – our major stress hormone, also gruesomely known as the 'death hormone'.

We need to raise awareness of the influence of stress on skin ageing and general health and longevity. Of course, no one is immune to everyday life and stress levels are par for the course. But here are some tips that can help lower our stress hormone levels.

THE BIG 7 STRESS BUSTERS

1: **Move freely.** When you're stressed, one of the best things you can do is move. Your body's biological stress response prepares you for a *physical* reaction, so give it what it needs. Even if it's running up and down the stairs or walking around for a while, get up from the computer, get out of the car. If you can't leave that meeting, at least clench your buttocks! Moving greatly helps to neutralise the high-alert stress state and coax metabolic changes back into balance.

2: **Breathe easy.** Consciously breathing more slowly and deeply is such an easy, yet effective technique to lower stress hormone levels instantly. Breathing all the way into your stomach activates your parasympathetic nervous system – the antidote to the sympathetic nervous system-mediated stress response. Our slow, deep breathing is essentially tricking our body into thinking we must be relaxed - our body can't help but oblige by dialling down our stress hormone levels.

3: **Control snack-attacks.** Don't reach for sugary snacks or quick-release starchy foods when you're stressed, as they'll elevate out-of-control glucose and insulin levels even more. Ditto stimulants such as coffee or energy drinks, which contribute to cortisol-release. If you're really peckish, have a handful of nuts instead.

4: **Stay positive.** Nurturing a mostly positive outlook not only makes life more enjoyable, but may also have anti-ageing benefits. A study involving nearly 1,000 participants revealed that optimistic people have higher levels of certain antioxidants in their blood (Boehm et al. 2013). Optimism is also linked to physical health (Rasmussen et al. 2009).

5: **Practise power-posturing.** It's been shown that open 'power postures' can actively help combat stress pretty much instantaneously. Think leaning back in your chair, elbows behind your head or standing upright, feet apart and hands on hips (channel Wonder Woman!). A study conducted by a team of psychologists found that just two minutes' power-posturing can significantly lower cortisol levels in the body (Carney at al. 2010).

6: **Keep smiling.** Laughing or smiling can partly override our body's stress response – even if we don't really mean it. By engaging those smile muscles, we're essentially tricking our brain into thinking we must be happy and relaxed, so our body switches off its stress signals. Similarly, studies confirm that treatments with BTX ('botox') can improve depression (Finzi et al. 2014, Magid et al. 2014) – bio-feedback by preventing frowning!

7: **Meditate more.** It's a tested and proven method of stress reduction that has been successfully employed by many different cultures through the ages. And don't feel it has to be 20 minutes or so of deep meditation - even a couple of minutes of simple mindfulness can make a difference. Studies confirm that mindfulness and meditation can lower cortisol levels (Brand et al. 2012, Fan et al. 2014). In one particular study, it was shown that daily meditation even induces telomerase, the enzyme that *lengthens* our telomeres (Hoge et al. 2013)! If you are a beginner, I recommend the '10% Happier' App to get started.

Get a great
night's sleep
Sleep deprivation has become a hallmark of modern Western society. Over the past five decades, our average sleep duration has decreased very significantly, mainly thanks to 'voluntary bedtime curtailment.' Are you perhaps trying to cut down on shut-eye, simply to fit more time into the day? Trust me – for your skin's sake, don't.

Good quality, restorative sleep is crucial for cellular repair and skin regeneration. Sleep deprivation on the other hand, is known to contribute to systemic inflammation and accelerated age-related processes as well as chronic health problems (Faraut et al. 2012, Nedeltcheva et al. 2014).

At night, we naturally release the sleep hormone melatonin. Levels start to rise in the evening and peak around midnight before slowly subsiding again and lack of sleep will mean our melatonin levels are impaired. Melatonin is a strong antioxidant that has even been shown to be able to help protect skin from the sun's damaging effects. Unfortunately, like so many other skin-friendly hormones, melatonin levels decline with age and sleep debt will hasten the fall off. Good sleep is also important for the nightly peak of our anti-ageing human growth hormone (HGH). If we don't get enough sleep, our natural HGH level is sub-optimal – and this also gets worse as we get older.

Yet another dangerous effect of sleep deprivation is impaired insulin sensitivity and glucose tolerance, which means increased generation of Advanced Glycation End Products (AGEs) known to accelerate the skin's ageing process. Several studies now also confirm that lack of sleep bolted onto other types of stress can impair skin integrity (Kahan et al. 2010). An animal study in wound healing (which is a good model for skin rejuvenation) found that sleep deprivation leads to a reduced number of skin fibroblasts, our collagen-producing cells (Gümüstekín et al. 2004). Sleep is even linked to telomere length and gene expression. In a fascinating genomic study, it was shown that sleep debt of only two nights led to a change in the expression of 500 genes – changes that were notably related to DNA damage and repair as well as stress responses (Pellegrino et al. 2012).

Lastly, a paper published in 2015 clearly links good quality sleep to both better skin and the ability to bounce back from stress. What the researchers found was that poor sleepers had significantly higher scores for internal skin ageing than good sleepers who slept for seven to nine hours each night (Oyetakin-White et al. 2015). Poor sleep quality was also found to be associated with an impaired barrier function of the skin and an overall lower satisfaction with one's appearance (Oyetakin-White et al. 2015).

> Sleep debt plus chronic stress will age your skin prematurely. Make stress moderation and sufficient good quality sleep a firm priority in your life.

•

SKINCARE – A TOPICAL ISSUE

The next step up on the *EUDELO staircase* is good quality skincare. I genuinely believe that a superior daily skincare regime is one of the best investments you can make in your skin's future. Including preventative and/or corrective skincare into your routine really can work wonders for your overall skin quality and texture, while improving elasticity, irregular pigmentation and fine lines. A study confirmed that one of the factors significantly associated with looking younger than one's age included more frequent use of skincare products such as cleanser, moisturiser and night cream (Mayes et al. 2010).

As I'm writing this, I'm thinking of the nurse I chatted to just a few minutes ago, who proudly told me she's using the cheapest moisturiser going – and nothing else. She wants to put the money she's saving on skincare towards a surgical facelift she's considering at some point in the future. This is just about the daftest interpretation of 'rainy day' money I've ever heard…

Good skincare has an entirely different function to a facelift. You simply can't replace one with the other. A facelift will stretch and lift the skin, making it *look* less wrinkly and saggy. But it will do nothing to improve your skin quality, texture and surface. Remember the *EUDELO 3-Key Principle?* Skin quality and health is one of those vital three keys and we ignore it at our skin's peril.

Great skin quality is integral to great looks and presenting the best version of yourself. Imagine a woman in her 50s, whose skin is glowing healthily and evenly – visible pores, irregular pigmentation and signs of dullness and tiredness all enviably absent. That woman will very likely look attractive for her age, even though her facial skin might not be as tight as her friend's after a facelift. Now imagine this 50-year-old friend whose skin is perfectly tight, but covered in brown spots and looking dull and tired. Large pores, crêpiness and leathery skin texture are all in evidence. Now, who do you think looks more attractive? You don't even have to answer that question…

The woman with better skin quality and texture will also

appear healthier. This is a science-proven, snap judgement that we're hard-wired to make. Remember the studies that confirmed that when people are shown just a small square of the skin surface, the ones with more even skin pigmentation are judged not only as younger, but more attractive *and* healthier too (Fink et al. 2012a, Matts et al. 2007).

The other reason why that nurse was talking nonsense is that good quality skincare can go a long way to delay – or even cancel out – the need for a surgical facelift. And even if you do have a facelift, healthy skin in good condition will heal much better after the surgery. Sometimes surgical colleagues send patients to me to get their skin quality improved prior to the knife to optimise healing and lower surgical risks. These guys quite rightly won't operate on anyone with really poor quality skin – that would be asking for trouble.

I'm really not against facelifts – far from it. But they have to be placed in proper context. You see corrective procedures right at the very top of the *EUDELO staircase* and surgery certainly fall into this corrective category. As it is, the *EUDELO staircase* is a non-surgical model, but were I to include surgical facelifts, they would only appear as a final step *after* non-surgical corrective procedures.

The bottom line then, is that good skincare is non-negotiable. The great news is that there have been some spectacular advances in skincare over the past few years. There are now highly effective products on the market, catering for every skin type. What we have at our disposal today is so much more sophisticated compared to only a few years ago.

Amazingly, even many specialist dermatologists aren't aware of this game change. They still firmly believe that prescription creams such as *wunderkind* tretinoin are the only ones that actually work, and all over-the-counter skincare is essentially a scam. Mistake! Now, don't get me wrong – I love tretinoin, it's marvellous. But there are now so many well-designed scientific studies confirming that over-the-counter skincare can be effective for stimulating collagen and inhibiting pigmentation, for example (Mehta-Ambalal 2016). I will talk about some of those later.

A little while ago, I gave a talk on skincare to an audience of dermatologists. Everything I presented was totally factual. Yet to my utter surprise, I was virtually lynched on stage. Many of those dermatologists were furious that I, one of their number, was giving credence to skincare. One rather emotional colleague blurted, "But you're a *doctor* – how can you advise about skincare?" I replied as calmly as I could, that because I am a qualified dermatologist and an expert in skin biology, my evidence-based advice is vastly safer and more effective than sales and marketing hype. "Do you actually believe it's better if our patients get their skincare advice from a sales assistant at the department store's beauty counter?" I asked them.

As a dermatologist, neglecting to discuss a patient's skincare is tantamount to an endocrinologist who ignores the influence of a diabetes patient's diet in my opinion. I'm astounded by the evident aversion to acknowledge skincare that many traditional

> Effective daily skincare is non-negotiable and crucial to slow down the skin's ageing process at a cellular level. A good skincare regime should include twice-daily cleansing, a high-grade antioxidant serum and SPF30-50 in the morning, plus a matrix stimulator such as vitamin A at night.

dermatologists express, especially given that they are so very well aware of the importance of emollients to conditions such as eczema and psoriasis. Many of my colleagues don't even speak about skincare with their acne patients, although using the wrong skincare can easily jeopardise their prescription treatment.

Funnily enough, one highly esteemed colleague quietly came to find me after my lecture and asked, "So you're saying there are actual studies looking at collagen production with skincare?" Hmm. I think there's quite a bit of educational work needed among dermatologists as a whole, although I can already see that the younger generation is far more open to the role of skincare.

Of course, not all skincare on the market is great. And in the increasingly heaving skincare jungle, it's now virtually impossible for laypeople to distinguish between a truly effective product and slick, yet misleading marketing. There are countless jars of stuff of all prices on beauty counters and the shelves of skin boutiques, that have zero scientific evidence behind them, yet nevertheless have persuasive marketing material to back them. You really do need an expert to design a good skincare regime for you.

As it's difficult to navigate your way through the skincare jungle and not everyone's able to book a personal consultation with one of the EUDELO experts in clinic, I'm curating a range of superior skincare on our website, EudeloBoutique.com. Here, you can also book a complimentary Skype consultation with one of our skincare experts, if you're unsure what to use. However, I'll give you some guiding principles on how to put together your own, effective skincare regime over the following pages.

Cosmetics versus Cosmeceuticals

These are the two main tribes of over-the-counter skincare products. The FDA's Federal Food, Drug & Cosmetic Act defines cosmetics as "articles intended to be rubbed, poured, sprinkled or sprayed on, introduced into, or otherwise applied to the human body ... for cleansing, beautifying, promoting attractiveness, or altering the appearance". Included in this definition are skincare products such as cleansers, shampoos, make-up and moisturisers. Products such as traditional hydrating moisturisers work superficially in the skin and as such are freely available in drug stores and high street department stores and are designed to be used at home without the supervision of any kind of skin specialist. They are not supposed to contain any ingredient that can change the skin's fundamental structure, function or biology – and this makes sense to some extent. Since their use is unsupervised, manufacturers want to reduce the risk of possible complications such as irritation, with the result that high street cosmetics are often quite bland, in my opinion.

A cosmeceutical product is a non-prescription formula containing more biologically active ingredients that have benefits beyond traditional moisturisers, such as the ability to influence changes in collagen metabolism and reduce wrinkles. The term 'cosmeceutical' is a fusion of 'cosmetic' and 'pharmaceutical' coined sometime in the 1980s and highlights the increasingly blurred boundaries between cosmetics and medicated creams in today's cosmetic science. Like cosmetics, cosmeceuticals are *officially* meant to act in the skin's upper layer (epidermis) only. Any topical application, which penetrates deeper into the skin and therefore has access to the bloodstream, is supposed to be classified as a prescription cream. However, this is a bit of a grey area, as we do know from clinical studies that good cosmeceutical skincare certainly has the potential for deeper benefits than purely epidermal effects – which is a good thing, if you really want to slow down premature ageing. There are, for example, studies that clearly show over-the-counter skincare containing retinol can indeed induce collagen production in the dermis and have significant clinical benefits (Babcock et al. 2015, Bouloc et al. 2015, Ho et al. 2012, Kong et al. 2016, Randhawa et al. 2015a, Sorg et al. 2014).

It is also useful to know that although the distinction between cosmetics and cosmeceuticals is legally recognised by other countries, that difference doesn't officially exist as yet according to UK and EU legislation.

So what works best?

Women – and increasingly men, too – are bombarded constantly by TV and magazine adverts selling the promise of 'youth in a jar.' They may use all the latest buzzwords – 'growth factors', 'peptides', 'antioxidants' and 'retinoids'. But to be honest, most of what you can buy in the high street contains nowhere near the right combination and concentration of stable, active ingredients and delivery systems to actually change the skin. Promises, promises...

Not surprisingly, a lot of confusion hovers over skincare: countless women end up wasting hundreds, if not thousands of pounds on moisturisers, serums and eye creams which simply do not work. If you want real anti-ageing benefits, such as increased collagen synthesis in the dermis, you need something stronger and more active – either a cosmeceutical or prescription product. You also need to use it under the guidance of an expert such as a cosmetic dermatologist with a specialist knowledge of cosmeceutical brands and prescription anti-ageing ingredients.

And a word about serums. I'm often asked, "which one's better, a serum or a cream?" To me, the question isn't relevant. Whether the product's defined as a serum or cream only indicates its base formulation. It says nothing about the actual active ingredients – and good actives come in various formats.

> Cosmeceuticals offer results-driven skincare and are best recommended by an expert. Get your cosmetic dermatologist to suggest a daily regime for you.

What matters most is the choice and combination of active ingredients in the right concentration *and* formulation – and this is what separates results-driven cosmeceuticals from many high street cosmetic brands. Then of course come the prescription-strength treatment formulas, which are regarded as the gold standards in their field. Here are some of the most beneficial ingredients for your skin.

The most active,
active ingredients

The list below is by no means complete, but these are among my favourite ingredients, in alphabetical order, that I regularly advise patients to use at home. Many of them I use myself too, as I rate them highly. Those that are prescription-only are marked Rx and over-the-counter ingredients, OTC. Before we then move up to the next step on the *EUDELO staircase*, I will give you a full example skincare regime.

• **Adapalene** (Differin®), Rx

This newer prescription retinoid is a synthetic vitamin A derivative, which is licensed for the treatment of acne. It also has added benefits in boosting collagen production and improving sun damage and premature skin ageing (Herane et al. 2012). In the UK, we have a cream (which I prefer for anti-ageing) and a gel (only suitable for very oily acne skin).

Since gold standard tretinoin cream (see below) without an added antibiotic is now difficult to source in the UK, many practitioners have begun prescribing adapalene instead. However, the scientific evidence for its effectiveness on sun damage and anti-ageing isn't yet as strong as for tretinoin. And, like tretinoin, it's contraindicated in pregnancy as it could damage the unborn child.

• **Alpha hydroxy acids** (AHAs), OTC

The Ancient Egyptians used AHAs – Cleopatra's asses' milk bath contained one of them, natural lactic acid. Now cosmeceutical staples, AHAs are fruit acids that soften and remove dead skin cells to exfoliate skin, leaving it smoother. They are well known to speed up cell turnover and skin renewal. However, what many people don't know is that they can even increase production of collagen and water-binding glycosaminoglycans (GAGs), and improve elastin fibre quality (Bernstein et al. 2001, Ditre et al 1996).

AHAs such as glycolic acid have the potential to irritate the skin if too much is used too quickly, so should be introduced gradually. Stronger concentrations of AHAs can be used to treat mild acne – they are particularly good for non-inflamed acne lesions such as blackheads and whiteheads (comedones).

AHAs are of course also a very popular ingredient in chemical peels.

• Antioxidants, OTC

These scavenge or neutralise free radicals, which is why they're such a key ingredient in skincare. Free radical generation with oxidative stress is a prime mechanism of skin ageing. Excess free radicals are triggered after sun and pollution exposure, but cell metabolism also generates free radicals every second of every day. This is why a high-grade antioxidant product is an absolute must in everyone's skincare regime.

The market is teeming with synthetic and botanic anti-oxidants, including vitamin C, vitamin E, phloretin, ferulic acid, resveratrol, ergothionine, flavonoid extracts and numerous others (Farris et al. 2005 & 2014, Humbert et al. 2003, Lin et al. 2005, Oresajo et al. 2008). A combination of synergistic antioxidants such as hydrophilic vitamin C and lipophilic vitamin E works best to protect different parts of the cell.

I usually recommend applying an antioxidant serum straight after cleansing each morning, underneath and as a backup to your sun protection.

• Arbutin, OTC

This hydroquinone derivative is a gentle lightening agent that targets irregular pigmentation (Zhu et al. 2008). It inhibits tyrosinase, the key enzyme of melanin pigment formation. I recommend to use any anti-pigment ingredient in combination with antioxidants and broad-spectrum, SPF30-50 sun protection. And most importantly – practise sun *avoidance*, as you can undo months of anti-pigment treatment in a single day of excess sun!

• **Azelaic acid**, OTC / Rx

Available over-the counter in lower concentration, this is another anti-pigment ingredient. It's also available at higher concentrations of 15% and 20% as a prescription product for rosacea and acne respectively. For that reason, it's a very useful multifunctional ingredient for those suffering with both breakouts as well as irregular pigmentation (Schulte et al. 2015).

• **Growth factors** (GFs), OTC

A variety of natural growth factors are produced by many different human cell types, as they regulate countless cellular processes and act as signalling molecules between cells. As specialised proteins, they play a role in modulating cell proliferation, blood vessel formation, collagen and elastin production and many other functions in our skin. Natural GFs are also vital for wound healing, a process which research has found to be a good model for reversing signs of skin ageing.

GFs used in skincare are one of the 'it' ingredients right now and there are a variety of different ones on the market (Malerich et al. 2014). In my opinion, GFs are a very interesting group of active ingredients in skincare, however, their clinical evidence is not (yet) as strong as that for antioxidants and retinoids. One notorious issue GFs have is their difficulty to penetrate the skin effectively due to their large molecular size. In contrast to some other anti-ageing ingredients, GFs are non-irritating and even the most sensitive skins can tolerate them.

• **Hyaluronic acid** (HA), OTC

This naturally occurring substance in the human body is found abundantly in the extracellular matrix of the dermis. It not only plumps the skin by holding water, but also possesses antioxidant properties and is involved in cell-to-cell communication and keeping the matrix well organised. The quantity and quality of our natural HA depletes as we age, which is one of the reasons our skin seems dryer and less plump. HA is a huge molecule, so to improve skin penetration via skincare, it's often fragmented into smaller molecules of varying size (Pavicic et al. 2011). Which size is best remains controversial...

However, while HA in skincare greatly helps to hydrate the skin's superficial layers (it can famously attract and bind 1,000 times its weight in moisture), it can't replace depleted natural HA levels in the dermis, whether fragmented or as native molecules. To boost levels in the dermis, we only have two viable options. Either use an active skincare ingredient that can trick cells into stepping up their own HA production; or inject HA with a needle (i.e. as fillers, HA skin boosters or mesotherapy, more about those later).

• **Hydroquinone**, Rx

Commonly prescribed for the treatment of melasma and other types of irregular pigmentation, hydroquinone inhibits the enzyme tyrosinase, the key enzyme in the pigment production process. Hydroquinone is a very effective, prescription-strength skin-lightening agent that should only be used under the direction of a doctor or prescribing nurse. Hydroquinone has developed a somewhat bad reputation due to potential risks such as ochronosis (a bluish-black discolouration of the skin). However, I feel that most of the problems associated with this ingredient are due to inappropriate, prolonged use on extensive skin areas.

Hydroquinone is often used in combination with vitamin A derivative tretinoin and an anti-inflammatory steroid in a mixture known as 'Kligman's formulation', which is extremely effective and remains the gold standard for treating hyperpigmentation (Kligman et al. 1975, Torok 2006). One of the brands we use in clinic is Pigmanorm®.

My recommendation is to use any hydroquinone containing product for only 3-4 months at a time, before going over to a non-hydroquinone maintenance treatment. As with any form of pigmentation treatment, maintenance is key, as otherwise the pigmentation will very likely simply return.

• **Kojic acid and other skin brighteners**, OTC
Derived from mushrooms, skin-lightening agent kojic acid inhibits the melanin-forming enzyme, tyrosinase. Kojic acid is also an anti-oxidant and has been shown to be able to prevent sun-induced wrinkle formation (Mitani et al. 2001). Like any anti-pigment ingredient, it should always be used in combination with antioxidants and broad-spectrum SPF30–50 sun protection (plus sun avoidance!).

Other over-the-counter skin lighteners include liquorice, mulberry and bearberry extracts, vitamin C, N-Acetyl Glucosamine (NAG), nicotinamide and various others (Sarkar et al. 2013). Another interesting anti-pigment ingredient is tranexamic acid. Traditionally used orally as a pharmaceutical compound to staunch bleeding, tranexamic acid has been reported to show promising results for melasma – a notoriously stubborn form of pigmentation (Perper et al. 2017). Tranexamic acid is used for pigmentation both topically, as well as orally and in combination with medical needling. Over-the-counter skin-lighteners are often found in combination in cosmetic formulas to increase their effect (Draelos et al. 2010).

• Peptides, OTC

This popular group of ingredients also known as matrikines can be roughly divided into three main categories: signalling peptides, neurotransmitter-affecting peptides and carrier peptides. Many of the most common group, signalling peptides (e.g. pentapeptides such as Matrixyl®) stimulate fibroblast cells to produce more collagen and elastin; others may inhibit the enzyme collagenase (matrix-melloproteinase 1, or MMP-1) whose job it is to break down collagen.

Neurotransmitter-affecting peptides such as Argireline® are said to mimic botulinum toxin (BTX, 'botox') by blocking nerve-to-muscle signalling and softening mimic lines. (Of course, they can't give results like BTX injections which are much more effective). Carrier peptides such as GHK copper complex deliver trace elements such as copper (a co-factor for several enzymes involved in collagen and elastin formation) into the skin.

Other peptides used in cosmetics might have additional actions such as anti-inflammatory effects (for example the tetrapepide, Rigin®). There are more than two dozen synthetic peptides on the market already and more are being developed as we speak. Although peptides don't yet have as many studies behind them as vitamin A derivatives, say, their evidence is steadily growing and they offer the advantage of growth factor-like activities but with better skin penetration because of their smaller molecular size (Aldag et al. 2016, Robinson et al. 2005). Peptides are well tolerated even by the most sensitive skins, so they're a useful alternative to more irritating ingredients such as vitamin A derivatives.

• **Polyhydroxyacids** (PHAs), OTC

These are AHAs with multiple hydroxyl groups which attract and hold water, making them more hydrating than traditional hydroxy acids. Due to a slightly larger molecule size and slower skin penetration compared to glycolic acid, they're also less irritating to sensitive skins, while still having good penetration properties (Edison et al. 2004, Grimes at al. 2004). Examples include Gluconolactone, Lactobionic Acid and Maltobionic Acid, the latter two also being known as Bionic Acids.

As well as providing AHA effects such as increased cell turnover and collagen/elastin stimulation, many PHAs have added antioxidant and anti-glycation benefits (Bernstein et al. 2004, Green et al. 2009, Grimes at al. 2004). Furthermore, they inhibit collagen and elastin-degrading MMPs and have been shown to help protect cell lipids and membranes from UV damage.

• **Salicylic acid**, OTC

Derived from the same active ingredient used in Aspirin®, salicylic acid is a beta-hydroxy acid (BHA) with multiple benefits. It unclogs pores, increases cell turnover, exfoliates skin and has anti-bacterial effects – all of which makes it a popular and effective acne ingredient. It's particularly useful for blackheads and whiteheads (comedones) due to its ability to penetrate pores, clearing debris at a deeper level.

In higher concentrations, salicylic acid is used to soften and remove thickened skin on cracked heels, say. Salicylic acid is also a popular ingredient in chemical peels (Arif 2015, Fabbrocini et al. 2009).

• Stem cell extracts, OTC

Stem cells are important, undifferentiated cells that have the ability to mature into a wide range of specific cell types. The skin is the largest repository of adult stem cells in the body and, as you'd guess, their primary function is to replenish the skin (Zouboulis et al. 2008). These self-renewing cells regenerate more and more slowly as we age, which is why skincare with ingredients that support and stimulate stem cells make an intriguing story.

Feeding our skin fresh, human stem cells would be the holy grail of anti-ageing – except skincare doesn't contain human cells. There might be stem cell *extracts* from apples, say, which contain bioactive substances thought to stimulate cell proliferation (Moruś et al. 2014). It's a very interesting concept, but more research is needed to verify the precise benefits of the different plant stem cell extracts currently used.

• Tretinoin, Rx

Also known as retinoic acid and Retin-A® (the latter is just one of the many brand names), tretinoin is the acid form of vitamin A. Tretinoin is not only highly effective for acne, but also remains the gold standard sun damage repair and anti-ageing ingredient and an all-time favourite of dermatologists (Darlenski et al. 2010, Kircik 2014, Griffiths et al. 1995, Grove et al. 1991, Weiss et al. 1988). I use it on my own skin a couple of times per week.

Tretinoin is backed by ample scientific evidence confirming collagen stimulation, inhibition of collagen-degrading MMPs and improvement of elastic fibre quality (Fisher et al. 1996, Kircik 2012, Kligman et al. 1993, Kong et al. 2016). Studies have also unequivocally shown improvement of sun damage, skin elasticity, pigmentation and wrinkles (Darlenski et al. 2010, Grove et al. 1991, Kong et al. 2016, Rafal et al. 1992). However, tretinoin is one of the most irritant forms of vitamin A and should be introduced slowly. Many people will use it intermittently, say two to three times per week to increase tolerance. It must not be used during pregnancy.

• **UV filters**, OTC

There will be a separate section on sun protection below, but here's a heads up. There are two main types of UV filters – physical (mineral) and chemical (organic) filters. Physical filters such as zinc oxide and titanium dioxide reflect and scatter UV rays on the skin surface, similar to a mirror. Chemical filters such as Mexoryl™ and cinnamates on the other hand work by absorbing UV light within the skin and converting it into a different type of energy (infrared light), more like a sponge. Aim for broad-spectrum SPF30-50 with a high UVA rating and always combine with topical antioxidants.

• **Vitamin A derivatives** (Retinoids), OTC / Rx

Retinoid is the family name for all vitamin A derivatives, both prescription versions such as tretinoin and adapalene, as well as over-the-counter compounds such as retinol and retinaldehyde. There are various over-the-counter vitamin A derivatives, but only prescription retinoic acid (tretinoin) fits the skin cell receptors. So the skin has to convert all other derivatives into retinoic acid before they can have an effect.

Three of the best-known non-prescription retinoids

are retinol (vitamin A), retinaldehyde (retinal) and retinyl palmitate (an ester of vitamin A). Starting with retinol esters such as retinyl palmitate, conversion takes place via retinol and retinaldehyde, to arrive at retinoic acid/ tretinoin. The diagram below explains it.

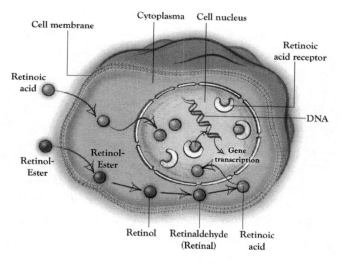

Fig. 17: Conversion of vitamin A derivatives in the skin.

Retinyl palmitate is the most commonly used retinoid in skincare, as it's easiest to formulate. But it's also my least favourite, as clinical effects are less good as with other vitamin A derivatives. Retinyl retinoate is a newer, synthetic hybrid retinoid ester with promising results (Kim et al. 2012).

Both retinol and retinaldehyde are highly effective, less irritating over-the-counter alternatives to tretinoin and I often recommend them to patients (Babcock et al. 2015, Bouloc et al. 2015, Fluhr et al, 1999, Ho et al. 2012, Kong et al. 2016,

Randhawa et al. 2015a, Sorg et al. 2014). They support collagen production, reduce sun damage, lighten pigmentation and soften lines and wrinkles.

Retinoids are among the best-investigated anti-ageing skincare ingredients on the market and ideally, everyone over 30 should be using one to support collagen production and a healthy dermal matrix. However, they can irritate, so should be introduced gradually and only used as tolerated. Everyone is different and some people might just tolerate them twice a week or so, preferably in the evening, which is fine.

• **Vitamin C, OTC**
Although it's an antioxidant, vitamin C (L-ascorbic acid) is in a category of its own when it comes to skincare ingredients. Essential for maintaining healthy, beautiful skin, vitamin C is a true multitasker (Farris et al. 2005, Humbert et al. 2003, Lin et al. 2005, Oresajo et al. 2008). It can neutralise reactive oxygen species, regenerate vitamin E, stimulate collagen production, reduce collagen-degrading enzymes and help protect our skin from sun and pollution damage. Vitamin C is also a vital cofactor required for making the triple helix structure of collagen.

Not surprisingly, many skincare formulations use vitamin C. It is, however, notoriously unstable in its pure form, and difficult to formulate in meaningful concentrations – some brands do a low-concentration 'dusting' just so they can mention it on the label. Often, you'll find, in my opinion, less effective derivatives such as ascorbyl palmitate are used instead of the pure, L-ascorbic acid form (Pinnell et al. 2001). While L-ascorbic acid is water soluble, tetrahexyldecyl ascorbate is a lipid soluble vitamin C derivative also used in skincare

(Fitzpatrick et al. 2002). The evidence behind the latter is not yet as strong as for L-ascorbic acid though. Make sure you ask your cosmetic dermatologist to suggest an evidence-based product.

I also noticed that there seems to be some sort of 'competition' going on as to which brand can claim the highest concentration of vitamin C on the market. While we need a certain level for optimal effects, in my experience, there is actually a sweet spot and higher is not always better (Pinnell et al. 2001). My favourite remains L-ascorbic acid in 10-20% concentration.

Prescription versus over-the-counter products

Which to use - an over-the-counter cosmeceutical (OTC) or prescription-only (Rx) product? It's completely up to your individual skin. In clinic, I sometimes start with Rx strength if the skin condition is quite severe and unlikely to respond to OTC levels – I'm thinking strong sun damage or melasma say. I might for example kick off melasma treatment with Rx Kligman's formulation, then use OTC kojic acid and arbutin as maintenance. The choice also depends on the patient's skin type and condition. Patients with oily skin for example tend to respond well to Rx vitamin A acid straight away, whereas in someone with a more sensitive skin, I might start with an OTC vitamin A first, to get them acclimatised before possibly stepping up to Rx.

Some patients themselves will have a personal preference for either Rx or OTC; and yet others might simply not want to splash the cash on continuous medical supervision and prescriptions, so OTC options might be their first choice.

There are many different scenarios, but ultimately the practitioner will help the patient decide what will work best for them.

Before putting together an exemplary skincare regime for you, let's speak about a couple of other skincare related issues that are important to know.

The 'good cop, bad cop' strategy

How well any of your products work is also down to commitment and adherence to the recommended schedule. My *'good cop, bad cop' strategy* is a perfect way of optimising that.

Our skin gets lazy with age (for example slowing down collagen production in the dermis) and we need to keep reminding it to keep up the good work. In my opinion, anyone in their thirties should be using collagen stimulating ingredients. These types of ingredients are known as *matrix stimulators*, since the dermal extracellular matrix (the space between fibroblast cells in the dermis) contains collagen, elastin and a gel-like substance rich in GAGs such as hyaluronic acid. Evening is a good time to use matrix stimulators such as retinoids, as the skin goes into repair mode when we sleep.

However, as you know, these vitamin A derivatives are highly active and can irritate if you overuse them. So when you start using them, it's important to introduce potentially irritating ingredients like retinoids gradually to give your skin a chance to get used to them. That might mean starting by using them only twice per week. A couple of weeks later, if you tolerate them well, you could step up to using them every other day. In two more weeks, you could even try using them nightly. Remember though, not everyone can tolerate using retinoids every day, which is fine, as you'll still get the benefits even if you use them intermittently.

So what do you use on the other days? An anti-inflammatory, soothing moisturiser's the perfect partner to your retinoid routine (added peptides or growth factors are fine, as they are non-irritating). Make sure it's a texture that suits your skin type – richer for dry skin, lighter and oil-free for oily and breakout-prone skin. Don't get tempted to slather on a rich moisturiser if you are prone to breakouts, even if your skin feels dry at that moment!

I always explain this to my patients as the *'good cop' (soothing moisturiser) / 'bad cop' (active retinoid) strategy.* They work in synergy and balance each other out. But you have to find your personal 'bad cop' limit – and finding your sweet spot may take trial and error.

> If you develop redness, dryness, flaking and/or itchy skin after retinoid use, don't automatically think you have an allergy – you've most likely simply overstretched your skin's tolerance (irritation and allergic reactions are not the same!). Stop for a few days to let the reaction settle, then start again, but more slowly.

> The *'good cop, bad cop' strategy* is a smart way of getting your skin used to retinoids. I have yet to see a patient who can't tolerate some form of retinoid using this tactic.

The SPF factor

If you mean to keep your skin looking younger for longer, there's one little adage you can't afford to ignore. Remember, prevention is better than cure. Sun protection is one of the most essential aspects of any skin preservation programme:

many experts agree that if you only do one thing for your skin, wearing sunscreen every day, year-round is it.

Why is sun protection so important? As we've already seen, the sun is one of the greatest causes of premature skin ageing and irregular pigmentation and can also lead to skin cancer (Krutman et al. 2017). According to Cancer Research UK, since the early 1990s, melanoma skin cancer incidence rates have increased by more than double (119%) here in the UK. Yet many people persist in cooking themselves in the sun, just to get a tan.

These days, most people know that sun-induced *burning* is highly dangerous: not only does it age the skin prematurely, but it also increases the risk of later skin cancer. However, what many people still don't realise is that for the fair-skinned, even *tanning* is a sign of cellular damage. In fair skin, tanning is in fact a cry for help. Our skin's DNA (genetic blueprint) has been damaged by the sun's rays, and the skin is desperately striving to protect itself from further trauma by producing more pigment.

> If your skin's fair, not only should you avoid burning, but tanning too. It's a sign of sun damage on a cellular level – your skin's cry for help.

Chronic sun damage is a cumulative process that builds over years and decades. Your skin 'remembers' every hour of sun exposure it has ever had, going right back to when you were born. Many people who are now developing skin cancer had sunburn or too much sun exposure in their childhood or teenage years back in the days when we weren't so sun savvy. The good news is that it's never too late to start protecting your skin from the sun.

And remember, it's not only episodic sun exposure (think

sunny holiday) but also long-term, low-level exposure unintentionally accrued during day-to-day activities. It's estimated that for the average person, this 'incidental' exposure accounts for 80% of their total sun exposure over a lifetime.

Sun protection means skin preservation. The best way to do that is to sit out of direct sunlight in the shade and eschew outdoor summer activities between 10am and 4pm. In addition, if you're committed to preserving your youthful complexion, wear a broad-spectrum, high SPF sunscreen every day, even in the winter.

But what does SPF really mean? It stands for 'Sun Protection Factor' and the number beside it defines the ratio of the minimum amount of UV energy necessary to produce redness (your minimal erythema dose or MED) when wearing sunscreen, compared to unprotected skin. Theoretically, SPF 30 will shield you 30 times longer than if you wore no protection at all, although this way of thinking has led to countless

> Make sure to get your vitamin D level checked, if you are using daily sun protection. Take a vitamin D3 supplement if your level is low.

sunburns, so don't rely on it! How quickly you would burn depends on various factors including your skin type, the time of day, the month and where you are in the world, so doing the SPF maths accurately is virtually impossible. Plus, the SPF rating is only relevant to *burning* UVB rays and doesn't say anything about *ageing* UVA. There are some indications of UVA protection such as the star rating system, but they can be misleading, as they are *relative* to the SPF of the product. So a 4-star UVA rating on an SPF50 product may actually provide better UVA protection than a 5-star UVA rating on an SPF15 product. The UVA circle logo is another indicator about the level of UVA protection you can expect in a product, but again only relative to its UVB protection level. A good broad-spectrum sunscreen should have a minimum 1:3 UVA:UVB protection ratio.

So what protection factor should you use? I recommend a broad-spectrum SPF30–50 (which will screen out 97 – 98% of UVB rays). Aiming high partly helps to offset one of sun protection's greatest contradictions – that under daily use conditions, we fail to achieve the factor on the package. There are a couple of reasons for this. Firstly - and studies have proved this – we simply don't apply enough product (Wulf et al. 1997). A product's SPF rating is determined under artificial conditions in the lab, using a predetermined amount of sunscreen which is often far more than we actually apply in any one helping in everyday life. Secondly, we don't re-apply it every two hours as needed to keep the protection level high (Bodekaer et al. 2008). You see? The SPF maths go right out of the window, here. So don't for goodness sake think that SPF12-15 in your high street moisturiser will save your skin. By the afternoon when the sun's at its highest, you'll have hardly any protection left.

Further protective ingredients you should look for on the tube are antioxidants. That's because ultraviolet radiation (UV) only represents about 10% of total solar radiation, while infrared radiation accounts for 50% and visible light for 40% (Schalka et al. 2014). Infrared light is known to contribute to premature skin ageing and visible light has been shown to cause pigmentation (Krutman et al. 2017, Randhawa et al. 2015b, Schroeder et al. 2008, Yoon et al. 2012). As UV filters can't protect us from infrared and visible light, we need to add the 'safety net' of antioxidants to scavenge free radicals generated by infrared and visible light (and the 2-3% UV-rays that even SPF30-50 fail to absorb. Remember, no sunscreen is 100% effective!). The most efficient way of creating a free radical shield is to apply an antioxidant serum and let it sink into your skin's surface before you apply your SPF.

For many people, a barrier to wearing a high protection daily sunscreen is that they think it will be inevitably thick and greasy. Forget those sticky, sand-magnet holiday lotions – things have changed. Savvy cosmeceutical brands have developed highly effective sunscreens with lightweight, non-greasy textures that feel great on the skin. There are even SPF30-50 moisturisers for breakout-prone skin – check EudeloBoutique. com to find my top products.

Advanced sunscreen products also moisturise your skin, so there's no need to apply extra moisturiser, unless of course your skin is very dry. In that case, make sure to apply your moisturiser first, let it sink in, then apply sun protection on top. If you have normal, combination or even oily skin, a sunscreen chosen to suit your skin type should be quite enough on its own.

Sun protection made simple? Aim for broad-spectrum SPF30-50 with a high UVA rating, plus wear antioxidants underneath. Apply the SPF twenty minutes before sun exposure and reapply every two hours, if you are in a hot climate. Choose a texture that suits your skin type and won't cause breakouts and blocked pores and apply it instead of your daily moisturiser, under makeup if you like.

"But what about my *other* treatment products?" I hear you

ask. If you're using an antioxidant serum (which by the way, is protective as well as having anti-ageing effects) wear it in the morning underneath your SPF moisturiser. Then use your vitamin A-derivative product at night.

Know your
skin phototype
———————

Melanin is our skin's natural, internal mechanism of protecting itself from the sun. This UV-absorbing pigment is produced by cells (melanocytes) in the epidermis on exposure to sun. The melanocytes then transfer the melanin to neighbouring keratinocytes, where it forms a protective 'parasol' over the vulnerable cell nucleus to try and shield its DNA from mutation-inducing UV light. The more melanin, or darker our natural skin type, the more natural protection we have from the sun. But don't think if you have dark skin, you're immune from sun damage, there's still a risk.

Not all melanin is created equally. In human skin there are two types of melanin pigment: black/brown eumelanin and lighter, red-yellow-brownish pheomelanin. When fair types try to tan in the sun, their skin generates more pheomelanin. And while eumelanin is a 'good quality' pigment that protects skin efficiently, pheomelanin is less stable and breaks down and even generates free radicals when exposed to UV light. So instead of protecting our skin effectively, pheomelanin actively contributes to UV-induced skin damage. Below is a guide to skin types according to the Fitzpatrick classification. I should point out that dermatologists often use the term 'skin phototype' to distinguish from other 'skin types' such as dry, oily, etc.

THE FITZPATRICK SKIN PHOTOTYPES

• **Phototype I** You always burn in the sun and never tan – the 'red, then white again' type. You may have pale reddish skin, blonde or red hair, light blue, green, or grey eyes and often freckles. **Sun hazard risk: Very high.** You're most vulnerable to skin cancer and skin damage, so take meticulous care to protect yourself from the sun.

• **Phototype II** You burn first, then gradually develop a light tan – the 'burn easily, tan poorly' type. You might have dark blonde hair, blue eyes and fair skin. **Sun hazard risk: High.** You need to be very careful in the sun to prevent skin cancer and skin damage.

• **Phototype III** You burn after longer exposure, but generally tan quite easily. You might have a beigeish skin tone, brown hair and brown eyes. **Sun hazard risk: Medium.** You have a typical mid-European skin type, but still need to take care to prevent damage.

• **Phototype IV** You tan very easily and rarely burn. You might have olive skin, brown eyes and dark brown hair. **Sun hazard risk: Medium-low.** Yours is a typical Mediterranean skin type, but you still need to take care in strong sunlight.

• **Phototype V** You have naturally brown skin that darkens even more in the sun and very rarely burns, if ever. You have dark brown eyes and dark brown or black hair. **Sun hazard risk: Low.** Your skin type is common in the Indian subcontinent. You may still ➡

need to protect your skin, especially if you're re-exposing it to strong sunlight after a long period.
• **Phototype VI** You have black skin with dark brown eyes and black hair. **Sun hazard risk: Very low.** Your skin is a typical central African type and doesn't burn in the sun.

How clean is your skin?

Before I tell you about the skincare regime everyone should be using, a few timely words about cleansers. I can't stress strongly enough how important proper cleansing is to your daily skincare programme. Cleansing removes dirt, old makeup, excess oil, dead skin cells and pollution remnants. But it's vital to use the right cleanser for your skin type.

Using the wrong type of cleanser can cause problems such as breakouts or dry, flaky skin. If you have naturally dry skin, your cleanser should cleanse your skin, but hydrate it at the same time – a non-foaming, creamy cleanser might be best. A well-formulated cleanser for oily skin will help reduce oil and pore-clogging impurities – foaming cleansers usually suit normal and combination as well as oily skin. Certain added actives such as salicylic acid or AHAs for oily skin can be very useful. However, I am not an advocate of anti-ageing ingredients in cleansers, as the vast majority will end up down the drain! Your skin simply can't absorb them that quickly.

In most cases, a good cleanser, water and your hands are all you need. I am not a fan of cleansing cloths, as I find the them unhygienic and unnecessary. So what about electric cleansing brushes? I don't think they're necessary for daily use, but two to three times a week they can be a great addition to your regime. As I mentioned in the section about pollution, they're able to shift toxic residues far better than manual cleansing alone, so I use mine when my skin has been exposed to more urban pollution than usual.

Now, I don't recommend waterless cleansers and wet wipes. If you're on a long-haul flight they can, of course, be handy. But they should never replace a proper daily session with cleanser and water. Cleansing wipes sit in

> If you suffer with any inflamed acne or rosacea lesions (spots or pimples), leave electronic cleansing brushes alone!

between rinse-off and leave-on products and in my opinion don't do either job particularly well. They don't cleanse as well as cleansing with a proper cleanser and water, and leave residues on the skin surface which can be irritating. I have seen countless skin problems caused by or contributed to by waterless cleansing.

While cleansing is crucial to your daily skincare routine, toners aren't strictly necessary. They were originally developed to remove irritating soap residues from the skin surface, but modern soapless cleansers have made them redundant for most skin types. Toners can even irritate dry and sensitive skin, especially those with an alcohol base. Only oily skin may benefit from special oil-reducing toners such as those containing salicylic acid and/or AHA blends. There are also some great home-peel pads available for oily skin that help remove excess oil and clear congestion.

Now, what about exfoliation? Most women and men experience dull skin as they get older, because their skin renewal slows down (remember - our skin becomes lazy, as we age). Dullness is caused by a build-up of excessive dead skin material, plus an uneven skin tone and blotchy pigmentation. These changes mean the skin surface reflects light poorly, making it appear duller and less youthfully fresh. So to get your glow back, some type of exfoliating scrub is often recommended by salespeople. But that's not necessarily the answer.

> Twice-daily cleansing with a facial cleanser tailored to your skin type and water is vital. Avoid waterless cleansers and wet wipes. Most people don't need toners, either.

Whenever I put together a tailored skincare regime for a patient, they're often surprised that I haven't included an exfoliating product, such as a scrub. "But what shall I use to exfoliate?" they'll ask. The thing is, many of our trusted anti-ageing ingredients, such as vitamin A derivatives and AHAs, will not only encourage collagen production and help with fine lines and wrinkles, but also exfoliate at the same time (a controlled, chemical exfoliation). So if you're already using one of these great, multifunctional ingredients, there may be simply no need to use a separate exfoliator. In fact if you do, you might end up with irritated skin. It's a case of look before you buff...

> Skincare containing vitamin A and / or AHAs exfoliate the skin chemically. An extra mechanical scrub isn't always needed – and may even cause irritation.

What do you really need? The cost of good cosmeceuticals may seem steep. But well-formulated products are the best investment you can make for your skin's future. You may even save money in the long term if you think about how much you've already wasted on products that weren't right for you or that you didn't actually need. I'm thinking of that 'pre-serum' serum the sales assistant in the super-specialised skincare boutique promised would make your moisturiser work better. Or the 12-step morning routine the vlogger with 12 million followers swore by. Many people also use products that actually contradict one another. They may be using a cleansing oil to wash with, say, but then find (and I wonder why?) that their skin's getting more congested. So now they add a salicylic acid toner only to find their skin's getting dry. So next up is a 'mega-moisture' serum that is supposed to ease their (self-induced) dry skin, but a few days later "hormonal" breakouts appear (nothing 'hormonal' about these...). So they start using home peel pads and so on and so on....

Let me just say I'm against overloading the skin with too rich, heavy and occlusive textures anyway, as they can clog up the pores and slow down the skin's vital, natural surface renewal. There are of course some exceptions such as eczema skin with impaired barrier function, which will benefit greatly from lipid rich emollients, as they stop the vicious circle of barrier disruption, water loss, dry skin, inflammation, more water loss etc. However, this is a small minority of people.

Generally, the current trend for heavy creams, balms and facial oils isn't a good one, in my opinion. People often overload their skin and 'suffocate' it with too heavy products. A trend I don't endorse, as it's doing your skin more harm than good. We end up seeing many of these people in our clinic with skin issues such as dull, lifeless skin and breakouts.

> Do not overload your skin with heavy cream, balms and oils – they clog up your pores and slow down skin renewal. Always use the lightest formulation you can get away with!

I'm also sceptical of the current trend (very popular in Korea for example) of applying layer upon layer (sometimes up to 17 layers!). You'll almost certainly compromise optimal absorption of active ingredients and could even risk the interaction of some products. So stick to a sensible number of layers, let's say three as a rule of thumb – even more so if your skin is oily – and use the lightest formulations you can without your skin feeling dry.

What feels like 'dry skin', is not always true dry skin anyway. A dry, tight feeling can be a sign of micro-inflammation, as we often see in rosacea prone skin. In these cases slathering on rich moisturisers is even more contraindicated, as they might make your rosacea worse. The solution is treating the micro-inflammation, not 'numbing' the sensation with heavy skincare! It's complicated, so best to let a cosmetic dermatologist put a tailored regime together for you.

At EUDELO we divide skin types into five categories, not four, as 'dry skin without breakouts' can simply not be treated the same way as 'dry skin with breakouts'. They all need very different skincare products. Sensitive skin is not a defined entity by the way, as it can have different causes and affect all of these five skin types (although it's of course less common in oily skin).

THE EUDELO SKIN TYPING SYSTEM:

- Normal skin
- Oily skin
- Combination skin (typically oily t-zone and dry cheeks)
- Dry skin without breakouts
- Dry skin *with* breakouts

Coming back to price, not all good skincare is ultra-high-priced, but good raw ingredients can be pricy, so if a cream contains several of these at truly functional strengths, the cost certainly mounts up. But don't confuse cost with quality. Not all 'prestige' products in chic department stores are worth their price ticket! My advice is to look beyond the fancy packaging for evidence-based products with proven benefits – ask your cosmetic dermatologist rather than the sales assistant for advice!

Below comes my essential skincare regime that everyone should follow. Yes, you might find it surprisingly simple. It can be easily adapted to address any specific concerns you have about your skin, but this should always be the starting point. And don't forget to apply all products on face, neck *and* chest (think 'hair line to nipple line'), as we want a congruent appearance of face and neck! And one last tip - once you have applied a product on face, neck and chest, wipe your palms on the backs of your hands, as they will benefit from this regime, too!

Using a cosmeceutical skincare regime like the one below is a great investment in your skin's future as well as ensuring it looks its best now. Cosmeceutical skincare can, of course,

YOUR DAILY SKINCARE ESSENTIALS

MORNING:

1. Cleanser suitable for your skin
2. High-grade antioxidant serum
   (e.g. vitamin C, vitamin E and/or other symbiotic
   antioxidants)
3. Sun protection moisturiser (broad spectrum
   SPF30-50)

EVENING:

1. Cleanser suitable for your skin
2. Anti-pigment serum, if needed
3. Matrix stimulating repair cream, as tolerated
   (start slowly), e.g. retinol/retinaldehyde.
   A simple moisturiser on the other days
   (may contain non-irritating anti-ageing
   ingredients such as peptides)
   - 'good cop – bad cop' strategy!
   The latter can also be applied *on top* of the matrix
   stimulator (wait 5-10 minutes between them), if
   added hydration is needed.
   Until your late 20s, you may skip the matrix
   stimulator.

also enhance and prolong the results of non-surgical aesthetic treatments, improve healing and reduce downtime as well as protect skin from further damage. So I just can't understand why so many aesthetic doctors and nurses aren't integrating good skincare into their patients' treatment plans.

I'm reminded of a conversation with a colleague some time ago. He's a highly regarded aesthetic doctor and a very skilled practitioner of aesthetic injectables. As we chatted about our clinics, I mentioned that every cosmetic patient we see gets a tailored, written skincare regime. I'm still shocked by his response, "Oh, we don't do much *skin* here'" he said, meaning skincare didn't figure for him. How on earth can an aesthetic practitioner *not* give skincare advice to their patients? Beats me. Time for the next step up…

•

DERMATOLOGY GRADE FACIALS — BEYOND PAMPERING

Dermatology grade facials are the next step on the *EUDELO Skin Enhancement Staircase*. If you're living a skin-friendly lifestyle and using good cosmeceutical skincare, these non-invasive treatments are the next logical step up on the commitment ladder. Although I've put them below the more intense, minimal-invasive regenerative procedures, dermatology grade facials actually do have a mild regenerative effect, too (plus there's nothing better to unclog your pores!). So if you want to do that bit more for your skin without the downtime, they're an excellent starting point.

There are hundreds of different facials available throughout the country, so how will you find the right one for you? I always explain it this way. There are three main categories of facials as I see it: Spa & high street (beauty) facials, medical facials and dermatology grade facials. And there's a considerable difference between them.

Spa and high street facials are the most basic. They're great for pampering and very relaxing. They generally involve the three main steps cleansing, exfoliating and moisturising in some form. Their mantra is hydration – hydration – hydration. They often involve layer upon layer of various serums, creams and masks, typically with ritualistic facial massage in a pseudo-spiritual environment. (Cue the whale music). They won't significantly affect skin biology and function so don't expect profound benefits.

Very few high street and spa facials include extractions – manually clearing blocked pores, blackheads and whiteheads. In fact, many spas and salons explicitly ask their therapists to refrain from extractions, as they can lead to inflammation and possibly scarring if they're not done absolutely correctly or the wrong products are applied afterwards. I view manual extractions as integral to a truly effective facial, but I wouldn't want an inexpertly trained or inexperienced therapist to do them on me, so the salon safe policy makes sense.

If you're after an hour of calm with a relaxing facial massage, then go for it. A word of caution though. Those with breakout prone skin should strictly avoid spa and high street facials even if they say they're (supposedly...) for acne or rosacea. They often make things worse – so walk away!

A few years ago, I was invited to a hen day and one of the scheduled treats was a facial in a very chic spa. Naturally, I didn't want to offend the bride-to-be, but there was no way I was going to have that facial – I knew it would make me break out. So I simply switched my treatment to a body massage, which was pure bliss...

Unlike traditional beauty facials, medical facials are more results-driven and designed to promote more long-term changes in the skin to encourage healthy and youthful looks. In contrast to spa and salon facials, they generally use ingredients that are more potent or concentrated to create a more intense treatment. They may involve more advanced forms of microdermabrasion, higher-level chemical peels, and/or high tech equipment such as certain types of laser (Freedman et al. 2008, Linder et al. 2013). So overall, they offer a more complex and potent combination of treatment steps, but may not be as relaxing as beauty facials. Medical facials may or may not involve manual extractions, which as I've mentioned, are important for optimum skin benefits.

Medical facials bridge the gap between beauty and aesthetic procedures and, with their mild regenerative benefits, are a wonderful way to improve the look and feel of your skin. They involve no downtime and for those with healthy skin, they're a great way of dipping a first toe into the regenerative treatment pool. However, be careful if you suffer from breakouts or any other skin issues, as most medical facials aren't dermatologist-developed so may not be ideal for problem skin.

Now for the most advanced facials - dermatology grade facials. These achieve maximum skin benefits, aid optimal regeneration and slow down the ageing process on a cellular level, while helping to restore skin health. Dermatology grade facials have - by definition - been developed by a specialist dermatologist, so in addition to all the regenerating benefits of a medical facial, they are entirely suitable and even therapeutic for problem skin with acne or rosacea breakouts, say.

Dermatology grade facials have a general structure that is tailored on the day to your skin's individual needs, making them versatile and completely bespoke. A good dermatology grade facial will always include manual extractions and thorough, device-assisted lymphatic drainage (Steventon et al. 2011). More about that below.

Not as relaxing as beauty facials, they're still more of an 'experience' and less invasive than minimal-invasive regenerative procedures which are the next step up on the *EUDELO staircase*. So whether you have healthy skin and want to slow the ageing process and look generally better, or have skin problems that need treating and want to address ageing concerns at the same time, dermatology grade facials are a highly effective option. I swear by them and have one every month myself. I also recommend them to all my patients including those with acne and rosacea.

THE 3 LEVELS OF FACIALS

1: Spa & high street (beauty) facials
Level: basic
Mostly about massaging and hydrating the skin. Very relaxing, but no significant effects on skin biology. Not suitable for those with problem skin such as acne and rosacea breakouts.
May include: cleansing, exfoliating, manual massage, mask and moisturiser.

2: Medical facials
Level: medium
More results-driven than beauty facials, and for those with healthy skin a great introduction to gentle regenerative treatments. Not dermatologist-developed, so may not be advisable for problem skin.

May include: all of the above, with more potent ingredients. Plus advanced forms of microdermabrasion, higher-level chemical peels, certain types of light/laser treatment etc.

3: Dermatology grade facials
Level: advanced
By definition, dermatologist-developed to achieve maximum skin benefits, aid optimal skin regeneration, slow down the ageing process on a cellular level and restore skin health. Suitable for both healthy and problem skin.

May include: All of the above, plus comedone and milia extractions, advanced lymphatic drainage, specific treatment steps for problem skin etc.

What happens during a dermatology grade facial?

Let me tell you about some of the elements we include in EUDELO's dermatology grade facials. This list is by no means complete, but you get an idea of what you might expect.

• ADVANCED MICRODERMABRASION
There are various devices on the market – for example wet microdermabrasion, hydradermabrasion, dermalinfusion – which are similar in concept to basic microdermabrasion in that they exfoliate and encourage skin to activate the epidermal basal layer. However, these more advanced techniques provide additional benefits (Freedman 2008). With

the help of vacuum pressure, the device also flushes the skin surface and pores, removing dirt, debris and impurities better than any other deep-cleansing method I know of. A unique treatment tip also pneumatically delivers serums into the skin, infusing it with specialised active ingredients – something traditional microdermabrasion doesn't do (Freedman et al. 2009). The infusion may include peptides, antioxidants, vitamins and hyaluronic acid to give the skin a major hydrating, nourishing and rejuvenating boost.

> Advanced microdermabrasion combines non-invasive exfoliation and mechanical stimulation with targeted infusion of nourishing cosmeceutical ingredients.

The treatment also improves blood circulation and so oxygen and nutrient supply to the skin. When your skin is hydrated and well 'fed', it functions better and feels softer, more plump and revitalised.

• CHEMICAL PEELS

Chemical peels exfoliate the skin even further, improving cell turnover and skin renewal as well as encouraging collagen and elastin formation (Linder et al. 2013). Ingredients such as glycolic acid, salicylic acid and other alpha and beta acids can be used to achieve this. The exact strength of the peel will be tailored to your individual needs, but because peels used in our dermatology grade facials are gentle to the skin, there's no downtime and skin-shedding as with deeper peels.

> Many dermatology grade facials include a no-downtime chemical peel to improve skin renewal and indirectly stimulate the dermal matrix.

• EXTRACTIONS

Comedones ('blocked pores', or blackheads and whiteheads) can be extremely stubborn and irksome. The good news is that this is one area where a dermatology grade facial will make a huge difference. It's a common misconception that blackheads are caused by dirt trapped in the pores: they're actually formed by a pore-clogging plug of excess oil (sebum) and skin debris (keratin). Unlike whiteheads, which are closed in by the skin, blackheads are open. Their black appearance is due to oxidation rather than dirt or poor hygiene.

When extractions are done well, they're amazing. Done badly though, they can inflame the skin, so therapists need to be highly trained and skilled to perform them. Good extractions will remove congestion without damaging or scarring the skin which can happen in the hands of a poorly trained therapist (or yourself...). And best of all - not only does removal of all that junk allow the pore to 'contract' and appear smaller, but extractions also prevent spots and pimples from forming. For pre-menstrual breakouts in women, extractions done around ovulation time, i.e. mid cycle, are particularly helpful (Steventon et al. 2011).

Certain pre-treatments such as salicylic acid infusions or a mild glycolic acid peel are often

Professional manual extractions are a vital part of all dermatology grade facials and are particularly important for breakout-prone skin.

Did you know that every single spot and pimple starts with a comedone? Sometimes they are invisible (micro-comedones), but they are always there first, so comedone extractions starve acne breakouts of their fuel.

performed prior to extractions, as they soften the dead skin material inside the pore so it comes out easier and with less pressure. As part of a full dermatology grade facial, the therapist may for example start by incorporating a salicylic acid and/or glycolic acid solution into the tailored hydradermabrasion phase of the treatment. Then vacuum-assisted automatic extractions will take place, followed by manual extractions of more stubborn lesions. This manual extraction is where skill and experience really comes in. Blackheads (open comedones) usually pop out with just a bit of the right kind of pressure. There's a very specific sequence of movements to this, not just squeezing: essentially, you have to get underneath the comedone from the sides, then push up. Whiteheads (closed comedones) often need a tiny scratch with a sterile needle (don't worry, it's painless!) to open the 'roof' and create an outlet when pressure is applied.

A similar method is used to extract milia (milk spots) where the therapist will remove a tiny hard pearl of trapped dead skin debris from underneath the skin. This usually works beautifully manually, but for particularly stubborn milia, ACP ('Advanced Cosmetic Procedure') involving a tiny needle and a small current can be used. (ACP is also great for removing skin tags and blood spots, by the way).

• SUPERFICIAL MICRO-NEEDLING

I'll talk about proper medical needling to stimulate the dermis layer later. What many of our dermatology grade facials involve is a more superficial needling to assist active ingredients to penetrate the skin. For this we use much shorter needles (0.2-0.5mm compared to 1.5-2.5mm for medical needling), which are essentially painless and don't involve downtime. You see, nature designed the skin's top layer (stratum corneum) to do a pretty good job of keeping foreign substances out. But by moving a sterile needle roller or electric needle pen over the skin, these very short needles breach the stratum corneum with thousands of tiny punctures that help serums penetrate the skin effortlessly. It's an easy way of encouraging actives to flood the skin far more successfully than a simple topical application could ever achieve.

The serums used with needling are tailored to your skin's individual needs. There might be a growth factor solution to improve skin elasticity; a mesotherapy cocktail of vitamins, minerals and HA to give dull, dehydrated skin a boost; or a skin-lightening solution to lessen irregular pigmentation.

> Superficial needling 'opens the door' to help active ingredients cross the threshold of the skin's protective barrier to boost their effectiveness.

• LYMPHATIC DRAINAGE

Lymphatic drainage is another integral phase of our dermatology grade facials, as mentioned. Lymph is a fluid that flows in a complex system of vessels, carrying away waste from our tissues. The lymphatic system with its vessels all over the body is entirely separate from our blood circulatory system and was in fact, discovered much later.

Lymphatic drainage massage encourages lymph to flow more easily and do the job of carrying away toxins and excess fluid better. It reduces fluid retention and 'de-puffs' the face. This is also very important for rosacea prone skin, which often has a known lymphatic drainage problem which in time leads to a thickened skin appearance.

Often underrated, the decongestant action of lymphatic drainage massage is integral to a dermatology grade facial and particularly important for rosacea prone skin.

We use two distinctly different techniques to encourage lymphatic drainage. Manual lymphatic drainage (MLD) uses specific, light pressure and rhythmic circular movements to stimulate lymph flow. The more advanced method is vacuum assisted lymphatic drainage with a specialist device.

• LED LIGHT THERAPY

There have been a number of reported benefits arising from light-emitting diode (LED) therapy. Different coloured lights have different applications. Red light for example, is anti-inflammatory and we might use it for rosacea skin. Red light has also been reported to help stimulate collagen production and new tissue growth. Some devices emit a combination of visible red light and near-infrared light with slightly longer wavelengths.

Blue light has been shown to have anti-bacterial effects and attacks the P. acne bacteria that contribute to acne breakouts. A combination treatment of blue and red light may prove synergistic, due to the interaction of anti-bacterial and anti-inflammatory effects. One big advantage of light therapy is that it's completely pain-free and involves no downtime.

But more is not always better. There is definitely a sweet spot where the light induces the desired results; while less may be ineffective, more might damage the skin. Think about infrared light. We know that the powerful infrared heat emitted from the sun contributes to skin damage and premature ageing. Yet a very well calibrated, small dose of red LED and infrared light has been proven to bio-stimulate skin and support its regeneration and rejuvenation (Barolet et al. 2016).

However, as a dermatologist I don't recommend relying on LED treatment alone for treatment of medical skin conditions such as acne or rosacea. In my experience, light treatment can be a useful adjunct for some patients, but highly effective and evidence-based prescription creams should remain the first line of treatment.

> LED light treatment can have different benefits depending on the wavelengths. Blue light is anti-bacterial, while red light is anti-inflammatory.

• BRAINWAVE ENTRAINMENT

I don't think many clinics offer this, but some of our dermatology grade facials are performed under state-of-the-art brainwave entrainment (Huang et al. 2008). I'm personally a huge fan, so I decided to introduce it in clinic, as the deep state of relaxation and lowered cortisol levels induced by brainwave entrainment complements the hands-on work in our dermatology grade facials wonderfully. Both work together to encourage repair and regeneration on a cellular level, ultimately supporting skin health and longevity.

Brain Wave Entrainment is a technique that causes our brainwave frequencies to synchronize with a periodic stimulus. In practice, we administer very specific, pulsing sound frequencies via headphones

> Brainwave entrainment enables your brain to go into deeply relaxing alpha and theta brainwaves. Levels of our stress hormone cortisol decrease, so greater cell regeneration is encouraged.

to stimulate the brain to move from its default beta wave state (alert state) to a slower alpha wave (deep relaxation) or theta wave (hypnotic) state. Brainwave entrainment works for almost everyone, and is effortless and extremely pleasant.

• OXYGEN BOOSTER

While you are having your dermatology grade facial (or regenerative procedure for that matter) at EUDELO, don't be surprised if your practitioner connects you to a microcirculation-enhancing device. This non-invasive device significantly boosts the oxygen and nutrient supply to your skin and improves its natural healing and regeneration potential.

The painless technology which works through unbroken skin is proven to boost microcirculation in the skin's capillaries for many hours after treatment, both at the delivery site as well as elsewhere in the body. When microcirculation is improved, oxygen and nutrient supply increases. Your anti-ageing efforts get an instant super-boost, with zero negative effects.

Ideal intervals All the above are examples of elements you might experience during a typical dermatology grade facial. We use our facials to combat a number of ageing-related concerns, from irregular pigmentation and fine lines to a dull, sallow complexion, enlarged pores and environmental damage from urban pollution and sun. At the same time, dermatology grade facials slow down the skin's ageing process and gently stimulate cell regeneration. One of the main distinguishing factors between these facials and medical grade facials is the added benefit that even dermatological skin concerns such as acne and rosacea will improve.

Dermatology grade facials are *functional* facials combining a multitude of therapeutic elements. As such they form an important part of a skin maintenance plan, as they are designed to support the health of your skin long-term and maintain it in optimal condition. If you can't find a dermatology grade facial near you, a medical facial is a good alternative (unless of course, you suffer with skin issues such as breakouts).

Make sure you have one of these facials every month – like with exercise, you need to be regular to get the best results. An interval of a month between treatments is ideal as our skin renews itself roughly every four weeks. However, this interval slows as we age, so with a monthly stimulation, we remind our skin to keep up the good work.

For a special event such as a wedding, say, you could follow a more intense course of for example three sessions in 10-day intervals or four sessions in 2-week intervals for a great pre-event boost to get your skin in top shape.

•

REGENERATING PROCEDURES – A STIMULATING TOPIC

We've now discussed the first three steps of the *EUDELO Skin Enhancement Staircase* – that's a skin-friendly lifestyle, daily cosmeceutical skincare and monthly dermatology grade facials all covered. If you're doing all these three things, you're doing your skin a very big favour. And it may well be that this is all you're prepared to do, which is absolutely fine. But if you're even more committed to looking after your skin and are ready to move up to the next level, regenerative procedures are the next step. Not that you're about to abandon the previous steps – remember all must be continued for you to progress. And yes, dermatology grade facials are already providing some regeneration benefits, but the next step will take skin regeneration into a different league. All these procedures are still non-surgical, so they make a great step up especially if you're in your thirties or older. And there's another reason why regenerative procedures are so popular.

Many women and men are understandably anxious about aesthetic interventions for various reasons. Not least, there's the worry you'll be thought vain or that the 'job' will be so obvious, you'll look like an overdone celebrity. Well, I'm with you there. Like you, I deeply dislike that overblown look – in fact it's one of my pet hates. That's why we have our *100% Natural Results Guarantee* at EUDELO. However, the beauty of this new, and exciting branch of aesthetic medicine, which we call 'regenerative aesthetic medicine', is that it employs innovative techniques designed to encourage the skin to restore and regenerate itself naturally. This process is known as bio-stimulation. We are gently coaxing the skin to regenerate. There is zero risk of ending up looking overdone - no-one will guess you've had a treatment. The only thing friends, family and colleagues will notice is how fresh and healthy you look and how radiantly your skin is glowing. They'll probably ask you what your secret is – but that's it. Tell them you've been getting 12 hours sleep every night, have started meditating, or have changed your skincare regime, if you don't feel comfortable telling them about your treatments. Believe me, they'll believe you! Having said that, I would encourage you to just tell them the truth – why not?

Regenerative procedures are a great soft entry for anyone

thinking about improving their looks without having what they regard as more "extreme" corrective treatments such as BTX and fillers. (If this is you, I still urge you to read the chapter about corrective procedures, so that you can make a genuinely informed decision!).

Regenerative procedures are, of course, also mandatory for anyone who wishes to get the ultimate 'wow' effect from corrective procedures. Remember *The Foundation Principle?*

> Regenerative aesthetic medicine is a new frontier in aesthetic medicine. It uses bio-stimulatory techniques to encourage the skin to restore itself naturally and slow down the ageing process on a cellular level.

Regenerative procedures are the foundation that corrective procedures sit upon – they help keep your skin fit and youthful. Don't skip a step on the *EUDELO staircase!*

The effects of regenerative treatments will appear gradually over a number of weeks. Don't expect overnight miracles - we're helping skin to help itself and that takes time. This gradual improvement also means the changes are subtle, which also makes the transition so much more natural.

What changes will you notice? After a regenerative procedure, the skin will develop a more refined skin surface with smaller pores and improved elasticity. Fine lines will soften as the skin regains more of its natural glow and lustre. Regenerative treatments encourage the skin to build more collagen and other matrix components, so they actually improve skin from within rather than just painting over the cracks.

Regular regenerative treatments keep the skin happier on a cellular level too, as they enable cells to behave more youthfully. This will ultimately slow down the ageing process by tackling the causes of premature skin ageing from the inside.

> Having regular regenerative procedures is like joining a 'skin gym' to keep it fit and well long term.

I must say, though, that it's not only laypersons who may not appreciate the importance of regular regenerative treatments. I actually got the idea for our *Skin Care Elite* programme while at an international anti-ageing conference. The vast majority of speakers were focusing on corrective interventions to make patients look younger, but very little was said about the need for concurrent regenerative procedures which improve skin on a cellular level. Now, I'm not against corrective treatments at all – far from it, especially when they're done conservatively like we do them at EUDELO. But I was amazed by my colleagues' lack of enthusiasm for skin regeneration and caring for skin on a more holistic level. So when I came back to London, I set up our *Skin Care Elite* programme as quickly as I could.

So what constitutes a regenerative procedure? They are, of course, non-surgical. Some of them are completely non-invasive, while others may require the use of very fine needles – I describe those as 'minimal-invasive'. But don't worry. For those where there are needles involved, we apply an effective numbing cream to ensure these procedures are painless. There might be a short downtime associated with these treatments - for example, your skin might look red for a couple of days. Below, I'll introduce you to a selection of great regenerative procedures. This list is of course, again, not complete, but these are some of my favourite ones.

Regenerative treatments are never a one-off treatment. A course usually consists of three to six treatment sessions (of one modality). For the following maintenance programme, there are a variety of schemes depending on the treatment. You might repeat the course a year or two later, or alternatively have a single top-up treatment every few months.

However, as ageing is a chronic process that never stops, the best outcome you'll have naturally is when you have some form of regenerative treatment each month. That's what our *Skin Care Elite* club is all about.

THE ELITE REGENERATIVE COLLECTION

These regenerative procedures will help your skin future proof itself on a cellular level.

- Platelet Rich Plasma Therapy (PRP)
- Mesotherapy
- Medical Needling (Collagen Induction Therapy)
- PRP-, GF-, Meso- and Bright Needling
- Gel Needling
- Carboxy Facials
- Cryostimulation
- Chemical Peels
- Laser Facials
- Other energy-based skin regeneration techniques

Platelet Rich Plasma Therapy (PRP)

Skin has an incredible ability to provide for its own healing and certain blood components act as one of the delivery systems for that process. Also known as the 'Vampire Lift' or 'Dracula Facial', PRP is a revolutionary regenerative aesthetic treatment that encourages the skin to build more collagen to renew and rejuvenate itself (Abuaf et al. 2016, Cho et al. 2011, Díaz-Ley et al. 2015).

As well as in aesthetic medicine, PRP's known tissue regenerative potential is used successfully in various other areas such as sports medicine, where injured tissues are injected to help professional athletes recover faster. PRP is even used in veterinary medicine.

The procedure involves taking a blood sample from your inner elbow. Using a specialised method and high-tech equipment we then isolate a fraction of plasma from your blood that is rich in platelets (platelet rich plasma or PRP). These platelets are an important reservoir of growth factors (GFs) which activate cells and are essential for tissue repair. Typically, we take 10ml – 20ml of your blood to create a PRP solution of around 2-4ml.

After a numbing cream is applied, the PRP fraction of your own blood is injected back into the skin - don't worry, the solution is a clear fluid. Once re-injected, the platelets release their various growth factors, including platelet-derived growth factor (PDGF), transforming growth factor (TGF), platelet-derived angiogenesis factor (PDAF), vascular endothelial growth factor (VEGF) and epidermal growth factor (EGF). Usually we inject PRP into the dermis layer of the skin, where the concentrated cocktail of GFs trigger surrounding fibroblasts to boost collagen and elastin production, so helping to repair and regenerate damaged or aged tissue.

Taking your blood, processing it in-clinic and re-injecting the concentrated PRP solution all happens within the hour: the solution must be totally fresh so that the platelets don't have time to discharge their GFs before re-injection.

The PRP injection can be done manually or with a 'meso-gun' – an automatic injection device also used in mesotherapy. PRP can also be needled back into the skin with a needle roller or automatic needle pen – more about these in the medical needling section. Alternatively, we might use a layering technique which injects PRP not only into the dermis, but also into deeper tissue layers such as onto the bone to try and slow down age-related tissue loss here, too. Our bones are wrapped in a thin connective tissue layer called periosteum - in many ways our bone's 'skin'. The periosteum plays a vital role in bone growth and maintenance. As mentioned, bones are not 'dead' material, but metabolically very active. Throughout our life, our bones are constantly being remodelled, but sadly our facial bones 'deflate' as we age. As the periosteum plays a crucial part in repairing damaged bone, the thinking behind placing PRP solution directly onto the periosteum is to stimulate the osteoblast cells of the periosteum to help slow down age-related bone resorption (García-Martínez et al. 2012, Pessoa et al. 2009).

A course of three to six PRP treatments is advised to get the best outcome. These are usually performed at monthly intervals, although there can be two to six weeks between sessions. PRP can be used on the face, neck, chest, hands or any other area in need of rejuvenation. It's very popular with our patients, as it's a very natural treatment which uses their skin's own resources.

> Rather than injecting synthetic ingredients, PRP (platelet rich plasma) treatment uses your very own growth factors to stimulate skin repair and regeneration.

Mesotherapy

For over 30 years, mesotherapy has been practiced in France, Italy, Germany and Spain in a wide variety of applications, not least aesthetic medicine. Here in the UK, we're catching onto the uniquely nourishing nature of mesotherapy and its ability to 'feed' your skin and improve its overall quality.

During treatments, a sterile, cell-boosting cocktail is introduced into the skin via a series of tiny, painless superficial injections. Depending on your individual case and area to be treated, your practitioner will carry out the procedure either manually or with an automatic mesotherapy gun. Some patients choose to have a numbing cream applied to make treatments 100% painless, while others are happy just to go ahead without numbing. The dermal injections are so superficial, you can hardly feel them anyway. Alternatively, the meso solution can be needled in using a needle roller or automatic needle pen, more about that below.

There are various good mesotherapy solutions on the market (and even more not so good ones…). We use a couple of different ones in our clinic so we can tailor the solution to whatever the skin needs on the day. One of them for example, contains a high-grade blend of more than 50 key skin optimization ingredients, ranging from vitamins and minerals to amino acids, hyaluronic acid, coenzymes, nucleic acid bases and antioxidants all proven to protect and nourish skin cells. Other solutions might contain ingredients with more emphasis on skin-lightening and yet others might concentrate on matrix stimulation and anti-ageing effects. There are also special mesotherapy solutions available for the body, which aim to improve cellulite or optimize scalp health and hair growth.

> Mesotherapy can be used not only to feed and nourish mature skin, but as a perfect preventative measure in younger patients, too.

Mesotherapy is performed as a course of four to six sessions at two to four week intervals before going on to a less frequent maintenance programme.

The great thing about mesotherapy is that it can be used to correct mature skin, but also as a preventative measure that nourishes and shields younger skin. Many of our patients book a course to re-nurture and rehydrate their skin after sunny holidays or during the winter.

Medical Needling (Collagen Induction Therapy)

As we age, our skin gets lazy and collagen production slows down. Medical needling – or collagen induction therapy (CIT) as it's also known – gives skin a gentle nudge to remind it to keep making fresh collagen. This is another, very natural regenerative treatment that helps the skin help itself. It involves a needle roller or an electric needle pen equipped with multiple ultra-fine, sterile needles and after numbing cream, the procedure can be painless. The needle roller (often called 'dermaroller' after one of the brands) is the traditional method; but automatic needle pens offer distinct advantages including improved results, reduced downtime and a lower risk of injury to the practitioner. However, not all pens are created equal, so it's important that your practitioner is using the safest one.

Medical needling creates tens of thousands of microscopically small punctures in the dermis. These intentional micro-injuries induce tiny, controlled wound-healing responses in the skin's deeper layer. Consequently, natural growth factors are released and fibroblasts are stimulated into synthesising new matrix tissue including collagen and elastin. In time, this will lead to a firmer, more elastic skin with a more refined skin surface appearance.

Studies confirm that needling provides both epidermal as well as dermal benefits with an increase of dermal and epidermal thickness of up to 658%, up-regulation of youthful collagen type 1 and significant clinical improvements (Fabbrocini et al. 2011, Hou et al. 2017, Ramaut et al. 2017, Zeitter et al. 2014). Medical needling not only rejuvenates the skin, but can also greatly improve the appearance of enlarged pores and acne or chicken pox scarring (Alam et al. 2014, El-Domyati et al. 2015, Fabbrocini et al. 2014, Hou et al. 2017). However, any active acne must be completely clear before needling treatment is started!

> Medical needling mechanically mimics the effects of fractionated laser technologies by creating microscopically small puncture columns in the dermis to stimulate collagen production and regeneration.

One of the advantages of medical needling is that we can induce positive effects deep in the dermis without stripping off the protective outer, epidermal layer of skin. The tiny superficial punctures on the skin surface close very quickly, within a maximum of 15 minutes (Liebla et al. 2012). This is a huge advantage, since the epidermis protects our body from water loss and entry of potentially harmful agents such as toxins and bacteria. And because no heat is created, there's also a very low risk of post-inflammatory pigmentation and scarring, which means that in contrast to other treatment options such as lasers, medical needling is considered safe for all skin colours (Cohen et al. 2016).

Medical needling is done in a course of three to six sessions at four to eight week intervals.

Advanced Medical Needling (PRP-, GF-, Meso- and Bright Needling)

For even better results, medical needling can be combined with infusion of a booster solution. These advanced forms of medical needling not only stimulate the skin mechanically, but also evenly infuse it with booster solution directly into the dermis where it's needed most (Budamakuntla et al. 2013, Nofal et al. 2014, Sasaki et al. 2017).

The booster solutions include cell-nourishing mesotherapy solutions (meso needling) and collagen-stimulating growth factor (GF) solutions. The growth factors used may come from a sterile commercial solution (GF needling) or may be derived from our own blood (PRP needling). You might have seen EUDELO's PRP needling featured in InStyle magazine as a recommended treatment to reduce pore size.

> The benefits of medical needling can be even greater when booster solutions of growth factors, cell-nourishing cocktails or pigment inhibitors are added.

If irregular pigmentation is a prime concern, medical needling can be combined with infusions of pigment lightening serum ('bright needling'). These skin brighteners may contain ingredients such as tranexamic acid, arbutin and/or kojic acid which are known to inhibit tyrosinase, the melanin pigment-generating enzyme. One of the advantages of this 'bright needling' technique is of course, that the pigment-inhibiting ingredients get much deeper into the skin than topical skincare can. This is particularly useful in forms of irregular pigmentation, where the pigment has dropped into the deeper skin layers, making it virtually unresponsive to creams and serums.

COLLAGEN DRINKS

When patients have regenerative treatments in clinic, we often offer them a collagen 'shot' to further boost the benefits of the procedure. We use a specially formulated drink containing high-grade bovine collagen, plus other symbiotic nutrients. Collagen shots have become something of a trend and I admit I was sceptical about them at first. But recent clinical evidence has made me change my mind. So how do they work?

Natural collagen is too huge a molecule to reach your skin intact after swallowing: to be absorbed by the gut, it would have to be digested into smaller units. Our shots contain small collagen fragments – peptides and amino acids – which are easily absorbed by the small intestine and distributed throughout the body via the bloodstream, where they remain for up to 14 days.

And here comes the fascinating bit. Because there are suddenly unusually high amounts of collagen building blocks floating around, your skin is tricked into thinking there must be some breakdown – a major injury, perhaps. The regenerative procedure you've just had will reinforce this message – think of the tens of thousands of micro-wounds induced by medical needling for example. So your skin responds to both these alerts by increasing its own collagen production – conveniently using the building blocks we've just supplied. This collagen stimulating trigger leads to tissue remodelling, skin regeneration and ultimately a firmer, more refined-looking skin.

Clinical studies have confirmed that collagen fragments are able to stimulate fibroblasts to produce not only more collagen, but also other vital matrix components such as elastin and hyaluronic acid and make the skin firmer, more elastic and even more hydrated (Asserin et al. 2015, Borumand et al. 2014, Proksch et al. 2014 a & b). We can exploit this natural response by giving you a shot of collagen to drink straight after your regenerative procedure in order to flood your system with collagen fragments and induce maximum production of your own, native protein.

There are countless collagen drinks on the market, many of them too low in dose or containing inferior types of collagen, so ask your aesthetic practitioner to recommend a good one. Also make sure it is not stuffed with sugar or artificial sweeteners. Personally, my preferred shot contains a superior-quality bovine collagen which is much more similar to human collagen than marine types. My dose recommendation is 10g collagen per day.

Gel Needling   Gel needling is a concept we pioneered at EUDELO and it combines hyaluronic acid (HA) skin boosters with medical needling. We've found that due to their synergistic effects, these treatments work more powerfully when combined than when performed alone.

HA skin boosters contain cross-linked hyaluronic acid in a sterile, injectable format making them somewhat similar to fillers, but much softer in consistency (their HA is runny like water rather than firm like a lifting gel). In contrast to native, non-stabilised HA molecules used in mesotherapy, the cross-linked HA in skin boosters lasts much longer and results in more pronounced clinical improvements in areas where the skin has lost plumpness.

> Gel needling combines HA skin booster injections with medical needling. It is particularly good for putting healthy plumpness back into crepey skin, so ideal for lower cheeks with accordion lines and 'bony' looking backs of the hands.

In addition to all the benefits of medical needling, HA skin boosters plump skin directly where needed and therefore is particularly useful for the lower cheeks, backs of hands, neck and chest, for example. You might have seen EUDELO's Gel needling featured in Woman & Home magazine.

For the ultimate outcome combine Gel needling with platelet rich plasma (PRP Gel needling).

Carboxy facials

Carboxytherapy is another bio-stimulative procedure where we use your own skin's ingenious ability to self-repair and renew to full advantage. Although both are regenerative treatments, carboxytherapy acts in a very different way to medical needling. You see, as we get older, our capillaries (tiny blood vessels) and microcirculation in the skin greatly decline. It's been reported that by the time we're 30, oxygen levels in our skin have dropped by 25%, and further to a hollering 50% once we're 40! This is devastating for long-term skin health and wellbeing. Carboxy facials boost our skin's microcirculation, letting more oxygen and nutrients reach the skin to support skin regeneration with collagen and elastin remodelling (Pinheiro et al. 2015) – and help offset yet another aspect of skin-ageing. So how does that work?

Tiny amounts of medical grade carbon dioxide (CO_2) gas are injected into the skin with a specialist device and a very fine needle. These superficial injections essentially trick your skin into thinking it's oxygen-starved, so it responds by dilating blood vessels and increasing blood flow to the area swiftly and powerfully. This increased circulation provides a surge of oxygen and other nutrients to the area treated for several hours.

In addition to the instant circulation boost, the temporary 'oxygen starvation' induced by carboxytherapy triggers the release of growth factors such as vascular endothelial growth factor (VEGF) which stimulates the production of *new* blood vessels (capillaries). These newly formed vessels, plus re-opened capillaries that had become dormant with ageing, assure improved microcirculation in the area long-term.

Make sure your practitioner is well-trained in carboxy facials specifically, as the optimal technique is very different from other forms of carboxytherapy. I originally learned from carboxy facial pioneer Dr Julia Sevi, who kindly shared all her

A greatly underestimated aspect of skin aging is that as we get older, our skin's microcirculation declines dramatically. Carboxy facials improve the flow of blood, oxygen and nutrients to the skin, making it healthier from the inside.

tips and tricks with me. Carboxytherapy is not only used for skin rejuvenation, but also for treating stretch marks, cellulite and scars, albeit with a different technique (Paolo et al. 2012, Pianez et al. 2012 & 2016).

Cryostimulation

Using the thermal shock of a very cold temperature to bio-stimulate the skin is known as cryostimulation – and I'm a major fan. But don't confuse it with cryotherapy / cryosurgery used to *destroy* cells when freezing verrucas, fat cells or sun damage. During cryostimulation, we only cool the skin down to about 5 degrees Celsius. This not only stimulates fibroblasts into producing more collagen and elastin, but also improves the oxygen supply to our skin, while leaving cells undamaged.

There are different types of cryostimulation devices on the market; whole body chambers and devices for local treatment. Interestingly, for whole body chambers, cooling of the head is particularly important (Louis et al. 2015). For cryo facials, we use targeted local cryostimulation devices. Some local devices utilize liquid nitrogen vapour (N2) while others use pressurised carbon-dioxide gas (CO2). Both methods work as long as the target skin temperature of 5 degrees Celsius is reached. Please note that a skin temperature of 5 degrees Celsius is very different

> Don't confuse cryostimulation with cryotherapy/cryosurgery. Cryostimulation cools the skin to 5 degrees Celsius to improve its microcirculation, oxygen and nutrient supply with no downtime. Cryotherapy/cryosurgery destroys targeted tissue by freezing it to below zero.

from an air temperature of 5 degrees Celsius (people always ask, "would I not get the same effect in winter?"). In fact, to reach the target skin temperature of 5 degrees Celsius, we use a cold stream of –78 degrees Celsius (CO_2) or –196 degrees Celsius (N_2)! Once you have experienced cryostimulation, you know it's very, very different from simple winter air... Pressurized CO_2 gas devices add a further dimension to the procedure, pressure (50bar), which boosts lymphatic drainage and thermal shock effects, and makes the experience even more intense – my personal favourite.

We've already seen that blood circulation and oxygen supply to our skin deteriorates significantly as we age. Cryostimulation helps slow this process by improving the efficiency of our skin's blood vessel network. During treatment, blood vessels contract and dilate which instantaneously boosts microcirculation to the skin for several hours after treatment and gives the network a strengthening 'workout', similar to training our muscles (Renata et al. 2010). Regular sessions improve local blood flow in our skin more long-term. With time the resulting higher pressure on the thin capillary walls will cause microvascular networks to branch out in order to accommodate the increased volume of blood circulation. That means that our skin's microcirculation, oxygen and nutrient supply will fundamentally improve – similar to carboxy facials, albeit to a milder degree with this completely non-invasive treatment. Cryostimulation also has anti-oedematous effects and improves lymphatic drainage (Sieron et al. 2010).

I have cryostimulation regularly myself, as it's incredibly elating and even triggers the release of endorphins, our natural 'happiness hormone'. And when using the cryostimulation device along the spine, we can even partly simulate the immune modifying effects of whole body cryostimulation (Lubkowska et al. 2010). What's not to like?

A word of caution, though. Make sure your cryostimulation is done with a device that continuously measures your skin temperature (contact-less) during treatment! Our skin needs it to be cold enough to trigger biological changes, but not so cold that it damages the tissue.

> Make sure your clinic uses a cryostimulation device that measures your skin temperature during treatment, as it's crucial to cool the skin to exactly the right degree.

Chemical peels   Fans of the TV show *Sex and the City* could be forgiven for linking chemical peels with Samantha's red-raw face scaring away the guests from Carrie's book launch. Even for non-*SATC* addicts, there are plenty of other things about chemical peels – not least the name – to scare you off, too.

The fact is, that acid peeling has been used in beauty treatments for centuries and there are many different types, most of which will not leave you shedding your skin like a snake. A peel can be a very effective way of softening fine lines and wrinkles, improving skin texture, minimising pigmentation and even reducing blackheads and whiteheads. However, chemical peels do not only improve the appearance of the skin, but also its fundamental health! A landmark study found that chemical peels are actually able to prevent skin cancer formation by removing sun-damaged cells (Abdel-Daim et al. 2010a/b).

These are the four main strengths and depths.

• **Very superficial peels** are non-clinical peels that you might have at a beauty salon or spa, or might even do yourself at home. Often containing low concentrations of plant enzymes, glycolic acid and/or other alpha hydroxy acids (AHAs), they help the very outermost layer of dead, horny cells to shed, but don't have any real regenerative effects.

I would not recommend this type of peel as one of your monthly regenerative treatments as it's simply not effective enough. However, home peel pads do a great job encouraging exfoliation and reducing oiliness.

• **Superficial peels** are mild chemical peels and the most commonly used type for improving skin texture and overall complexion. They work by removing part of the stratum corneum and sometimes the upper epidermis. They can improve discolourations, surface roughness and texture, but also stimulate collagen production via communication between epidermal and dermal cells. With a superficial peel, you'll achieve a more refined skin surface with a fresher, more vibrant skin tone and improved skin texture.

Peeling agents used in superficial peels include AHAs such as glycolic, malic and lactic acid; and beta hydroxy acid (BHA) salicylic acid. AHAs really are multifunctional superstars and scientific studies have confirmed peels with AHAs such as glycolic acid are able to increase collagen production in the dermis (Omi et al. 2010, Okano et al. 2003, Yamamoto et al. 2006). Hydroxy acid peels are also great for patients with comedones (blackheads and whiteheads) and a tendency for breakouts (Kaminaka et al. 2014). Salicylic acid can also be a useful acne-management adjunct (Arif 2015), although for best acne results, peels should of course be used in combination with prescription treatment. There are also new generation retinol peels that I find particularly useful for ageing skin.

To achieve the best results, a course of treatment (four to six sessions at one to two week intervals, say) is always recommended for superficial peels. The treatment is quick and isn't painful, although you might feel tingling or slight stinging with AHA peels (with retinol peels you often don't feel anything). You may be a little pink afterwards and in some cases experience mild flaking a couple of days later. But generally, there's no significant downtime.

> Most superficial peels don't involve downtime. Hydroxy acid peels are great starter peels and also well suited to younger patients or those who prefer their skin not to be visibly flaking after treatment.

• **Medium-depth peels** affect the epidermis and upper dermis (papillary dermis) and are often performed by a doctor or nurse. The peeling agent is designed to induce damage that triggers a healing response leading to skin-remodelling. Two of the most common agents are trichloroacetic acid (TCA) and Jessner's solution, a mix of lactic acid, salicylic acid and resorcinol. Glycolic acid in higher concentrations can also result in a medium depth peel. Although darker skins generally have to be careful with medium and deep peels (as there is a risk of irregular pigmentation), there are specialist medium depth peel solutions available that specifically address pigmentation including melasma, and are suitable for dark skin. I have seen some extraordinary results with these.

> Medium depth peels act on the epidermis and upper dermis and work particularly well for more mature skin with visible sun damage.

Medium depth peels are often done as a one-off session that has the potential to result in a similar or even better outcome than four or six sessions of superficial peels. However, medium depth peels involve more downtime than superficial peels. Redness, swelling, flaking and potentially some crusting may occur. The flaking often occurs with a delay of two to three days after treatment. Medium depth peels also have a higher rate of potential complications such as reactivation of cold sores, long-lasting skin discolouration and in extremely rare cases scarring. For that reason, make sure to have any medium depth peels in a clinic that is equipped to deal with potential complications.

As an alternative to the stronger one-off peels, there are gentler types of TCA peels available that need to be repeated – for example three to four sessions at one to three week intervals. After completing this course, you can achieve similar results to higher-strength, one-off TCAs.

A medium-depth peel reduces the signs of sun damage with wrinkling and irregular pigmentation and improves skin quality and texture. For certain medium depth peeling agents, you'll feel some stinging, but the treatment is generally well-tolerated without anaesthetic. For other types of medium depth peeling agents, you won't feel anything at all when the peel is applied.

After any peel, it's essential to wear daily broad-spectrum sun protection with SPF30 – 50 for around four months – if you don't already do this as a matter of routine!

• **Deep peels** act on the deeper layers of the dermis and are mainly used to improve more severe skin conditions. The most commonly used agent here is Phenol, which denatures biological polymers and can have a really dramatic rejuvenating effect around the eyes, for example. But deep peels aren't for the faint hearted - downtime is significant, with oozing and crusting, and risks are much higher than for all other types of peels.

Deep peels should only be performed by an experienced doctor. They are performed only once and are sometimes done under general anaesthetic (as part of a face lift, say) as they can be quite painful.

With the advent of modern lasers – especially fractionated ones – deep peels are now used less often in medical aesthetic practises due to their higher risk of complications such as post-inflammatory pigmentation and scarring.

Chemical peels, despite being very low-tech, can be highly effective on a clinical and cellular level, and are in my opinion greatly undervalued.

• **Peel boosters** are customised to each patient and added to certain peels to address specific concerns. Depending on the brand of peel used, the booster might be retinol for ageing skin, or vitamin C and kojic acid for irregular pigmentation. Another interesting peel booster I've worked with are agents that help prevent and repair sun-induced DNA damage. Adding DNA-repairing enzymes and ferulic acid for example have been shown to significantly decrease thymine dimers (signs of UV-induced DNA traumas) caused by sun. Yet other peel boosters encourage the peeling agents to penetrate deeper into the skin. Superficial needling can also further enhance the benefits of certain peels.

Laser facials

These are among my current favourite regenerative treatments, as despite the amazing benefits, many of them induce zero downtime. There are different devices and techniques on the market - I will talk you through ours as an example. For the laser facials at EUDELO, we use fractionated Q-Switched Nd-YAG technology (Neodymium YAG), which you may also have seen called the 'Hollywood Facelift' or 'Clear Lift 4D' in the media (Beri et al. 2015, Gold et al. 2014, Luebbberding et al. 2012, Yue et al. 2016). This laser emits short, yet enormously powerful bursts of light that reach underneath the skin's surface. Here, the light causes a photo-acoustic effect to create microscopic punctures in the dermis, which stimulates collagen and also helps fragment unwanted pigmentation in the skin.

Another distinctive characteristic of this laser is its fractional pattern, which means the laser beam creates microscopic 'columns' of skin regeneration, leaving pillars between untouched which greatly lowers the risks of treatment, such as scarring. The laser technology is non-ablative, meaning it leaves the

> With fractional, non-ablative laser facials we can stimulate collagen production in the dermis without damaging the skin's surface layers. No-downtime laser facials are among my favourite regenerative treatments.

skin surface intact. It leads to regeneration selectively in the deep backbone of our skin, the dermis, exactly where we need it for real anti-ageing benefits. Inducing a controlled dermal wound without injuring the overlying epidermis causes all stages of healing response and skin repair to happen beneath the unharmed skin's surface – which means no downtime.

You can see the picture emerging that many regenerative treatments work by creating tiny wounds in the skin that trigger repair and remodelling. Our laser's mechanism of action for example is somewhat similar to medical needling, but with the amazing difference that the thousands of micro-wounds and healing responses it causes don't even touch, let alone puncture, the skin's surface. This of course, makes this type of laser facial a true 'lunchtime procedure'. And, as pigment isn't its primary chromophore (molecular target), it's safe for all skin types including dark skin. That's because this laser shatters the unwanted pigment with shock waves, unlike conventional pigment lasers that are attracted by and heat up pigment specifically. Best of all, it's 100% painless, even without numbing cream. A course of six treatments at two week intervals will give the best results.

Other energy-based regeneration techniques

There is a huge variety of energy-based regeneration techniques on the market and I'd like to mention a couple of commonly used ones. We've already talked about LED treatments in the dermatology grade facials chapter. Radiofrequency (RF) is another treatment, which has become increasingly popular in recent years and uses RF energy to heat the dermis and tighten the skin without damaging the top layer. Most commonly used for non-surgical skin-tightening on both the face and body, most RF treatments are completely non-invasive, but a few use needles. There are various RF technologies on the market such as unipolar, bipolar or multipolar depending on the number of electrodes used, and future developments will continue to keep RF widely used for skin tightening (Beasley et al. 2014, Krueger et al. 2013).

Some devices may use a mix of both RF and ultrasound (I'll talk about ultrasound skin-tightening below). Yet other devices use near infrared light (NIR) to heat dermal tissue non-invasively (Gupta et a. 2014), stimulating collagen and elastin production to encourage firmer, more elastic skin. Your skin temperature should be measured during treatment to ensure it's high enough to bring about significant benefits without risking problems such as burns.

> Energy-based treatments such as radiofrequency and near-infrared light heat the dermis to stimulate collagen production.

All of these energy-based bio-stimulative treatments naturally require a course of several sessions (up to 6 to 12) and will induce benefits gradually over some months. Again, look at it like joining a skin gym – great results are rarely achieved in a single session!

Symbiotic effects

Now you have an insight into how some of my current favourite regenerative treatments work, you can see that we aim to stimulate the skin from a variety of different angles in order to get the best, cumulative results over time. So when planning your annual skin regeneration programme, make sure you make full use of the symbiotic benefits regenerative treatments can offer. One of our most popular annual *Skin Care Elite* routines is for example: three PRP needling sessions to boost collagen production, then three monthly carboxy facials to optimise oxygen and nutrient supply to the skin, followed by three laser facials for collagen stimulation and then another three carboxy facials.

It's my very strong belief that regular regenerative treatments together with good daily skincare are one of *the* best investments you can make in your skin's future. They're something no-one who cares about their skin should be without. But how do they fit in with more corrective aesthetic treatments? I totally understand that in addition to the fundamentals of preventing and preserving, patients often want instant transformations – those little tweaks that enhance naturally great features or soften not so great ones. Not that we should correct our imperfections to conform to some standardised view of perfection – remember, I'm on a mission against those unnatural, 'done to death' looks. We don't want to create a crowd of alike looking women, but celebrate diversity. However, if you're keen to realise your personal 'best you', I'm right with you. In fact, I'm one of you. That's why in the next chapter, I'll explain how best to combine your regenerative treatments with corrective treatments modern aesthetic medicine has to offer.

•

CORRECTIVE PROCEDURES – THE ULTIMATE WOW FACTOR

If you're even more committed to keeping your skin in its best shape, or are looking for that instant wow factor, it's time to step up to the topmost level of the *EUDELO Skin Enhancement Staircase*.

Non-surgical corrective treatments such as wrinkle-relaxing BTX injections and dermal fillers take aesthetic intervention a stage further and can dramatically address signs of ageing, including loss of facial contour. Corrective procedures can also be used for advanced indications such as non-surgical nose and chin shaping. Body shape and contour can of course also be addressed with non-invasive aesthetic treatments, however, as this would go beyond the scope of this book, I will not speak about those here.

> Forget everything you've heard about BTX and fillers. The way we use non-surgical corrective treatments is changing!

Three of the most popular corrective procedures are wrinkle relaxing injections (botulinum toxin or BTX such as Botox® or Bocouture®), fillers and volumisers. These injectable treatments can help us to achieve the more dramatic, yet still completely natural-looking results, which are fundamental to my philosophy. Certain concerns such as loss of facial volume will *only* improve with corrective procedures – you'd never get your youthfully plump cheeks back with skincare or even regenerative treatments. And while some people draw a line under injections, hear me out first!

There are so many myths and misinformation floating around about cosmetic injectables that I'm 100% convinced you'll learn something new by reading what I have to say. Don't skip the following chapter. Read it, take all the information in – and *then* make your decision. Even if a corrective procedure isn't for you right now, you never know how you'll feel in the future. Keep your options open – and keep an open mind. You can only make a truly informed decision after reading this chapter.

There is a huge demand for injectable treatments these days, yet the bombardment of both positive and negative press about these procedures can leave you confused about what to believe. Research confirmed that in a representative sample of 1,000 women aged between 25 to 70 years, about 50% contemplate cosmetic procedures, yet less than 10% go ahead (Ehlinger-Martin et al. 2016). That doesn't surprise me. Hopefully this book will help women (and men!) considering cosmetic treatment to make an informed decision and do what's right for *them*.

Research has also revealed that the time women take to consider aesthetic procedures is much longer than thought: some think about having BTX and fillers for 10 years before stepping through that clinic door. The *average* length of the 'consideration phase' varies from country to country – in the UK, it's around two years.

When to start   I'm often asked what *is* the best age to start having 'botox' and fillers. It completely depends on your skin age, rather than chronological age. Most people may need to start with BTX in their end 30s or 40s, although some have such a strong habit of over-using their frown muscles in their 20s, that BTX might be needed already before the age of 30.

I also recommend starting earlier rather than later with fillers to prevent lines from etching themselves into the skin irreversibly. Early intervention also means you'll get away with lighter fillers and repeated conservatively done injections give a more natural result long-term.

Last but not least, starting early enough with BTX and fillers will even slow down the ageing process. As with everything, prevention is better than cure. Start early enough, and little tweakments over time will usually prevent the need for more drastic corrections later. It's all about prevention and early intervention (P&E!). We often see this in clinic – people who started little tweakments early tend to age much better than those who left it too late, and will need less treatment later on.

In this context, it's interesting to know that women are considered to be at the peak of beauty in their mid-thirties (reassuringly not earlier...), just before signs of facial ageing begin to appear (Ehlinger-Martin et al. 2016). So starting to do something in your early 30s certainly is a good idea. What I aim to do with the following chapters is to equip you with all the facts about corrective tweakments so that you can make an informed decision without leaving it too late to get the best results.

Wrinkle relaxing injections with botulinum toxin (BTX)

Botulinum toxin (BTX), better known as Botox®, is a prescription-only injectable treatment which has many indications both medical and cosmetic. But its most famous use is for softening lines and wrinkles (Carruthers et al. 2013, Dorizas et al. 2014, Small 2014, Sundaram et al. 2016). Since its line-erasing action was first noted in 1987, Botox® has become a household name. But what many people don't realise is that Botox® is just one of the brand names of the active ingredient BTX. Botox® is in fact a brand of BTX type A manufactured by a drug company called Allergan. You may also hear it referred to as Vistabel® which was the name used to distinguish it from the medical brand when it was first licensed for cosmetic use. There are other BTX brands, such as Dysport® and Azzalure® too. Bocouture® is a next-generation botulinum toxin from Germany that has been purified, with a lower load of non-essential proteins.

I have extensive clinical experience with both Botox® and Bocouture® and like both very much (that's why I speak more about these two brands than maybe others). Essentially, I can achieve great results with both of these, and feel that the clinical differences are more in the practitioner's hands than with the choice of product, as a scientific study I participated in confirmed (Prager et al. 2010). (Naturally, I can't vouch for other, inferior quality or counterfeit products that come into this country...) So from now on, I'll consistently refer to any type of botulinum toxin-A as BTX to make sure you understand I'm talking about the active ingredient, not any particular brand.

> Botulinum toxin (BTX) softens mimic lines by reducing wrinkle-forming facial over-movements.

It's fair to say that BTX has revolutionised the anti-ageing market. It has been widely credited with changing the face of the aesthetic industry by kick-starting the now established specialist area of aesthetic medicine. Before its arrival, the options available to those seeking a more youthful appearance were limited largely to surgery or collagen and fat injections. Even though the concept of cosmetic enhancement wasn't new when BTX came on the scene, what aesthetic doctors struggled with was how to effectively treat mimic lines such as crow's feet and frown lines.

BTX has been used in cosmetic treatments for more than

25 years now, even longer for medical indications. Its long history of medical use means that in the right hands, this well-researched drug is extremely safe. You might also be interested to hear that in medical indications such as torticollis (a painfully twisted neck) the dose that is injected is much, much higher than in cosmetic treatments, which is reassuring from a cosmetic safety profile point of view.

And while BTX has been used cosmetically for decades, the way we use it has been adapted and greatly optimised – in forward-thinking clinics at any rate. But more about that, shortly.

BTX FOR EXCESSIVE SWEATING

Hyperhidrosis – or excessive sweating – is a miserably debilitating condition. The significant limitations it imposes mean quality of life is compromised, as patients are unable to feel confident and comfortable going about their everyday lives. It most commonly affects the underarms, palms of the hands and soles of the feet.

BTX injections are an extremely effective option for the armpits and effects last for 6-12 months (de Almeida et al. 2014). Prior to the procedure, a special numbing cream is applied to make the treatment completely painless. Feedback from patients is extremely positive. We're told repeatedly that it's a life-changing treatment.

One of the things that has made BTX so popular is that serious side effects are extremely rare. Even if (usually mild) unwanted effects do occur, BTX is effective for around three to four months, so any problems are short-lived and often only last for around six to eight weeks. However, as with any aesthetic intervention – especially corrective ones – it's absolutely crucial that the person treating you is not only appropriately qualified and trained, but also highly experienced. As I've mentioned, BTX is a prescription-only medicine and can only be prescribed by doctors, dentists and prescribing nurses (that is nurses with additional prescriber's qualifications). It's a sad fact though, that because the treatment is seen as cosmetic, there are numerous examples of non-medics such as beauty therapists injecting people with this drug. Not only is this illegal and unethical, but also downright unsafe. So don't have your BTX treatment in a beauty salon or hairdresser's (yes, that happens!) but in a clinic where it's administered by an experienced medic.

> BTX such as Botox® and Bocouture® are prescription drugs, so make sure only a qualified medical professional in a reputable clinic treats you with these.

How do BTX treatments work? Basically, when BTX is injected into a muscle it will stop it contracting temporarily or soften contractions, depending on the dose. This is why BTX is an excellent treatment for dynamic or mimic facial lines – it normalises the over-movement that is causing mimic lines. So the great thing about cosmetic BTX is that it gets to the root cause of the line by preventing the muscle from over-moving. For this reason, BTX can also play a useful wrinkle-prevention role in people who habitually over-use certain facial muscles, but don't have visible lines yet. For example, some people frown without even noticing. Staring at a computer screen all day won't help either…

BTX has another biological benefit, too. It has been shown that muscle-induced chronic repeated crinkling of the skin increases the release of the enzyme collagenase in our dermis. Collagenase degrades collagen, so by preventing recurrent skin creasing, we're also reducing collagenase and with that preventing collagen loss. If constant creasing stresses our skin on a biological level, BTX gives it the rest it needs to improve its collagen levels.

It takes on average about five days for BTX to start kicking in. The effect on the muscle is fully reversible and, as we've seen, lasts around three to four, sometimes up to six months, so patients usually come for top-ups two to four times a year. However, many patients report that in time, the intervals between clinic visits get longer as the facial muscles 'learn' not to crease and wrinkle as much. So essentially, BTX can re-train your muscles.

> Constantly over-engaging facial muscles causes repeated skin creasing, which leads to collagen breakdown via induction of the enzyme collagenase. BTX inhibits this pathological process.

STORIES FROM THE CLINIC

When I see patients for their first assessment, I often notice that those with pronounced dynamic lines really do engage their muscles excessively even as they're talking to me. When I point this out to them, they're completely unaware they're doing it. Helping them to bring that over-movement back into normal parameters benefits their skin short-term and long-term.

I've also seen that with BTX treatments every three to six months, facial lines improve even more over the coming two years or so. You'll see a good degree of correction already after the first treatment, but then with repeated treatments the benefits tend to get even better.

Ideal lines for BTX treatment include crow's feet, frown lines between the brows and worry lines across the forehead. These three areas are licenced BTX indication, however many other areas are treated in everyday practice (off-label). We can for example perform a gentle, non-surgical brow lift with BTX, soften smoker's lines and relax the downward pull of the mouth corners so you lose that grumpy look. More advanced indications are reduction of 'turkey neck' bands and creating a more defined jaw line – the 'Nefertiti Lift'. Lastly, in patients with a square face caused by overactive jaw muscles (think clenching or grinding teeth at night), BTX can significantly reduce the bulk and dramatically slim the lower face, which can be transformational for female faces.

It's important to know that for BTX to be optimally effective, you should start treatment when the lines are still dynamic and not yet static. You can test this in the mirror by gently stretching the wrinkle between two fingers. If it disappears completely, it's still dynamic and can be easily treated with BTX. But if you can still see the line, etched into the skin, it's become static and additional treatment may be needed. In these cases, we can offer a soft filler or

> Don't leave it too late! BTX works best before mimic lines become static and are visible even when the face is relaxed. BTX also plays a useful role preventing habitually hyperactive facial movement which causes skin creases.

HA skin booster as a follow-up treatment two weeks after BTX.

BTX treatment can be done in different ways. It can be administered in comparatively high doses that 'freeze' movement completely, but this looks unnatural in my opinion. Alternatively, lower ('baby botox') doses of BTX soften movement without freezing muscles completely. This low dose can be delivered via a series of multiple tiny injections at certain points all over the face – the 'sprinkle botox' method. If you lower the dose even more, you get ultra-low-dose 'meso botox'. We prefer these low-dose BTX regimes at EUDELO. We want to normalize hypermobile muscles, but want you to retain your natural facial movements. It's that 'no-one would know you've had botox' look.

We also much prefer a full-face treatment, rather than isolated treatment of let's say the forehead. Full-face approaches give the most harmonious, overall look. Treating an isolated area means leaving other muscles hypermobile and possibly even overcompensating for the reduced movement of their 'colleagues.'

Gentle, low-dose injection schemes seem to be a more European approach to BTX, while in the US and South America in particular, there seems to be a tendency for stronger 'freezing.' But I'm starting to see a turning point, here. I once had a Brazilian patient who asked me to freeze her forehead so much that it "looks as shiny as a mirror". Needless to say, I refused.

'Sprinkle botox' is an innovative way of softening mimic wrinkles. Very small doses are injected into multiple sites, so lines are relaxed without freezing facial expression. The result looks completely natural.

For BTX injections we use very fine needles, not much bigger than acupuncture needles. Usually, these injections only cause very little, if any, discomfort, so a numbing cream isn't usually needed.

STORIES FROM THE CLINIC

A habit we've standardised at EUDELO is to always mark up the face with a skin pen before we treat with cosmetic injectables. Not because even after years of aesthetic practise we still feel insecure about injecting precisely! In my experience, results are always superior with thorough planning and meticulous marking.

So, to sum up, well-administered, low-dose BTX isn't about freezing your face or making you look weird. It's about re-training *healthy* movement patterns. Who thinks an unremitting, 24/7 frown is a normal, healthy expression? It's a pathological habit – and it's not a good look. We can reverse that.

Dermal fillers

Along with BTX, dermal fillers are one of the most popular injectable aesthetic interventions (Ballin et al. 2015, Gutowski et al. 2016, Moradi et al. 2015). Most people know fillers as treatment options to fill wrinkles and this remains a great indication, especially for static types. However, in recent years, fillers have become much more than just treatments for lines and wrinkles. In fact, we've moved away from indiscriminately pumping up lines and filling folds as it was done in the old days. The much more exciting and cutting-edge way of using fillers is for replacing facial volume and to restore more youthful facial contours. More about that later, but first let's talk about what fillers actually are.

A word of extreme caution to start with. Unlike BTX, dermal fillers aren't prescription-only medicines, but classified as medical devices. This makes the task of monitoring who's doing the injecting and what exactly is being injected a far more daunting one.

> Filling and contouring injections can not only soften lines and wrinkles, but also restore more youthful facial contours.

Unlike the US, where only a handful of products are approved by the Food and Drugs Administration (FDA) for cosmetic use, the UK currently lacks any kind of meaningful regulation for fillers. There are countless fillers on the market here and new ones are constantly being released. That's why it's crucial to know which ones have the best safety records and give the best results. The potential side effects and problems with fillers are far greater than those from BTX, so it's vital that you not only ensure you're having your treatment performed by a properly trained, highly experienced aesthetic doctor or nurse, but that you fully understand which products they're using as well. This book will brief you with a good background knowledge of the different types of fillers, so that you can ask your aesthetic practitioner the right questions before treatment.

Injecting filling substances into the face to offset ageing is nothing new. Fat transfer procedures were carried out as far back as the 1890s, but results were often inconsistent and unreliable. Paraffin and silicone injections were used in the early 1900s, but poor safety records and complications meant these treatments didn't catch on. It wasn't until the introduction of collagen almost a century later that the term 'dermal filler' fully emerged. The first injectable collagen treatment designed for facial rejuvenation was derived from bovine collagen. Along with Botox®, collagen paved the way for the non-surgical aesthetics revolution. Although patients needed an allergy test before undergoing treatment, collagen injections grew in popularity, especially in the US where, according to the American Society for Aesthetic Plastic Surgery (ASAPS), they were still the 13th most common procedure performed in 2008.

However, in the last decade, collagen's popularity has declined with the emergence of a plethora of other fillers, in particular hyaluronic acid fillers, which are now considered the gold standard and certainly my favourite type of filler. You'll find out why in the next few pages, but first, back to basics. Why use a filler at all?

Dermal fillers are the main solution for static lines and gravitational folds. Basically, they lift depressions in the skin. Fillers can be used in all sorts of facial areas, from deep nose-to-mouth lines, to superficial 'lipstick bleed' lines around the mouth. The effect is instantly visible, although there may be some temporary swelling and bruising. Occasionally we might need more than one session to obtain an optimal outcome. How long the effects last depends on the patient, their age and lifestyle, the exact filler used and the area injected, but the average is around six months for lines and wrinkles (longer for contouring injections). The thicker and more viscous the filler (for deeper lines or facial contouring) the longer it generally lasts. In very mobile areas of the face, a filler will last longer in combination with BTX, as over-movement of facial muscles can make a filler dissolve quicker.

HOW TO LOWER THE RISK OF BRUISING

Bruising is a common side effect of fillers. Although new techniques such as using blunt cannulas can reduce this risk, even the best injectors can cause bruises as we're still puncturing the skin. Bruising may take between five days and three weeks to fade fully: anti-bruising creams containing vitamin K can help them vanish a little quicker. The good news is, you can help reduce the risk even further before you have treatment with the following tips.

• **Avoid taking blood-thinning painkillers** such as Aspirin® in the two weeks before the procedure. But check with your GP (General Practitioner) first that they are happy for you to stop.

• **Avoid potentially blood-thinning supplements** such as fish oil, gingko biloba, vitamin E and ginseng for two weeks prior to the procedure. Arnica supplements can help with healing post-procedure, but should not be taken before as it is also thought to increase bruising risk.

• **Pre-cooling the skin** with a cool pack wrapped in gauze before the procedure may also lower the risk of bruising by contracting blood vessels. However, don't cool the skin while it's bleeding, as cooling slows down blood clotting.

When dynamic mimic lines have turned static – think those permanent creases between your brows that don't even soften when you fully relax your frown muscles – we often use fillers as a second step after BTX. These secondary static lines have developed because essentially, you left the treatment of your mimic lines too late. Frown lines are initially all dynamic, which means they're only visible when you frown. This is the perfect time to treat them with BTX. But if you leave them untreated too long and they turned static, BTX alone won't do a great job and you'll need an additional filler treatment, usually a couple of weeks later.

Don't get me wrong – BTX is still very important as it treats the underlying 'root cause' of the line – i.e. chronic over-movement of certain muscles – and prevents further deepening. For this reason, treating a mimic line with filler only would be like painting over the cracks without fixing the underlying problem.

Having said that, there's some extremely interesting research emerging around 'myo-modulation' with fillers. This new evidence shows that hyaluronic acid fillers can also dampen overactive muscles to some extent. Obviously, BTX weakens muscles much more powerfully: if you injected a high enough dose, you can pretty much paralyse a muscle temporarily. But it's fascinating to see how facial muscle activity can also be modulated gently with clever filler placement, and how excessive movement can be visibly reduced in some patients after filler treatment. I'm really excited about these new developments. It's thrilling what aesthetic medicine can do these days.

TYPES OF FILLERS

• **Temporary fillers.** Most dermal fillers used in the UK today are temporary or 'resorbable' products, made from various kinds of materials. Hyaluronic acid (HA) fillers are the most widely used and have an excellent safety profile. HA fillers are today considered the gold standard. Also known as hyaluronate, HA is a naturally occurring substance present in every living organism. We have an abundance in our skin – in fact 50% of our body's total HA is found there – so it's highly biocompatible and rarely causes allergic reactions.

An important member of the glycosaminoglycans (GAGs) family, due to its high water-holding capacity, one of HA's key roles is to maintain the plumpness and moisture that helps keep skin smooth and elastic. With its ample presence between the cells in the dermis, we now know that HA not only holds water and provides a constructive framework in the dermis, but is also involved in cell-to-cell messaging while supporting nutrient exchange between blood vessels and the dermis. Furthermore, HA acts as a free radical scavenger, so it's a highly important multi-tasking component of our skin. However, HA levels decline with age and its quality also deteriorates.

As we've already seen in the cosmeceuticals chapter, certain skincare products provide topical HA to hydrate the skin's superficial layers. HA fillers however, work in a different way. We inject a solution containing sterile, transparent hyaluronic acid gel into much deeper skin layers. Just as with natural HA, the HA filler is degraded over time by enzymes in the body called hyaluronidases. A hydrating and free radical scavenging effect may well be an added bonus, but the main aim of these fillers is to literally fill up lines from underneath and contour the face. They also have an age-slowing potential as treatments can help induce your own collagen production (Turlier et al. 2013, Wang et al. 2007).

HA fillers come in different thicknesses, viscosities and lifting capacities which makes them a versatile choice for treating different facial zones. A thinner product is well-suited to fine lines and wrinkles or for subtle lip enhancements, whereas a thicker one is ideal for addressing deeper folds. An even thicker filler (also called 'volumiser') is used to contour the face and replace volume loss, more about that in the next section.

The other important thing to note is that unlike other types of fillers, HA can be reversed by injecting the enzyme hyaluronidase which effectively dissolves them within 24–48 hours. So, if for some reason you want rid of your HA filler, this can be done quite easily. Another scenario might be that we need to dissolve a filler in case of a (rare) complication such as development of a nodule. Although fillers overall have low rates of complications such as infection, nodules, hypersensitivity or necrosis, adverse reactions with filler treatments are a little more common than with BTX and we need to be prepared – as I have experienced first-hand with my own under-eye treatment.

> Hyaluronic acid remains the gold standard filler ingredient. HA fillers are temporary fillers. They are also reversible, if need be.

Hyaluronidase is a prescription drug, though – another reason to go to someone who is medically qualified and appropriately trained to manage complications should they arise. A beautician or other non-medic simply wouldn't be in a position to trouble-shoot like this. So don't risk your health to save cash and remember, if something sounds too good to be true price wise, it usually is.

HA fillers come in all sorts of price ranges and some products from abroad can be noticeably cheaper. At EUDELO, we decided to use only the highest quality HA products as these come with the greatest clinical evidence behind them. Trusted HA brands include Belotero®, Juvederm®, Restylane® and Teoxane® amongst others. The Belotero® range by Merz and Allergan's Vycross® ranges are my personal favourites.

• **Long-lasting fillers.** There are other types of filler that don't contain HA and last longer than HA fillers. Some practitioners call them 'semi-permanent', but I don't think this is a good term – 'long-lasting' is more accurate.

Long-lasting products such as Radiesse® and Sculptra® work differently to HA fillers – they are so-called 'stimulatory fillers', as they stimulate new collagen formation more strongly than HA fillers (Breithaupt et al. 2015).

Sculptra® is made from poly-l-lactic acid (PLLA). The injected poly-L-lactic acid is broken down within the skin over a period of months, however new collagen gradually appears and the clinical effects can last up to two years (Vleggaar et al. 2014). I know respected colleagues who like to work with Sculptra® and the results can indeed be impressive. However, personally I'm not a big fan, due to a higher risk of nodules and less predictable results in my opinion.

Radiesse® contains synthetic Calcium Hydroxylapatite (CaHA), which has been safely used for over 25 years in a variety of indications in the human body. The CaHA microspheres are composed of calcium and phosphate ions which occur naturally in human tissue. Once injected into the skin, the CaHA particles form a 'scaffold' for the patient's own tissue to grow new collagen between. The gel carrier dissolves within a few months and the CaHA particles gradually break down and are metabolised by the body after about a year, so only the new collagen structure is left. Clinical effects last up to two years, in some cases even 30 months (Bass et al. 2010, Emer et al. 2013).

At EUDELO, we use HA fillers for the vast majority of treatments because of their great benefit-to-risk ratio and potential reversibility. With advanced techniques, we can achieve most things we want to for our patients using HA fillers, especially since the introduction of cannula-assisted injections. However, there is one facial area where Radiesse® does a particularly great job. With less water-attracting properties compared to HA, Radiesse® gives the jaw line a nice 'crisp' definition and I like to use it for doing just that.

- **Permanent fillers**. These may include solutions such as liquid silicon and rounded polyacrylamide (acrylic) beads in a hydrogel carrier, but they're not very commonly used today - in fact I'm strictly against them, as they have a higher risk of complications (Ledon et al. 2013, Marinelli et al. 2016, Smith 2008). Even if you don't experience an adverse effect, feel the aesthetic result is perfect and are glad you don't have to keep coming back for top-ups, your face naturally

> I advise against permanent fillers. They carry a more unfavourable benefit-to-risk ratio compared to temporary fillers and if you don't like the result, you're stuck with them.

changes with time. Ideally, aesthetic treatments are adjusted to keep up with facial changes; but a permanent filler may look oddly out of place ten years down the line. And you're stuck with that, like it or not. So be smart, stay safe and keep your options open.

HA skin boosters   Bio-revitalisation with hyaluronic acid ('HA skin boosters') is a great treatment for improving skin texture and plumpness. As mentioned in the Gel needling section, HA skin boosters are essentially very soft HA fillers containing cross-linked/stabilised HA that are injected over large skin areas. As such, HA skin boosters sit between conventional HA fillers and non-cross-linked HA used in mesotherapy.

Bio-revitalisation with HA skin boosters is particularly suitable for finer lines, crisscross lines, crinkling of the skin and overall loss of elasticity. Essentially, skin boosters are great for areas where your skin has lost plumpness and gained crêpiness, such as the lower cheeks. Clinical studies, one of them conducted by myself, confirmed that HA skin boosters will improve not only the appearance of the skin, but also skin elasticity, firmness and roughness (Kerscher et al. 2008, Reuther et al. 2010, Streker et al. 2013, Williams et al. 2009a).

One of my favourite areas for HA skin boosters are the hands. You see, age-related volume loss also affects the backs of hands. That's why hands can start to look bony and sinewy when we get older – a 'deflating' experience that's easy to fix with HA skin boosters (Williams et al. 2009a). And in contrast to thicker fillers, there is no risk of ending up with a dreaded 'pillow hand'. In my opinion, it's important to maintain the natural appearance of visible movement of tendons, rather than burying them under a thick layer of filler, which looks weird and unnatural. And don't forget about the neck and chest - also great indications for HA skin boosters. Remember, a congruent impression is important, so we mustn't treat the face in isolation, ignoring other exposed skin areas such as hands and chest.

Some of my favourite HA skin boosters are Belotero Soft by Merz, Restylane Vital and Vital Light by Galderma and Volite by Allergan. Depending on the product, revitalisation with HA skin boosters is done as a one-off session or a course of three (to six) sessions at two to four week intervals. For even better results, HA skin boosters can of course be combined with growth factors/PRP and medical needling (GF Gel needling / PRP Gel needling).

Volumisers and facial contouring

While most people only know about dermal filler in the context of lines and wrinkles, the more progressive way of injecting fillers involves a full-face approach which considers age-related changes in facial volume which, believe me, start much earlier than you think! With a full-face approach, we aim to restore facial volume and contours to those of a more youthful-looking profile.

Starting from mid-life, the fat pads in our cheeks start deflating, as mentioned earlier. At the same time, fatty tissue migrates south, creating a tendency for heaviness and sagging in the lower face. As if all this wasn't enough, even the underlying body structure diminishes, which means the whole face loses its support. A shrinking support structure leaves the face looking tired and less attractive, while the overlying skin envelope essentially becomes too big and starts sagging. This of course, will lead to the secondary problem of folds and creases.

With stiffer, more lifting fillers (*contouring fillers* or *volumisers*) we can give this lost support back to our face. This technique has totally transformed aesthetic medicine and full-face results often come close to those of plastic surgery – or even better, as we can restore the face's youthful volume rather than stretching the skin to fit a shrunken scaffolding. Think about it – what would you rather do? Stretch your skin over your increasingly gaunt cheeks to smooth out the wrinkles? Or restore the original youthful contour, so that your skin fits your face better once again? A no-brainer, I'd say.

Restoring youthful cheek contours is the most commonly performed facial contouring treatment. Advanced contouring indications include filling of temple hollows, chin augmentation, jaw line treatments and tear trough correction for that deep under-eye depression. My own rather weak, recessed chin has had a little 'helping hand' and thanks to a contouring filler, looks much more in balance with the rest of my face now. Scar revision, correction of facial asymmetry and nasal deformity are also all advanced filler indications.

> From mid-life, our entire face starts to deflate. Fat tissue and bone resorb, which means that the face loses its underlying support structure and its envelope of skin becomes too big and starts to sag and crease.

A WORD ABOUT CANNULAS AND NEEDLES

Traditionally, dermal fillers were injected with a needle. But increasingly, we're using fine, blunt tubes called cannulas during treatment. This means we use a sharp needle to create a tiny entry hole, insert the blunt cannula into it, then deliver the filler through its tube. The cannula causes less tissue trauma and has a lower risk of bruising. Cannulas are also great to treat larger skin areas such as the cheeks, as we can reach different parts of the face from one entry hole – a bit like key-hole surgery. Most importantly, cannulas carry a lower risk of accidentally injecting filler into a blood vessel and thus causing a lack of oxygen supply to the skin with subsequent necrosis. So for certain anatomical 'danger zones' – facial areas with important blood vessels – working with a cannula is crucial (Braz et al. 2015).

But however much I love working with cannulas, there are certain areas where a needle is more precise, so in most filler sessions, I'll use a 'best of both worlds' combination of both needle and cannula. This requires expert knowledge and years of experience, which is another reason why it is so important to choose the right clinic and practitioner – don't compromise.

While cosmetic treatments used to be all about chasing lines and wrinkles, the past few years have focused more on re-contouring the face. Remember the EUDELO *3-Key Principle?* Lines and wrinkles only occupied one of the three key areas of facial ageing, arguably the least important one. Apart from improving skin quality and skin health, replacing lost volume and re-contouring the face is the third key and crucial for a truly successful rejuvenation outcome.

In fact, reducing lines and wrinkles should be the *finishing* touch to well-supported features. Following our earlier house analogy, softening lines and wrinkles would be the decoration of the house, i.e. the cherry on the cake. Nobody would start decorating a house if the structure isn't sound and it's about to collapse. First things first – get the structure right and put supporting beams in (all built on a firm foundation of regenerative treatments to improve skin quality of course!), only then worry about final touches such as reducing lines and wrinkles. This is what progressive aesthetics is all about.

Fig. 18: First things first – get the structure right with supporting beams and a firm foundation, only then worry about decorating the house.

Coming back to our face - if you lose facial volume, that crucial first impression your face gives out changes too. Where once it looked youthful, lively, friendly and approachable, it now looks drawn, tired, sad and even grumpy. While I've heard people say they're not bothered about a few lines and that they even add character, no-one has ever said they don't mind looking gaunt and tired. This is such a fundamental truth, it's really important to bear in mind.

> Contouring fillers are an indispensable tool in modern aesthetic medicine. There are very few people from mid-life onwards who won't benefit from this treatment as it addresses the root cause of lines and sagging, and recreates a more youthful facial profile.

I think we can all agree that naturally sculpted cheekbones, lush lips and a firm jawline contribute to an attractive profile. If you have lost them with age or are not naturally endowed with these features, contouring and volumising fillers can help. Contouring fillers or volumisers are essentially more 'robust', better lifting versions of wrinkle fillers and are injected deeper under the skin, often directly onto the bone to softly shape the face. The procedure is usually very straightforward, painless with a numbing cream and can even be a 'lunchtime' procedure. Contouring effects last around 12 months, in some cases up to two years, but that depends on a variety of factors, including the choice of filler, and varies from patient to patient (Few et al. 2015). In time, your body's own enzymes will degrade the HA filler – just as happens with your native hyaluronic acid.

We've also observed that with repeated treatments – say

once a year – people's faces tend to age far better than they would without contouring, possibly due to increased collagen production and stimulation of lifting facial ligaments. This means that there is a preventative element in addition to the corrective effect of the treatment. Now let's look at how volumisers contour specific areas.

• CHEEK CONTOURING

Cheeks are one of my favourite areas for sculpting, as age-related volume loss in the cheek area has such a negative impact on how attractive and youthful we look (Ramanadham at al 2015, Rohrich at al. 2007 & 2008). In my experience, extensive endurance exercise such as long-distance running may hasten this decline even more. As well as experiencing age and lifestyle related changes like this, some people's flatter cheeks are hereditary and would naturally benefit from having their contours improved.

The good news is that cheeks can be enhanced non-surgically, simply by injecting a contouring HA gel underneath the fat tissue (Baumann et al. 2015, Few et al. 2015). This is also known as the 'Y-Lift' as it turns the bottom-heavy triangle of age into a more upwardly, youthful heart shape again. Most women know intuitively that sculpted cheeks enhance their appearance – that's exactly what we try to emulate with blusher or bronzer!

The absolute key to this treatment is not to over-treat and create the 'pillow face' look that so many people seem to have fallen foul of. This, frankly is one of the worst things we can do. While cheek contouring greatly benefits most men and women from their mid-life onwards, it's crucial for the practitioner and the patient to understand the limits of this lift.

Of course, contouring the cheeks will lift the face – however, it's not a miracle cure for facial sagging. Often a combination approach is needed – for example, cheek contouring plus focused ultrasound assisted lower face tightening. But most importantly, accept the simple fact that while we can make you look better and slow down the ageing process, it's not (yet?) possible to halt ageing completely. If you ask me, ignoring this reality is one of the chief reasons for the over-filled pillow cheeks I so often see these days. Better to look older than odd.

> If you can clearly see that someone's cheeks are volumised, they're overdone. Correctly and subtly-done treatments look so natural, you'd never guess. So don't push your practitioner to inject more and more – trust their judgment (unless they look weird themselves…).

If done well, there is really no reason to fear the pillow-face when having cheek contouring done. It's all in the 'dose'. Even by just adding for example 0.2ml of a HA contouring filler into two points on each cheek, you'll lift the skin, support the facial ligaments that hold up your cheeks, and even slow down the ageing process – without becoming a human hamster. So that would be less than 1ml for the entire treatment – not much at all, if you compare it to the average 5ml teaspoon. With small volumes like that, the risk of ending up with a pillow face is zero.

> Repeated low-volume injections of contouring HA fillers to the cheeks can support lifting facial ligaments and slow down sagging.

One of our most popular treatments, the EUDELO *Pillar Lift*, is based on this type of natural-looking, balanced facial contouring. We carefully inject subtle supporting 'pillars' of specialised HA into the cheeks to 'shore up' the face, like buttresses. Add some line smoothing injections and HA skin boosters to the mix, and there you have it – the EUDELO *Pillar Lift*.

• NON-SURGICAL NOSE RESHAPING

This innovative HA filler/volumiser treatment is particularly popular in Asia. Not every nose is suitable for treatment, but for certain patients it can prove a great alternative to rhinoplasty surgery (Humphrey et la. 2009, Liew et al. 2016).

Non-surgical nose shaping can be used to correct prominent humps and bumps on the bridge of the nose (it essentially hides them) and to even out its shape and refine its profile. As well as making the nose look straighter, the treatment can also be used to elevate or uplift the tip of the nose. Conversely, if a prominent, upturned 'ski slope' nose is the problem, it can make that less obvious.

Treating the nose with fillers is a highly advanced technique and not without risk: there are important blood vessels in this area and their accidental obstruction may have serious consequences, such as necrosis. If you're having your nose treated, make double sure you see an experienced aesthetic doctor or nurse.

> HA fillers can hide prominent bumps and straighten the bridge of the nose without the need for surgery.

• ADDING DEFINITION TO THE CHIN AND JAWLINE

Some people are very conscious about their small or recessed chin and would love a more balanced profile. Others may have lost bony support in the jaw area with age, contributing to development of sagging and jowls. Injecting a contouring HA gel into the chin area redefines the lower facial contours and greatly balances features. Depending on how it's done, chin shaping can make a person look more feminine and heart-shaped, or more masculine and square-shaped. Chin augmentation can even make a prominent nose seem less large. Chin contouring is in my opinion a hugely underrated treatment that can benefit both men and women (Bae et al. 2013, de Maio 2015, Suryadevara et al. 2009).

We can also treat the jawline with contouring HA fillers or CaHA containing Radiesse®, making it appear firmer and better defined. And imagine the power of combining cheek contouring with chin and jaw defining treatment – way to go! I've had this combined procedure myself and it's made a huge difference.

> Chin shaping can make a huge difference to your entire facial profile. It balances facial features, if the chin is recessed, and can make the person look more feminine and heart-shaped, or more masculine and square-shaped depending on the aim of the treatment. Chin shaping is one of *the* most underrated treatments there are in my opinion!

It's not surprising that non-surgical chin and jawline shaping is the first treatment many men start with, as the contemporary male look includes sharp contours of the face with a strong chin and well-defined jawline (de Maio 2015).

We've just talked about *boosting* facial contours. But what if I told you that it's now also possible to *take away* unwanted bulk from under the chin and jawline without surgery? It's all thanks to another type of injection, which, incidentally, makes a great partner to HA contouring. What I am talking about are fat dissolving injections (Anand 2016, Dayan et al. 2016, Hersant et al. 2015, Jones et al. 2016). For an even more powerful jawline approach, we may combine HA contouring fillers with fat-dissolving injections and focused ultrasound skin tightening (more about those in the next chapters).

● FILLING DEEP UNDER-EYE HOLLOWS

Tear troughs – those deep hollows under the eyes – can make you look very tired and even sad. They can be lifted with a soft HA filler, but not everyone's a suitable candidate. If there's also puffiness (oedema) or prolapsed fat beneath the eyes, results from fillers may not be satisfactory and surgery might be a better option. But if the skin in your eye hollows seems to be lying directly on the bone with hardly any fat padding between, an HA filler or HA skin booster can make a major difference to those tired-looking dark shadows (Hill et la. 2015, Huber-Vorländer et al. 2015, Rzany et al. 2012). However, this is an advanced indication, so make sure your practitioner is highly experienced in this area.

> Lifting deep under-eye hollows 'wakes up' the face and makes it look less tired.

● LIP SHAPING

With age, the general facial deflation we experience also affects the lips. They gradually become thinner, less 'rosebud' plump and may develop fine vertical lines both on them and around the contours. Understandably, there's a certain amount of fear around lip augmentation, especially the dreaded 'trout pout.'

But it doesn't need to be obvious! Done subtly, lip augmentation is a fantastic procedure that can look totally natural. We're essentially just re-plumping the lips and replacing the volume they've lost – no more, no less. So no, in the hands of a good practitioner, gentle lip shaping won't make you look 'done' ... and is central when trying to look the best version of yourself (Fischer et al. 2016, Solish et al. 2011)!

Apart from overfilling the lips until they're unnaturally enlarged, one of my pet hates is over-accentuating the border between the red of the lip and the surrounding skin. Some practitioners even do this intentionally to try to create a visible, sharp 'step' or contour here. Frankly, I think this is a dead giveaway that you've had a 'lip job'. Oh, I know where they're coming from: of course, flattening, ageing lips lose their defined border, hence that increasing need for lip liner. But when do younger lips ever have an obvious, in-your-face ridge around them? So why would I try to create it?

I'll tell you what it is – just as with pillow face cheeks, trout pout lips are based on misguided over-compensation. We're humans, not machines. We can't fully reverse age-related changes – and nor should we try. This is where the EUDELO philosophy comes into its own. We want you to look the best version of you and confident whatever your age, not coerce you to try to stop the clock no matter what. Desperate age-denial does no one any favours: it merely leaves you looking 'done' and gives the aesthetic industry a bad name into the bargain.

> Gently re-plumping lips gives back the lost volume that makes them look youthfully fresh – an essential part of aesthetic treatment. It also softens lines both on lips and feathering around the contours. Forget the trout pout, with the right touch results are 100% natural – your own lips, minus 15 years.

Where lips are concerned, I much prefer recreating a youthfully plump lip *body* rather than trying to achieve some sort of 'designer' *shape*. I go gently, replenishing volume without going overboard; and instead of treating the lips in isolation, I also replace lost plumpness around them, which is essential, as research confirmed (Beer et al. 2015). This refines the lips and reduces lipstick bleed lines in a much more natural way, without the need for an obvious 'step' outline.

At our clinic, we offer the EUDELO *Feather Lip Smoothie*, a treatment which rejuvenates lips by boosting hydration and adding a subtle roundness for a soft, natural look, as featured in The Sunday Times' Stylist magazine. We do this by injecting a HA skin booster with a flexible cannula. Inspired by keyhole surgery, we create a tiny entry point for the cannula next to each mouth corner. This avoids pricking a needle directly into the sensitive red of the lips, so there's a lower risk of bruising and less swelling after treatment.

> Over-filled lips with an obviously steep contour between them and the surrounding skin are dead giveaways for fillers. Avoid both!

The most advanced lip treatment that we've just introduced is the EUDELO *Lip P-Booster*. This is a treatment that not only plumps, but has an anti-ageing action, too. The first step is to create rejuvenating platelet rich plasma (PRP) from the patient's own blood, as explained in an earlier chapter. This growth factor rich solution which, when mixed with an HA-containing gel to give an all-important, instant plumping effect, helps slow down further lip deflation over time. You might have read about EUDELO's *Lip P-Booster* in Tatler and Cosmopolitan Magazine.

The *Lip P-Booster* infuses PRP derived growth factors with a soft HA gel in and around the lips to gently plump the whole area and slow age-related deflation at the same time.

As with all our lip treatments, an extra strong numbing cream is applied to the lip area, so the procedure is comfortable. The specially prepared *Lip P-Booster* is injected using a blunt cannula, which softly enters the lips from the mouth corners just as for the *Feather Lip Smoothie*. Via the same entry point, we also target lines around the lips to boost plumpness and smooth lipstick lines. With repeat treatments every four to six months, you should see not only the immediate plumping effects of HA, but the cumulative benefits from the PRP infusion.

• THE FULL-FACE APPROACH

You might have heard the term 'liquid face lift', which is used for a combination of non-surgical rejuvenating procedures such as BTX wrinkle relaxers plus multi-syringe facial contouring and line-softening with HA fillers and volumisers. While I'm not keen on the term 'liquid face lift', the concept is good as it combines different rejuvenating modalities for a full-face approach – which is certainly the future of aesthetics.

Two 'liquid face lift' techniques you may also have heard of are the *8-Point Lift* and the more detailed *MD Codes™*. These concepts have been developed by pioneering plastic surgeon Mauricio de Maio. The 8-Point Lift involves small amounts of HA filler injected into eight key points on each side of the face. Injecting these 16 points re-contours the full face and rejuvenates its overall appearance in a balanced way. The MD Codes™ are an advanced version of the 8-Point Lift.

This time, the face is divided into smaller areas, such as the cheeks, chin, temple and brows. Here, each anatomical unit has its own number of specific filler injection points, again resulting in re-contoured facial features.

Taking some aspects of these techniques as a starting point, I went on to develop the EUDELO *Architect*. This innovative treatment combines four non-surgical modalities to address all main problems of the ageing face and results in dramatic, yet completely natural-looking rejuvenation of the entire face. Based on today's understanding of facial balance and approaching the entire facial structure harmoniously whilst in

---

THE EUDELO ARCHITECT:
4-IN-1 FULL FACIAL HARMONY

1: **Full-face contouring** with a hand-picked combination of HA volumisers - evidence based star products chosen to work together in perfect concert.

2: **Re-training unhelpful muscle movement patterns** such as over-expressive frowning or depressor muscles that pull the mouth corners downwards with a EUDELO proprietary low-dose BTX scheme.

3: **Non-invasive skin tightening and lifting** with micro-focused ultrasound with high-resolution ultrasound visualization, a highly advanced corrective and regenerative treatment to stimulate collagen production.

4: **Reducing lines and wrinkles** with soft HA fillers and HA skin boosters – the crowning stroke.

motion and in rest, the EUDELO *Architect* not only restores youthful contours, softens lines and wrinkles and tightens and lifts the skin, but also re-trains unhelpful muscular movement patterns. It almost goes without saying that the treatment is tailored to each individual.

Back to our happy house analogy, the EUDELO *Architect* not only decorates the house to the highest standard, but ensures strong supporting beams and a firm foundation are in place to provide a fully comprehensive approach.

When I explain facial contouring to patients, I often compare it to a coat-hanger. Think of taking your jacket off a hanger and hanging it on a hook instead. It sags and creases, doesn't it? Sadly, that's what happens to our face with age. Whereas once it was supported well by underlying bone, muscle and fat, some of that scaffolding gets lost over time. Loss of volume plus gravity causes the overlying skin envelope to sag and our entire face looks older and sadder. Now think of putting your jacket back on the hanger. Supported by just two key points where the shoulders should be, it regains its shape, so the creases don't show.

The facial contouring part of the EUDELO *Architect* (and the EUDELO *Pillar Lift* for that matter) works rather like that. By strategically adding small aliquots of volume into specific key points, we improve facial support and make the entire face look fresher and more youthful, in such a balanced and natural way, no one would ever know.

Facial contouring is, of course, a 'couture' treatment, tailored to each patient – there's no 'one size fits all', no 'painting by numbers'. A good aesthetic practitioner will be able to adjust the treatment to your particular face shape, specifications and aims. And it goes without saying that facial contouring is

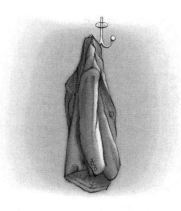

Fig. 19: Supporting two key points where the shoulders would be, lifts and smoothens the entire coat.

not something you want to get from a novice – an advanced approach like this involving multiple injections requires extensive knowledge of facial anatomy, physiology and muscular movement patterns.

Remember A medical aesthetics clinic is not a self-service supermarket – it's hardly a good idea to go into the consulting room with a shopping list of what you'd like to be done. It's called aesthetic *medicine* for a reason – you wouldn't tell your GP what to prescribe, would you? Trust your practitioner's diagnostic skills and treatment recommendations. I strongly recommend listening to what your doctor or nurse says they feel your skin needs – they're the experts and they're examining your face objectively. In my experience, patients are often unaware of the real problem, or that lines and wrinkles are merely an effect, not the cause.

And would you believe me, if I told you that more lines can potentially even make faces *more* attractive? Let me prove it. Think of someone you know and visualise their face. Now imagine them going from a neutral, relaxed facial expression into a broad smile. Their face just lit up irresistibly, no?

So how can that be, if smiling makes their crow's feet look more pronounced and their nose-to-mouth lines deepen? One of the main reasons our smiling faces look more appealing is that instantly, our cheeks are plumped and our chin elongates. And this is exactly what we can recreate with facial contouring (without the added lines...)!

And the best thing of all? The total peace of mind that because facial contouring with HA fillers is non-surgical and we can dissolve HA if need be, it's fully reversible if you don't like it (never happens though). Personally, I break into a cold sweat just thinking about waking up from having a surgical face lift and hating the result. There's no going back – imagine that! Don't know about you, but I'd much rather pay for a treatment that's gradual, fine-tuneable and potentially reversible.

So to sum up, facial contouring is a truly amazing, non-surgical, full-face rejuvenation technique based on today's understanding of facial balance. The latest techniques address the entire face harmoniously, rather than just chasing isolated lines and wrinkles.

> One of the best things about HA fillers is that they can be reversed, if needed. If you don't like them, lose them. Priceless!

Dissolving fat   I am very excited to tell you that it is now possible to *take away* excess facial fat on the lower face without surgery or liposuction! The treatment consists of injecting deoxycholic acid, a naturally occurring molecule that works a bit like a biological detergent, into fat deposits under the chin and along the jawline (Anand 2016, Dayan et al. 2016, Hersant et al. 2015, Jones et al. 2016). The fat cells are gradually liquefied and destroyed permanently, and the liquefied fat is then eliminated naturally via your lymphatic system. Brand names you may have heard about that do this are Aqualyx®, Kybella® (in the US) and Belkyra® (in Canada and Europe). A treatment of two to four sessions at four to eight week intervals is typical for under the chin. I really like fat dissolving injections, as they can be fine-tuned very nicely.

Another method to reduce the appearance of a double chin is cryolipolysis, i.e. freezing the fat to minus degrees in order to destroy the tissue (Ingargiola et al. 2015, Krueger et al. 2014). The most well-known device for this is CoolSculpting®. Targeted fat cells are crystalised (frozen), then they die. The dead fat cells are digested by surrounding specialist cells and naturally eliminated from the body over the following weeks and months.

Both cryolipolysis and injections with deoxycholic acid can also be used for stubborn fat pockets on the body, say 'saddle bags' on the thighs, but discussing body treatments would go beyond the scope of this book.

In contrast to these two evidence based methods, fat dissolving mesotherapy doesn't work as well in my opinion.

Thread lifts
_____

A thread lift is a non-surgical, but slightly more invasive aesthetic procedure compared to fillers and BTX. Here, surgical sutures are inserted into the soft tissue of the face to help lift lax skin and counteract sagging. The procedure is done under local anaesthesia, occasionally with light sedation.

Two general types of lifting threads are used. Free-floating barbed threads have barbs that lock into place once the thread has been positioned – think of them opening like tiny umbrellas. With suspension threads, the far end is tied to deeper facial structures as anchoring points. These anchoring points are stable anatomical points that won't give way. Via an entry point, often behind the hairline, a thick hollow needle is inserted to position the threads under the skin. The upper end of the threads is tugged upwards so the skin envelope is lifted. In addition to lifting threads, there are also threads that are inserted in the dermis, in a lattice-work pattern, for skin rejuvenation. Between ten and several dozen threads are inserted per treatment, depending on the indication.

Some threads dissolve over time, while others don't. Materials used include ordinary suture type materials (similar to stitches used in surgery) such as polypropylene mono-filament Prolene (non-resorbable), nylon (non-resorbable), polydioxanone PDO (resorbable) or others such as polylactic acid PLA (resorbable). In the case of resorbable threads, by the time the material has dissolved a few months later, it's thought that fibrotic tissue that has formed around it keeps lifting the skin after the suture itself has gone. I am not sure to what extent this is a reliable effect (to a visibly relevant degree!), as quite a few patients report no lasting effect with resorbable threads beyond the first few months.

Thread lifts are having a fashion moment right now and increasing numbers of clinics are introducing them to their patients. The concept of a face-lift without surgery is indeed attractive to both men and women. But whereas thread lifts redistribute the skin envelope, they don't replace lost facial volume as done with facial contouring, and excess facial skin is not removed as with surgery. For that reason, some patients may experience a puckering or rippling of their skin where the sutures have been pulled tight. This may be hidden in the hairline, but occasionally the puckering is visible.

At the time of writing, we are not performing thread lifts at EUDELO, as I have some reservations about them. One of the reasons I'm hesitant at the moment is that I've seen too many not so great results and even puckering cases. Furthermore, when results have been good, I've often felt they weren't long-lasting enough given the relative invasiveness of the procedure. Lastly, I also feel uncomfortable about 'blindly poking around' deep facial structures. When I'm deciding whether or not to introduce a new treatment to EUDELO, I always ask myself if I'd have it myself. If not, then why would I want my patients to have it? In the case of thread lifts, the *current* answer is no. That doesn't mean I might not change my mind once the thread lift technique has matured though.

Energy-based devices

In recent years, there has been an influx of various types of energy-based devices on the aesthetic market. From laser and IPL to radiofrequency and ultrasound, these machines use light or other types of energy for a broad range of indications, including facial rejuvenation, body shaping and skin tightening. I've mentioned some of them already in the regeneration chapter, but I'll explain a little more here, as some treatments clearly fall into the correction category. For others there might be an overlap. I won't talk about body shaping devices, however, as they're beyond the scope of this book.

Lasers and IPL   Laser and IPL devices have become an indispensable tool in aesthetic medicine, as technologies are getting better and better (DiBernardo et al. 2016, Li et al. 2016, Pozner et al. 2016, Stewart et al. 2013). A laser is essentially a high-energy beam of light with unique properties. Laser light consists of photons (small light particles) all of which have the same wavelength, or colour. Different wavelengths from different types of laser are absorbed preferentially by certain types of tissue (the target structure, also referred to as chromophore). So, lasers can be used to *specifically* target different chromophores in the skin, such as melanin pigment, haemoglobin (in blood vessels) or water. This is called selective photothermolysis. It's important to understand that lasers are designed to treat a specific indication or skin concern: a laser targeting pigmentation is different from one used to treat facial redness and broken veins, or yet another which resurfaces skin by targeting water. Lasers aren't the omnipotent magic wands they're often portrayed as, but they're excellent in their very specific areas.

> A laser emits a single wavelength or colour, while IPL emits a broader spectrum. Both are very useful in treating specific skin problems such as vascular skin changes (e.g. facial thread veins).

Intense Pulsed Light (IPL) systems differ from lasers in that they emit a broader spectrum of light and deliver multiple wavelengths (or colours) simultaneously to the tissue. However, these wavelength ranges are still used to target specific skin structures such as pigment or redness, which makes them great for specific tasks, too.

Laser and light-based technology has developed significantly in recent years and can be used to address a wide range of different indications. As well as skin rejuvenation, concerns such as pigmentation, unwanted hair and tattoos, scars, facial redness and teleangiecstasis (broken vessels) can all be treated successfully. Some light-based devices are used to treat skin diseases such as psoriasis and acne; however, I would always recommend combining that with prescription creams.

THE THREE MOST IMPORTANT SKIN STRUCTURES TARGETED BY LASERS AND IPL (I.E. 'CHROMOPHORES') ARE:

- **Melanin** for treatment of irregular pigmentation and hair removal
- **Haemoglobin** for treatment of facial redness and thread veins
- **Water** for resurfacing / rejuvenation (i.e. treatment of fine lines, scarring and improvement of skin texture)

You may hear lasers being referred to either as *ablative* or *non-ablative*. In very simple terms, this refers to how much damage they cause to the top layer of skin. An ablative laser (also called resurfacing laser) such as an Er:YAG (Erbium YAG) or CO2 laser will remove or ablate the skin surface in order to trigger a wound-healing response so that remodelling and rejuvenation takes place. Results can be dramatic, especially with the deeper-reaching CO2 laser, but ablative lasers are generally more aggressive and involve more downtime, risks and complications compared to non-ablative lasers.

> 'Ablative' lasers remove the surface layer of the skin, while 'non-ablative' lasers leave the surface unharmed.

Whilst ablative lasers remove the surface layer of the skin, non-ablative lasers work on the mid-layer or dermis, while leaving the surface intact. Non-ablative lasers are generally less invasive and carry less downtime, which has made them popular with patients who don't want that lengthy recovery period. But whereas there's less risk and downtime, in simplified terms, you may need multiple sessions with a non-ablative laser to achieve an equivalent result to an ablative laser.

Another laser term you might have heard is 'fractional' or 'fractionated'. These devices are a newer concept of targeting only a 'fraction' of the skin at a time by delivering multiple, microscopically small treatment *columns*. These treatment zones are separated by bridges of untreated, healthy skin, which helps to heal the tiny wounds the laser causes. This again means reduced downtime and lower risks (Borges et al. 2016). The fractional concept exists for both ablative and non-ablative lasers. With regard to the former, I would always advise a fractional over a fully ablative laser for safety reasons.

One of the first fractional lasers to be marketed was the

Fraxel® device, but there are now a number of machines – both ablative and non-ablative – that use fractionated technology, although just like with 'hoover' or 'botox' people often (incorrectly) refer to other brands with this brand name.

Now let's briefly look at laser and IPL hair removal, since these are such popular treatments. You might have heard them called 'permanent hair removal', although the term is misleading. While lasers and IPL devices can result in long-lasting hair reduction, they can't promise to remove hair permanently, as you'll still need occasional top-up treatments to keep skin hair-free.

How effective laser and IPL hair removal is depends on a number of factors including the patient's skin and hair colour: treatments are generally most effective for patients with pale skin and dark hair. This is because the light targets the pigment in hair and the more contrast there is between skin and hair, the more effectively the energy is channelled into the root of the hair. Since laser/IPL light can't 'distinguish' between hair and skin pigment, the effects on darker skin are less good and the risk of unintendedly burning the skin and leaving post-inflammatory hyperpigmentation (PIH) is higher.

> Fractional lasers deliver microscopically small treatment columns into the skin. The surrounding areas of untreated tissue accelerate the healing process and reduce downtime.

A newer development in long-lasting hair reduction are IPL home devices. Here, the technology has been adjusted to be safe for home use; light energy emitted is generally lower and often via additional filters. With these home devices, you'll need more frequent sessions to achieve and maintain results equivalent to clinical hair removal treatment, but they are a great alternative to in-clinic treatments. I use one myself at home.

• PLASMA SKIN REMODELLING

Plasma is an increasingly popular technology used in aesthetic medicine, in particular for upper eyelid tightening. As you might know, plasma is the fourth state of matter in which electrons are stripped from atoms to form an ionized gas (Elsaie et al. 2008). High-temperature plasmas have been used in surgery for over two decades. However, it is now increasingly used as a non-surgical method to rejuvenate skin. Plasma produces a controlled thermal damage in the skin in order to elicit a wound healing response with skin remodelling. Unlike laser and IPL devices, which deliver energy to specific targets, or chromophores, plasma non-specifically heats tissue upon contact (Elsaie et al. 2008). The technology can be used at different energy settings for different depths, from more superficial epidermal to deeper dermal effects (Elsaie et al. 2008).

Plasma devices can be used from local skin areas such as lipstick bleed lines or upper eyelids, to full-face treatments (Kilmer et al. 2007, Potter et al. 2007, Scarano et al. 2016). As plasma technology leads to full ablation of the skin, my personal preference would be to use plasma energy on small skin areas only. The upper eyelids for example can be a good indication in some patients (some practitioners call this non-surgical blepharoplasty), also because post-treatment redness that may last for weeks, can be hidden more easily.

• ULTRASOUND SKIN TIGHTENING

This is an amazing treatment that can lift and tighten skin on the face, neck and chest without downtime. Ultrasound waves have of course, been used diagnostically throughout the medical field for more than 50 years, so their safety is well established. However, very different therapeutic ultrasound devices harness the power of these waves to deliver profound collagen-boosting effects in both the skin and the superficial muscular aponeurotic system (SMAS), the layer of fibrous tissue that surrounds facial muscles. This ultimately leads to a lifting effect on skin and muscle layers, so a good therapeutic ultrasound device can not only tighten skin, but lift facial features too. This method is referred to as high intensity focused ultrasound (HIFU) or micro-focused ultrasound (MFU) and is one of my favourite treatments for a sagging of lower face, although it's also very effective for lifting eyebrows.

If you use a powerful enough device, it's usually a one-off session that only needs repeating every couple of years. It goes without saying that I combine this treatment with replacing lost volume in the mid-face, if needed. Ultrasound tightening and facial contouring with fillers are indeed a great combo. And there's another treatment modality that complements ultrasound skin tightening beautifully, too. You have heard about it before. It's of course fat dissolving injections. If there's quite a bit of heaviness in the lower face with fat under the chin and along the jawline, I recommend melting some of that fat first, before performing the ultrasound tightening, as the ultrasound will then have a much easier job of lifting facial features. Another one of my dream teams!

Clinical studies have established ultrasound skin tightening as safe and effective in over half a million treatments worldwide – and counting (Fabi et al. 2013 & 2014, Harris et al. 2015, Hitchcock et al. 2014). However, my

> High intensity focused ultrasound is a very effective, non-invasive skin tightening and lifting technique that works well for the lower face.

strong advice is to have treatment with a device that not only delivers HIFU/MFU, but also incorporates simultaneous ultrasound *visualisation* (HIFU-V/MFU-V). This allows the practitioner to visualise the exact tissue layers they're treating (as they are treating!), ensuring the energy is delivered precisely where it's supposed to go (Fabi et al. 2015, MacGregor et al. 2013). Delivering energy into the right layer of tissue might sound easy, but believe me – it's not. Most ultrasound skin tightening devices offer different treatment heads with different penetration depths and advise using a certain transducer for targeting the dermis and another for targeting the SMAS layer. However, everyone's face and tissue is different and the thickness of the dermis and exact

> In my opinion, simultaneous ultrasound treatment *and* visualisation is non-negotiable for both best results and avoiding unwanted effects. Don't compromise on the visualisation feature!

depth of the SMAS layer greatly varies from person to person (and even from one area to the next in the same patient!). For the best lifting results, we need to target the SMAS layer accurately and I can say from experience that its depth is definitely not always the same. So visualising all tissue layers *while* we are 'shooting' is of paramount importance!

The other reason I like ultrasound skin tightening is that it is not only a corrective, but also a regenerative procedure that stimulates collagen production. At EUDELO, we like to use HIFU-V/MFU-V to intervene early and treat patients who are starting to show loss of firmness and elasticity, rather than wait for significant lower face sagging and jowls. Remember, it's all about P&I – prevention and *early* intervention.

A PARADIGM SHIFT

We've now discussed both regenerative and corrective procedures in depth and have seen what can be achieved with today's aesthetic medicine toolbox. Naturally this list can never be complete (and it's a moving target!), but I have selected what I currently consider the most important treatments for you to know about. Now I want to come back to the paradigm shift currently happening in aesthetic medicine that I mentioned right at the beginning of this book. This paradigm shift is highly significant and will change both the way we view cosmetic procedures and the looks of the men and women who opt for them.

First, let me remind you that we don't necessarily aim to make people look *younger* – but we do want them to look more *attractive*. And yes, there's a difference. The more we obsess about making a patient look younger, the higher the risk they'll end up looking 'done.' Naturally, if you're aiming to make someone's face more attractive, they may well look more youthful, too. But there's much more to it than that!

Attractiveness doesn't just revolve around age, but also involves whether a person's face looks symmetrical, has balanced features, and whether they have more masculine or feminine qualities. If a woman has quite a square face, for example, slimming her lower face will make her look more feminine and thus more attractive. Making her eyes look bigger will also distract attention from her chin, creating a more feminine first impression. Conversely, making a male patient with soft facial features look more attractive may mean giving his chin and jawline *more* definition.

It's all highly individual, but these subtle changes are tricks of the trade we have only really mastered over the past few years and many practitioners – let alone patients – may not yet even be fully aware of the possibilities. Making someone more attractive may also mean tweaking biological features that are not ideal, such as my hereditary deep tear troughs and weak chin, or correcting facial asymmetries.

> Modern aesthetic medicine aims to make people look more *attractive* rather than just looking *younger*. We want you to enjoy being the best version of yourself, so don't compare yourself to others!

This primary pursuit of attractiveness sits perfectly with aesthetic medicine's current paradigm shift. As I mentioned earlier, we're moving away from simply chasing isolated symptoms such as lines and wrinkles. What we really want to do is improve *subconscious impressions* and change *emotional indicators* of the face. These are concepts that forward-thinking plastic surgeons Steven Dayan and Mauricio de Maio amongst others have helped to popularise and they are fundamental to the EUDELO *system*, too (Charles Finn et al. 2003, Dayan et al. 2012, Michaud et al. 2015). So what does this mean for you?

Let's take frown lines as an example. We've long known that the main benefit of relaxing lines between the eyebrows isn't so much that the patient will look less lined, but that the patient will look less angry. Not constantly scowling will not only make this person look more attractive, but also less threatening and more approachable, possibly even triggering a cascade of seemingly unrelated positive influences in their life. Time and time again, I've seen to my utter joy that aesthetic medicine really can indirectly help change someone's life for the better. If you look better, you'll feel better and carry yourself more attractively on a holistic level.

Research has confirmed that relaxing frown lines not only changes the way we appear to others, but can benefit us psychologically via bio-feedback (Alam et al. 2008, Heckmann et al. 2003, Hennenlotter et al. 2009). If we frown less, our brain is tricked into thinking we must be happier. That's why relaxing frown lines with BTX has also been shown to benefit patients with depression (Finzi et al. 2014, Magid et al. 2014).

So treating someone with BTX can not only make them appear less angry and standoffish, but may also help them to feel better in themselves. A clever treatment with BTX can also make their eyes look bigger and less close-set. (I'm talking about a very subtle change here, not the infamous 'surprised American look,' as my sister-in-law once put it).

As our primal brain tends to perceive small, close-set eyes, depressed eyebrows and an angry scowl as aggressive and threatening, the subconscious first impression is a negative one. This means you may be unintentionally projecting an emotional state that doesn't reflect your true feelings. By tweaking these features with BTX, we're essentially modifying the subliminal response that evolution has hard-wired into us over millions of years. Even the slightest change – often barely detectable to the conscious eye – can significantly benefit first impression and non-verbal communication between individuals. And that is exactly what the new wave of aesthetic medicine is all about.

The subtle, strategic changes made by certain non-surgical aesthetic procedures can alter split second first impressions to your advantage. These changes might be minor modifications you're not even consciously aware of, or that only a trained eye could point out. But they can significantly alter the way the world perceives you.

> Less is more! Minimal aesthetic changes to the face can significantly improve deep-seated subconscious impressions people have of you, without leaving you looking 'done.'

And it doesn't stop with frown lines. I think we agreed earlier that flat, gaunt-looking cheeks can make people appear tired and exhausted - something contouring fillers can change instantaneously. Also, patients look significantly less weary and sad when their deep under-eye hollows are lifted with a soft filler. Furthermore, gently plumping skinny lips and lifting the corners of the mouth will make a person look much less tense and stressed. Raising drooping brows and opening the eyes will further support a positive projection of our personality and how we're perceived. The ageing process can also change muscular action patterns in our face in a way that can make us look as though we're perpetually snarling. All these issues and negative impressions can be addressed with smart aesthetic 'tweakments'.

You might not be able to put your finger on it after an aesthetic adjustment, but something is different. Somehow, you just look brighter and fresher. Perhaps people will compliment you on something seemingly unrelated. "What a great lipstick colour", or "that top really suits you", they might say. Or simply, "you look happy!"

A study published by Dayan and co-workers in the *Journal of Dermatological Surgery* in 2010 even revealed that aesthetic treatments (in this case, softening nose-to-mouth lines) can subliminally improve how your social attributes are perceived (Dayan et al. 2010). Social skills, academic performance, finance, occupational success, relationship success, and even athletic success all appeared better after this subtle aesthetic treatment (Dayan et al. 2010). The key, of course, is that cosmetic treatment is undetectable. If you look 'done', the potential benefits can be *reversed* and the way people perceive you can be more negative than before!

> The new aesthetic medicine paradigm is shifting away from treating isolated 'symptoms' such as lines and wrinkles, towards a full-face approach, which includes subtly changing negative emotional traits and improving subconscious impressions.

And it gets even better! When researching for this book, I came across the fascinating concepts of 'facial mimicry' and 'emotional contagion'. This means that we tend to automatically change our own facial expression and even emotional state in response to emotional expressions of *others* (Dimberg et al. 2012, Kelly et al. 2016, Pawling et al. 2017, Prochazkova et al. 2017). And that can happen even if the portrayed emotions are not real. Get your head around this – *your* frown lines might put other people in a bad mood!

> For the first time in human history we can now make people look *better*, as they get older!

Changing emotional features and enhancing first impressions does of course work best in a full-face approach. So rather than obsessing over isolated areas such as lines and wrinkles, think 'attractive' inside and out – and you get the general picture of what the new aesthetic paradigm seeks to achieve.

YOU MIGHT ALSO
WANT TO KNOW...

•

PAIN RELIEF

Often our patients ask us, "does it hurt?" The honest truth? While all non-surgical aesthetic interventions are either non-invasive or minimally invasive, as we move up the staircase, some of the regenerative and corrective procedures would be a little uncomfortable without pain management. However, there are very effective ways to take away that pain.

Many clinics will apply a numbing cream containing lidocaine to make treatments more comfortable. Topical lidocaine stops nerve conduction, causing temporary loss of sensation. However, there are huge differences in effectiveness depending on how this is done.

I strongly believe that the clinical staff should apply numbing cream so that it's done properly and in good time – at EUDELO we apply ours around 45 minutes prior to the procedure. We found that a shorter application time is less effective. Another trick to optimise pain relief is to cover the numbing cream with cling film. This occlusion helps the cream to penetrate faster and deeper, making the anaesthetic effect more powerful.

Handing you a tube of numbing cream and expecting you to apply it randomly at home or in the clinic bathroom – or worse, not offering you numbing cream at all – is not good clinical practise in my opinion!

Different numbing creams can also differ greatly in effectiveness, depending on the active ingredient(s), their concentration and other factors. Good old Emla® cream for example, is in my experience quite weak compared to newer preparations such as LMX4®. Our ultimate weapon is a 30% lidocaine cream specially mixed in Germany. However, we only apply the latter to small skin areas to avoid unwanted systemic effects.

That's because ignoring safely rules can prove fatal. In 2005, a 22-year-old woman from North Carolina died of a lidocaine overdose. Following instructions she'd been given by staff at a local hair-removal clinic, she generously applied numbing gel to both of her legs at home, then covered them in plastic wrap. On her way to the clinic, Berg passed out. She went into convulsions, then a coma and eight days later she was dead. A very powerful reason why both having treatment and numbing in a reputable clinic is essential.

> There are highly effective numbing creams on the market, which can make treatment virtually painless.

Another reason to carefully think about who is injecting you is that some patients react with an allergy to the added lidocaine in fillers – something your clinic needs to be able to treat immediately and confidently.

Because today's advanced numbing creams are so effective, and most dermal fillers now also contain their own dose of lidocaine to further minimise pain during treatment, dental blocks (numbing injections like at the dentist) are rarely needed these days.

•

MEDICAL DERMATOLOGY & SKIN CONDITIONS

In this book, we've been discussing skin ageing and common age-related concerns. However, there are a number of very common medical skin conditions such as adult acne and rosacea, which are seen in aesthetic clinics (rightly or wrongly...) on a daily basis. You will remember that the first key of facial analysis is skin quality and skin *health*. Complete skin health is supremely important for 'great skin', so we should take these common skin issues seriously and give them the attention they deserve. What's the point of having amazing bone structure and barely a wrinkle if you suffer with recurrent breakouts? On the other hand – being merely disease-free is not good enough either. Only by optimising skin quality after solving skin health issues can you achieve complete skin wellbeing. A vibrant, smooth, even skin that glows healthily and looks simply ... well - great! And that's what our clinic, *EUDELO Dermatology & Skin Wellbeing* stands for – *complete* skin wellbeing.

Don't ignore blemishes or pimples, even if they only erupt at a certain time of the month or as transient blotches on your skin. These are skin health issues that need to be treated properly – and I don't mean by

> Being disease-free is not enough, true skin wellbeing goes much further!

peels or lasers in a beauty salon or medi-spa! Breakouts benefit incredibly well from prescription creams, ideally supervised by a dermatologist. Likewise, redness, pigmentation or sun damage are not 'things' you have to put up with. In most cases, they're treatable and shouldn't be accepted as a fact of life, even if you've had them all your life. Some patients may assume their issues are too mild to bother a doctor with – which isn't the case at all. Also, don't be discouraged from seeing a dermatologist if you've already seen other doctors to not much avail. If this sounds like you, very likely you simply haven't found the right doctor for the job. Our dermatologists see patients like this all the time. Rest assured – help is out there.

> Don't ignore breakouts or have them treated in a beauty salon. Breakouts are a skin *health* concern that should be treated with prescription treatment, ideally by a dermatologist.

And while it's extremely important to get even mild skin health concerns diagnosed and treated medically, it does not mean that this medical treatment can't be combined with cosmetic treatments. All I'm saying is that cosmetic treatments *alone* shouldn't be used to address skin health issues. We need to start taking our skin health more seriously. As you may have guessed, treating skin health issues as 'cosmetic' problems is one of my personal bugbears.

This is also vital when getting lesions such as skin tags, moles or pigmented warts removed. Any skin lesions should be diagnosed by a dermatologist before they are touched! I've seen videos on YouTube, where a highly suspicious looking "skin tag" was removal by a beauty therapist – and I literally felt sick. How bloody dangerous! There's no way they could be sure they're not dealing with skin cancer. No skin lesion should be removed without proper diagnosis by a trained dermatologist armed with a dermatoscope.

STORIES FROM THE CLINIC

In the past year alone, we had two patients at EUDELO who booked with one of our therapists to have what they thought was a "skin tag" removed. When the therapist called in one of our dermatologists to check the lesion, a melanoma skin cancer was diagnosed! A therapist in a high street salon would have most likely removed the lesion – insufficiently and none the wiser. Don't risk your life by getting anything removed without proper diagnosis by a dermatologist.

In many countries around the world, visiting a dermatologist is to skin what seeing a dentist is to oral health. Sadly, in the UK, we're lagging behind in our understanding of how important regular skin health checks including routine mole checks really are.

> Just as you have a dentist, everyone should have a dermatologist they see for any skin health issues and routine checks.

Some common skin health concerns
_____

• **Acne** and its breakouts, spots and pimples is one of the most common skin health issues we see at EUDELO. Even though spots are very common in teenagers, don't ignore them as a normal part of growing up. Even mild acne can have a significant negative impact on confidence and has even been linked to depression. We're also seeing a large increase in cases of adult acne which can persist into your 30s, 40s and beyond. Breakouts can leave scarring, another reason to get medical treatment early. Try not to fix them yourself with over-the-counter remedies or cosmetic treatments.

I often see patients in clinic who feel their breakouts are too minor to be called 'acne'. However, acne is merely the medical term used for spots, pimples, blackheads and whiteheads. Any pimple however small is therefore an acne lesion.

The excellent news is that we have highly effective treatments for acne breakouts, including prescription creams, acne antibiotics and isotretinoin, a vitamin A acid tablet. But what I often see is that GPs and other non-dermatologist doctors tend to prescribe a single acne cream, which often disappoints. In my professional experience of treating thousands of acne patients over the years, most respond better to a clever combination of different prescription creams: one cream in the morning and another in the evening, say, or different products on different days of the week. A tailored regime like this yields far better results.

If you suffer with acne into your adult years and are also concerned with wrinkles, you might be interested to hear about prescription creams that not only control spots, but give great anti-ageing results, too (e.g. tretinoin cream). Then there are those that improve both breakouts and pigmentation issues (e.g. azelaic acid cream).

It's also imperative to take the patient's skincare into consideration and build a personalised regime around the prescription creams. I'm always amazed to learn that most GPs – and even most dermatologists – don't talk about skincare with their breakout patients. To me, that would be like an endocrinologist ignoring what a diabetic patient eats. The wrong skincare can aggravate or even cause acne, so if you suffer with breakouts, get specialist advice on what products to use and avoid.

For cases where topical treatment alone is not enough, there are highly effective acne antibiotics available. And if those are not working, the vitamin A derivative isotretinoin (Roaccutane® is one of its brand names) is a valuable treatment which switches off acne for good in the majority of patients. Isotretinoin used to be prescribed in higher daily doses with a high chance of side effects, such as severely dry skin and lips. We now know that this medication can still be very effective in much lower daily doses (the exact dose depends on the patient and their bodyweight) which makes treatment far more tolerable, although a little longer in duration. Some patients might not even take the medication every day, but three times per week or so. At EUDELO, we have a lot of grateful patients who, after years of struggling, have finally seen the last of their acne breakouts.

Isotretinoin is also used for sun damaged skin and research has shown that low intermittent doses of isotretinoin can increase collagen production and improve the skin's appearance (Rabello-Fonseca et al. 2009).

You might have seen reports about a possible link between Roaccutane® and depression in the press, so let me update you on the latest evidence. The reported connection between isotretinoin and depression is controversial. While some studies reported increased rates of depression (especially with high doses), others either showed no such increase or even revealed *reduced* depression scores as patients began to feel better about their skin and so themselves. Amidst all this confusion, I was delighted with the recent publication of a big systematic review and meta-analysis (the mother of all studies and the highest degree of medical evidence), which found no isotretinoin-depression link (Huang et al. 2017). So those patients who do feel their mood lowering on this medication seem to be very unfortunate outliers. And of course, it's always difficult to distinguish between depression caused by the acne itself – which is common – and medication-induced depression.

This mentioned study also reflects my own extensive professional experience with isotretinoin. At EUDELO, where we tend to prescribe a low-dose treatment, we have not observed any link between isotretinoin and depression. If anything, people who felt low because of their skin reported feeling better since starting treatment.

Of course, anything that's effective has a potential for side effects – that goes without saying. But we also have to think – what are the alternatives? These might include for example, years and years of systemic antibiotics, which themselves are connected to various adverse effects. I can honestly say that if one of my three children were to develop acne, which we can't control with other treatment, I would happily have them started on oral isotetinoin. And, by the way, I've taken it myself in the past when I suffered with an overlap of adult acne and rosacea. I hope I've reassured you.

Remember that isotretinoin is a highly effective medication and the only one that can switch off acne for good, rather than merely controlling it. I'm incredibly thankful that we have this at our disposal. Never forget that acne is a disfiguring, potentially scarring skin condition with proven negative effects on the patient's quality of life. In fact, acne itself has been shown unequivocally to be connected to depression and suicidal thoughts in a significant number of affected patients. So in my professional opinion, we can spare more patients from depression by treating their acne than risk potentially inducing it in a small minority of very unfortunate cases.

A very useful adjunct for any acne sufferer is a dermatology grade facial. One of the most beneficial steps to acne control is the thorough extraction of comedones, as discussed earlier, because all spots start as comedones. Remember though, that dermatology grade facials are totally different from beauty facials in salons and spas which anyone with a tendency to breakouts should strictly avoid. Oh, and one more thing. Before we even think about treating potential acne scarring, all active acne lesions must be completely cleared!

• **Rosacea** is another very common facial skin problem in adults that is often mistaken for acne both by patients and supposed skin experts. It's more common in women than men, and fair skin types are particularly susceptible – which is why it's also known as the 'curse of the Celts.' Rosacea can show up with vascular changes (typically redness, flushing and broken capillaries) and/or inflamed lesions (spotty breakouts such as papules, pustules, bumps and 'blotches'). The eyes may also become dry and gritty-feeling and the lids may get inflamed. The skin on the nose may develop a condition called rhinophyma, where the skin reddens and thickens, and pores appear enlarged.

Rosacea often appears mid-life. Patients often tell me they never had acne as a teenager, but now they're in their forties they've started getting breakouts (as well as lines and wrinkles…). Not fair!

> Rosacea is a common skin condition that's often confused with acne breakouts.

Happily, there is a range of effective treatments for rosacea. You will need different types of treatment for the inflamed and the vascular symptoms. Any inflamed lesions such as spots, bumps and blotches should be treated with prescription creams and once again, a combination regime works better than a single cream. Please note that steroid creams are contraindicated for patients with rosacea, as they can aggravate or even cause rosacea ('steroid-induced rosacea'). If topical treatment alone is not sufficient, anti-inflammatory or antibiotic tablets may be added. In some cases, vitamin A acid (isotretinoin) tablets are very useful and in my experience, an ultra-low-dose regime works best for rosacea sufferers.

For temporary relief of rosacea-related redness, we can prescribe a highly effective cream called Mirvaso®, which greatly reduces redness for up to 12 hours. I like to prescribe it as an emergency 'skin saver' for special occasions, but don't routinely recommend using it daily. For longer-lasting effects,

> Laser or IPL treatment for rosacea-related redness and broken vessels must *only* be started once all spots, pimples and bumps are cleared!

vascular rosacea with facial redness and broken vessels (teleangiectasias) benefits from laser or IPL treatment. However, any inflamed lesions must be cleared first, so don't even think about having a laser or IPL treatment if you're still getting breakouts.

As well as following your prescription programme, it's also important to check your lifestyle habits. Beware of potentially aggravating factors such as sun, spicy food, alcohol (particularly red wine) and hot beverages. Your daily skincare regime is also crucial, since the wrong products can cause flare-ups. It can be very tricky to find the perfect skincare regime for rosacea, and in my experience most high street brands get it wrong. Let your cosmetic dermatologist help.

Interestingly, most rosacea patients report that they suffer with "dry, sensitive skin" that at times feels tight and uncomfortable and is often reactive. With this in mind, sufferers attempt to soothe their skin with rich creams or oils which may however aggravate rosacea breakouts! The reason is that perceived "dry skin" in rosacea is not true dryness, but a sign of micro-inflammation in the skin, as briefly touched on in the skincare chapter. That's why it's crucial to treat the micro-inflammation of rosacea with prescription creams rather than 'numbing' the sensation by plastering on rich skincare! Treating the micro-inflammation will also lessen the perceived need for heavy moisturisers, a win-win situation.

As sun exposure can also aggravate rosacea, your daily skincare regime should include a suitable sun protection product with SPF30-50. While high protection products used to be heavy or sticky, there are now much lighter formulas on the market. My preference for rosacea skin are pure mineral filter products, but make sure they come in a lightweight base.

> Both acne and rosacea need a specialist, tailored skincare regime. And remember with rosacea, what feels like dryness is often micro-inflammation – rich creams can aggravate rosacea! Make sure your cosmetic dermatologist advises you.

• **Eczema** or atopic dermatitis is an intensely itchy chronic skin condition that can affect not only the body, but also the face. It is particularly common in babies and children pre-puberty, but adults may suffer too. A US study of over 27,000 adults aged 18 to 85 years old found that more than 10% suffered at least one eczema episode in the past year, which is surprisingly high (Silverberg et al. 2013). Progressively drier skin that happens naturally with age can contribute to eczema development.

In addition to prescription creams, a twice or more daily application of a lipid-rich emollient is crucial. This will help normalise the skin's barrier function, relieve dryness and lower the frequency of flare-ups. Fragrance-free skincare is preferable for eczema skin.

While daily emollients are a mandatory maintenance treatment for eczema prone skin, anti-inflammatory prescription creams are needed during flare-ups. Besides topical steroids there are also steroid-free anti-inflammatory creams available from your dermatologist. A mistake I often see is patients using very low-strength steroid creams (as they are worried about using something stronger) such as hydrocortisone, but for prolonged periods. However, in many cases it may actually be better for the skin to use a slightly stronger steroid, but for a shorter time period (or intermittently – ask your dermatologist about 'weekend-therapy'). There is no need to be scared of steroid creams, as long as they are used correctly! Also note that for eczema skin, prescription *ointments* are preferable to prescription *creams*, as ointments are more hydrating and tend to contain less preservatives. If topical treatment is not enough, anti-inflammatory tablets and/or light treatment may be used.

While most cases of eczema are endogenous (i.e. not

caused by an allergy), diet may play a part in some patients and a blood test for food allergies or other allergens might be advised. If a contact allergy is suspected (for example to fragrance or certain preservatives in skincare), then a special allergy test called a patch test may need to be arranged. Other environmental factors such as over-cleansing and the dry air of central heating or air conditioning may also aggravate eczema.

> Daily application of lipid rich emollients is mandatory for eczema prone skin.

• **Seborrhoeic dermatitis** (seborrhoeic eczema) most commonly affects the central face, especially in men. It's often particularly bad around the eyebrows and nose creases. The skin might look red (sometimes with a yellowish hue) and flaky and can occasionally itch mildly, but not as severely as with atopic eczema (which is a helpful distinguishing factor). The condition can also affect the scalp with dandruff-like flaking and the chest, too.

Seborrhoeic dermatitis is a chronic skin condition, but it can usually be well controlled with prescription creams and shampoos. These are often a mix of anti-inflammatory and anti-fungal products. Occasionally we see patients with an overlap of seborrheic dermatitis and rosacea, which can be a therapeutic challenge, as anti-inflammatory creams we use in seborrhoeic dermatitis may be contraindicated in rosacea.

• **Psoriasis** is a chronic, scaly skin condition, which often affects the elbows, knees and scalp. In more severe cases it can be widespread over the entire body, including the nails. The face can also be affected, sometimes in overlap with seborrhoeic dermatitis ('seboriasis'). Infections such as a sore throat or certain drugs such as beta blockers can trigger psoriasis flare-ups.

> Psoriasis can affect the face and be present with or without co-existing seborrhoeic dermatitis.

Although psoriasis is a genetic condition that we can't cure for good, we can control it with various topical and systemic prescription treatments, as well as light treatment. Mild facial psoriasis can be treated with anti-inflammatory prescription creams and regular application of emollients is also important.

• **Skin tags** or fibromas are very common, harmless little soft skin lesions, which can grow on tiny 'stalks', often on the neck and the trunk. Their size can vary from smaller than a grain of uncooked rice to the size of a pea, or larger. They're associated with friction – either skin against skin, or clothing – and are often found in areas such as the neck, armpits, groin and under the breasts. Overweight individuals and patients with blood sugar control issues tend to get more of them.

Skin tags can appear individually or in large crops and may catch on your clothes or simply look unsightly. They can be removed quite easily and the ideal method depends on their size. However, proper diagnosis by a doctor, ideally dermatologist, is important to avoid overlooking a sinister lesion.

• **Angiomas.** Sometimes harmless little vascular lesions called 'cherry angiomas' come up on the skin. Also known as blood spots, Campbell de Morgan spots or, unkindly, senile angiomas, they are very common, bright red and sometimes slightly raised blemishes that mostly appear on the midriff.

Most people over 30 years of age have at least one and their number tends to increase from around the age of 40. Their cause is unknown.

A spider nevus or spider angioma on the other hand is a centrally dilated blood vessel with smaller capillaries radiating from it like the legs of a spider. They can appear as a single lesion (on the cheek, for example) or in larger numbers, and are the result of the dilation of pre-existing tiny blood vessels.

While the vast majority of angiomas are harmless and nothing to worry about, in very rare cases the appearance of multiple lesions may be linked to internal diseases, such as thyroid or liver problems or an internal malignancy.

Although both cherry angiomas and spider nevi are benign, many people want to have them removed for cosmetic reasons. Treatment is straightforward and methods used are vascular laser, IPL or electrocautery, all of which essentially 'heat seal' the angioma.

• **Thread veins** on the face (teleangiectasias) are permanently dilated, tiny blood vessels. There are a variety of reasons why you might have them, including chronic sun damage and rosacea. They often appear around the nose and on the cheeks.

While many facial thread veins might need treatment with a vascular laser or

> Cherry angiomas appear as little red spots on the trunk, whereas spider nevi with their radiating 'legs' are more common on the face.

> Facial thread veins can be caused by sun damage and rosacea. These conditions may need to be addressed medically before the thread veins themselves can be treated.

IPL device, individual, medium-sized telangiectasias on the face can successfully be treated with ACP ('advanced cosmetic procedure'), a form of electrocautery, where electro-currents generate heat in a needle-shaped electrode, which seals the dilated vessel.

Where thread veins appear on the legs, light-based treatments may also be used, but the recurrence rate on lower legs is much higher. The gold standard for treating thread veins on the legs remains micro-sclerotherapy, the injection of a solution such as polidocanol that seals the blood vessels. If you suffer with thread veins on the lower legs, you may also want to get checked for varicose veins.

• **Milia** or milk spots are harmless, very common lesions that affect all ages. Milia appear as small, deep-seated white, hard bumps (like tiny white beads below the skin), often on the upper cheeks and around the eyes. Milia are superficial cysts filled with keratin material (skin protein) and not pus as it might appear.

Some people simply inherit a tendency for milia, but overloading the skin with heavy skincare is also a common reason. Newborn babies not uncommonly develop milia, although in contrast to adult milia these tend to disappear on their own. When they appear inside the mouth they are called Epstein's pearls.

> Milia often crop up around the eyes and can easily be extracted during a dermatology grade facial.

Milia are not connected to lack of cleanliness or drinking milk. Milia can crop up individually or in large numbers and although they are benign and have no other symptoms, patients often request their removal. They can be manually extracted by a specially trained aesthetician, or removed with ACP.

• **Pigmented warts.** As we get older, many of us will develop pigmented warts or seborrhoeic keratoses. These often appear on the trunk, sometimes in large numbers, but may also appear on the face. Although they're called warts, unlike viral warts and veruccas on the hands and feet, they're not contagious. A seborrhoeic keratosis can be tiny or grow up to two inches across. They may be flat or have a rough and warty surface that looks 'stuck on' and may thicken and darken over time. Not surprisingly, they're often considered unattractive.

Seborrhoeic keratoses are easy to remove and the exact technique – whether surgical scraping, ACP, plasma treatment, freezing or ablative laser – depends on the type and size of lesion. While they're usually easy to spot, on occasion seborrhoeic keratoses can be difficult to distinguish from sinister pigmented lesions such as a melanoma skin cancer, even for doctors. To diagnose lesions like this, examination with a dermatoscope is indispensable (remember, the dermatologist's 'desert island' piece of equipment!).

> Pigmented warts are very common on the trunk and easy to remove. But they need to be diagnosed by a dermatologist as they can on occasion mimic a melanoma skin cancer.

A non-pigmented variant of seborrhoeic keratosis, known as stucco keratosis, appears as small, dry, skin coloured 'stuck on' lesions on the lower legs.

Yet another variant is dermatosis papulosis nigra – multiple, slightly raised brown lesions of 1-5mm diameter that occur in black skin, often on the cheeks and forehead. Dermatosis papulosis nigra is very common, especially in women, with around 35% of African Americans reportedly affected. You may have noticed them on the well-known actor Morgan Freeman.

• **Sebaceous hyperplasia** or 'overgrowing oil glands' are often found on the forehead and cheeks of adults. They appear as yellowish lesions of 1-3mm in diameter and examination with the dermatoscope reveals a central pore surrounded by yellowish lobules. Sebaceous hyperplasias are benign and harmless, but can at times be difficult to distinguish from a basal cell carcinoma (BCC) skin cancer, so correct diagnosis by a trained dermatologist is once more important.

> Overgrowing oil glands can mimic a basal cell carcinoma skin cancer and need to be diagnosed by a dermatologist using a dermatoscope.

ACP, cryotherapy (clinical freezing), plasma treatment, or an ablative laser are all therapeutic options for removal. To lower the rate of recurrence and new lesions, vitamin A acid prescription creams such as tretinoin can be useful.

• **Verrucae and warts** are benign skin lesions caused by the Human Papilloma Virus (HPV). They can take on a wide variety of shapes and forms, for example 'warty', rough-surfaced growths on the hands or lesions that tend to merge and grow inwards on the soles of the feet, which may make walking uncomfortable. All these are viral and potentially contagious on contact.

Cryotherapy (clinical freezing) can be useful to treat them as well as topical products containing high concentrations of salicylic and/or lactic acid. Stubborn lesions may need curettage and cautery (C&C, surgical scraping and electrosurgery) performed under local anaesthesia. Sometimes they disappear without treatment as our immune system fights the virus, but this may take a long time.

Plane warts (verruca plana) are tiny flat variants of viral warts. They often arise in multiples on the face, hands or shins and are discrete in appearance, with a smooth, skin-coloured surface. Plane warts may pseudo-koebnerise – which means that trauma from scratching or shaving can spread the virus to other skin areas.

> Warts and verrucae are viral skin lesions that can appear on the skin in different forms and shapes.

Filiform warts (verruca filiformis) are less common viral wart variants. These tiny, long, thin, skin-coloured lesions protrude from the skin like little twigs, often on the face. Plane and filiform warts are both easy to remove with ablative techniques such as ACP, curettage (surgical scraping) or freezing.

• **Scars.** Some people develop raised, overgrowing scars (hypertrophic scars or keloids) after surgery, trauma or even minor inflammations arising from folliculitis or acne. While hypertrophic scars are lumpy but remain in the original skin area, keloid scarring spreads beyond the original trauma site. Hypertropic scarring is much more common than true keloids, although patients often incorrectly refer to any raised scar as a "keloid". Keloids are more common in black compared to Caucasian skin (Allah et al. 2013).

> Hypertrophic scars and keloids are two different types of raised scarring that patients often lump together.

The earlier overgrowing scars are treated the better the chances of a good therapeutic outcome. As with any scar, they won't disappear completely, but we can flatten them significantly and improve their appearance with treatment. A common treatment for both hypertrophic and keloid scars are injections with potent steroid solutions.

• **Chronic sun damage** is a common skin problem, even in the UK. The most common signs are countless solar lentigines – 'freckles' all over the skin, especially on the face, shoulders and upper back in adults. Often patients believe these signs of sun damage are simple "freckles", so let me explain the difference.

Childhood freckles are called ephilides in medical language and are caused by a genetic predisposition. Those true freckles are small, round and symmetric, much more prominent in summer and fading or completely disappearing in winter. With increasing age, freckles become less noticeable. Solar lentigines (sun spots, age or liver spots) on the other hand, often appear in middle age as a result of sun damage. They are larger and more irregular in shape than true freckles, are often found on exposed skin such as the face and hands (never in places where the sun don't shine, such as buttocks!) and tend to stay prominent even in winter.

> Freckles in children may look cute, but in adults they're a sign of chronic sun damage.

Actinic keratoses (AKs) are another common type of sun damage in adults, often occurring on the face, ears and scalp (especially if men are bald), hands and forearms. They are in fact, pre-cancerous lesions and especially common in fair skin and older people who have accumulated a fair bit of sun exposure throughout their lifetime. As I've mentioned before, your skin remembers every hour of sun right back to your childhood. It clocks up those hours and once it's had enough, depending on your skin type it may start to develop pre-cancerous lesions such as AKs and other problems.

AKs often feel like a little patch of rough skin – imagine touching a cornflake and you get the picture. Or you might notice a lesion that keeps scabbing over, or flakes even though you moisturise it thoroughly. Because AKs are pre-cancerous lesions, it's important to treat them promptly. This can be done with specialist prescription creams, curettage (surgical scraping) or freezing.

> Rough skin patches can be pre-cancerous skin lesions (AKs, or actinic keratosis) that require medical treatment.

• **Moles** are brown spots on our skin that most of us pay little attention to. They occur when our pigment building cells (melanocytes) grow in clusters. Some moles are present from birth, but most appear later. Moles come in all sorts of shapes and sizes, and healthy moles are of no concern. However, abnormal moles (dysplastic moles) need urgent attention, as they can turn into a skin cancer. If you notice a suspicious looking mole, seek medical advice immediately, ideally from a dermatologist. Understanding what suspicious moles look like is the best way to prevent skin cancer.

I strongly recommend you self-examine the skin on your entire body, top to toe, once a month. The best way to do this is when you come out of the shower. Ask a friend or family member to check your back, scalp, ears and other areas you can't easily see yourself. And don't forget to look between your toes. The easiest way to identify worrying signs is by using the alphabet rule below, which lists a few of the symptoms that

SUN SAFETY RULES

Being sensible when out and about will help to protect you from sunburn and significantly reduce your risk of accumulating sun damage and developing skin cancer. Use these tips to enjoy the sun safely:

1. **Get shady.** Avoid sun exposure during the middle of the day when UV radiation levels are highest. If you're outdoors, stay in the shade.
2. **Slip on protective clothing.** Cover up, ideally with long-sleeved shirts and trousers and wear a wide-rimmed hat. Large sunglasses provide additional protection for the delicate skin around the eyes.
3. **Slap on sunscreen.** The first two tips are imperative. However, also don't forget to apply sunscreen. Make sure it has an SPF of 30 – 50 for UVB protection and a UVA circle logo or 5-star UVA rating.

might indicate a dysplastic mole or melanoma skin cancer.

Skin cancer is the ultimate, most serious manifestation of sun damage and can prove fatal. The earlier it is detected, the better the outcome, so I strongly recommend a yearly mole check and skin cancer screening, ideally with a dermatologist. If you have a particularly high number of moles, a high sun-exposure history (you've lived abroad, worked outdoors or have outside hobbies, say), are fair-skinned or have other risk factors for skin cancer, more frequent check-ups may be necessary.

Mole checks involve a full, top-to-toe body inspection including the scalp and under the feet. If there is anything

THE ALPHABET SKIN CHECK RULE

Once a month, use the ABC rule as you check your skin top to toe for signs of suspicious moles.

Asymmetry: Do the two halves of a mole differ in shape?
Border: Are the edges of a mole irregular or blurred? Do the outside edges of the mole show notches or look ragged?
Colour: Is it uneven, patchy or does the mole have different shades of black, brown and pink?
Diameter: Is the lesion more than 5mm in diameter? (that is about the size of the back-end of a pencil)
Evolution: Has your mole changed in any way, for example in size, shape, or colour? Or has it become raised or itchy, or is it bleeding or oozing?

Also look for any skin lesions that have appeared and won't go away. Does that scaly patch or scab refuse to heal? If in doubt, check it out! If any of the signs above are positive, make an appointment with your doctor as soon as possible to have it checked.

remotely suspicious, the lesion will be scrutinised with the dermatoscope. Often a diagnosis can be made using this device in a completely non-invasive way. However, if a biopsy is needed so the lesion can be examined under a microscope, a local anaesthetic will make this painless.

I strongly feel that moles should not be lasered. I appreciate that many cosmetic clinics offer this, but as a dermatologist I can't endorse this practise. If you wish to lose the mole, even if it's just for cosmetic reasons, surgical removal with histology (microscopic tissue study) for peace of mind is the safer method.

> Everyone should have a routine annual mole check, ideally with a dermatologist.

Skin cancers

There are three main types of skin cancer, which are divided into two groups: melanoma skin cancer ('black skin cancer') and non-melanoma skin cancers ('white skin cancer'). The two main non-melanoma skin cancers are 'basal cell carcinoma' (BCC) and 'squamous cell carcinoma' (SCC).

By far the most common type of skin cancer is the BCC, or 'rodent ulcer'. The main cause is cumulative sun exposure and fair skin types are naturally more at risk. The good news about BCCs is that they don't have the ability to spread into the inner organs, so don't impact life expectancy. However, if not removed, BCCs will keep growing locally, so an early diagnosis when removal is still straightforward is important. A BCC can appear in different shapes or forms, such as skin-coloured, red or pigmented lumps and bumps, ulcerated or bleeding lesions and eczema-like patches. Basically, any non-healing skin lesion should prompt you to see a doctor - ideally a dermatologist. In contrast to BCCs, squamous cell carcinomas (SCCs) can spread into inner organs although that's thankfully not very common.

But by far the most dangerous type of skin cancer is melanoma. This is a malignant skin tumour which can arise from normal skin or in a pre-existing mole. Melanomas are aggressive and can spread into inner organs and potentially prove deadly. They can appear even in young people.

According to the British Association of Dermatologists (BAD), skin cancers constitute the most common group of cancers in the UK. Worryingly, the rate of melanomas in the UK is above the EU average and skin cancer rates in affluent areas are even higher compared to more deprived ones. Overall, cases are rising and according to the BAD, melanoma is the fastest-increasing cancer of them all. The good news is that if a melanoma

> The most common types of skin cancer are basal cell carcinoma, squamous cell carcinoma and the most dangerous, malignant melanoma. Excess sun exposure increases the risk of skin cancer.

is caught early, the prognosis in most cases is fine. That's why every person should keep a close eye on their skin and report any suspicious moles to their doctor as soon as possible.

Thankfully after clinical and dermoscopic examination, we can reassure the majority of our patients. However, if a mole remains suspicious we are able to take it out painlessly under local anaesthesia and send the tissue off for histological analysis under a microscope.

STORIES FROM THE CLINIC

A patient once came to see me for wrinkle relaxing injections. On examining her skin, I noticed a melanoma skin cancer on her neck, which could have killed her if left untreated. We arranged prompt surgical removal and I am pleased to report that she remains fine to date.

CHOOSING THE
RIGHT CLINIC

We've spoken about the remarkable results arising from the aesthetic medicine paradigm shift and its 'less is more, overall impression over symptoms' approach. And we've seen what modern concepts such as the EUDELO *3-Key Principle*, *Foundation Principle* and *Staircase Principle* can achieve. Now it's time to talk about something even more fundamental – safety. As with all medical treatments, aesthetic medicine is a discipline that naturally comes with potential risks, such as infection and hypersensitivity reaction.

As this book focuses on the new concepts in aesthetic medicine that allow you to look great, not done, discussing potential risks and side-effects in detail would be beyond its scope. This should, of course, be part of everyone's pre-treatment consultation with their practitioner. Nevertheless, I do want to give you some advice on how to choose the right practitioner so that

> Non-surgical interventions discussed in this book may be aesthetic in nature, but they are also medical procedures. For safety reasons, they should not be approached in the same way as a haircut or manicure.

your treatment results will be as safe and successful as can be. As one of my colleagues, New York dermatologist Dr Heidi Waldorf once said, "it's not the paint or the paintbrush, but the painter who creates a masterpiece". Couldn't have put it better myself.

In any other area of medicine, you would expect firm government regulations to be in place to ensure safety and standards are met. Yet when it comes to aesthetic procedures, the regulatory arena has become a minefield, putting patients at risk from unscrupulous, non-medical practitioners. The non-surgical sector is the biggest growth area in aesthetic medicine, yet the lack of sensible regulation surrounding it has made it difficult for patients to find safe and ethical practitioners. Since the government made the somewhat controversial decision not to impose statutory regulation on this booming market, everyone from vets to dental hygienists, beauticians and podiatrists have been trying to take a bite out of the cosmetic injectables 'pie'.

It is important to remember that BTX is a prescription-only medicine. This means that only doctors, dentists and nurses who have a prescriber qualification can legally offer this treatment. Doctors, nurses and dentists are all held accountable by their professional governing bodies – the General Medical Council (GMC), the Nursing & Midwifery Council (NMC) and the General Dental Council (GDC) respectively. So a good starting point is to make sure your practitioner is on their professional governing body's register. However, not all nurses have a prescribing licence, so double check yours has. There have been issues with remote prescribing. This is where a loophole in the law has been exploited, so that non-prescribers can get their hands on BTX by getting a doctor to prescribe this drug for their patients over the phone. This is thankfully no longer an acceptable practise and all of the professional governing bodies who hold medical and dental practitioners to account have spoken out against it, making it clear that their members risk losing their right to practise if they engage in it. However, even since remote prescribing was outlawed, reports of non-medical practitioners injecting BTX keep surfacing. This is of course illegal but patients might not even be aware that their practitioner is breaking the law. So it's vital to make sure your practitioner is a medically qualified prescriber before you let them inject you with BTX.

While the legal situation for prescription-only drugs such as BTX is (in theory) clear, it's worryingly less cut and dry for dermal fillers. Fillers are classified as 'medical devices' rather than prescription medicines, so strictly speaking it's not illegal for a non-medic to administer them. Does that mean I'd recommend seeing a non-medically qualified practitioner for a volumising treatment? Hell no!

> Don't compromise when you decide which practitioner you see for your aesthetic treatments. Remember, it's not the paint or the paintbrush who creates the masterpiece – it's the painter themselves.

In my personal opinion, you would be barking mad to show such a lack of concern for your personal health and safety.

In the right hands, fillers are great aesthetic treatments with a very good benefit-to-risk ratio. But as with everything that delivers results, there's always a possibility for unwanted effects. No effective treatment has zero risks – that simply doesn't exist. In fact I'd go as far as to say that zero risk equals zero success, too. Think about Aspirin®. It's available over the counter and in most cases, perfectly safe and well-tolerated without problems. But some people are allergic to Aspirin®️ and may develop a reaction. And so it is with all effective treatments.

One of the possible post treatment complications are infections which might require a prescription treatment to settle. Being a medical prescriber therefore, is also important here. Also, imagine you're having lip fillers, which have a known tendency for triggering cold sores. A medical prescriber can prescribe you anti-viral tablets to prevent or treat cold sore flare-ups. And should you need to dissolve a hyaluronic acid filler, hyaluronidase – the enzyme that does this – is a prescription-only medication, too. Another example. As mentioned, most fillers now contain local anaesthetics and it's possible to develop an allergy to them. Only a trained medic will be able to deal with this kind of emergency on the spot. It's a rare complication, I'll grant you, but it's also highly unpredictable and can happen to anyone. Looking at all these examples, you can see how crucial it is to have your aesthetic treatments in a reputable medical clinic.

A superior knowledge of facial anatomy is also essential to minimise risks. With many aesthetic procedures, we're putting a needle into very precise locations with complex anatomical structures. Without specialist knowledge and training you can cause actual harm. The most worrying fact is that many non-medic injectors don't even know what they don't know. I have learned this from first-hand conversations with non-medics planning to inject fillers. They were blissfully ignorant about their lack of true understanding of facial anatomy and possible complications. Truly alarming. So summing up, my advice for BTX and fillers is to only go to a practitioner who is medically qualified, has a prescribing licence and furthermore is *highly experienced* in administering these treatments, so can deal with complications, should they arise.

BOTOX PARTIES

Never have a treatment at a 'Botox Party' or treatment in someone's home. This is not a safe environment. Injectables aren't toys. Having them done in a clean, clinical environment that's fit for purpose – without peer pressure or under the influence of alcohol – is non-negotiable.

While more and more people are thankfully aware of the potential risks of cosmetic injectables, many still underestimate the danger of lasers and IPL devices. A burn from either of these can be serious and if the eye is hit, lasers can even cause blindness; which makes it even more shocking that in October 2010, the UK government decided to de-regulate lasers and IPL for cosmetic use. After speaking to an insider, I believe that this has happened because the Care Quality Commission (CQC) was simply overloaded and unable to cope, so something had to give. This means that although the CQC continues to regulate healthcare professionals using lasers and IPLs to treat "disease, disorders or injury," the beauty sector now falls outside its remit, leaving non-medical practitioners to treat clients without being accountable. Needless to say, this de-regulation also triggered a boom in so-called medi-spas and laser treatments offered on the high street in salons and even department stores.

Registration with the CQC is unfortunately not required for purely aesthetic clinics. However, some aesthetic clinics are registered, if they also offer medical consultations and/or minor surgery. If you find such a clinic, at least you know there is an independent, highly experienced, centralised organisation scrutinising what they do - peace of mind, perhaps. Of course, there are many non-CQC registered clinics, which are excellent too, but they're naturally more difficult to check. As I've mentioned, there are various self-regulatory aesthetic 'kite mark' schemes, but these are non-centralised and seem to be competing with each other to become the market leader – so the jury is still out on these.

Experience is key

While my advice for BTX and fillers is to only go to a practitioner who is medically qualified, be aware that being a registered doctor, dentist or prescribing nurse doesn't necessarily mean they have the appropriate expertise to perform aesthetic interventions well. Unfortunately, there are many, many practitioners who offer aesthetic treatments straight after going on a weekend course. Expertise only comes with a whole load of practise.

On-going training is also essential. To train once, then keep treating without continuously updating your knowledge is nearly as bad as insufficient training in the first place. I'm particularly wary of practitioners who proudly proclaim that they've been injecting for 25 years, yet you never see them at conferences. Are they still using the same old techniques? Things have changed dramatically in the last quarter century, so unless they've quietly been updating their knowledge, best beware. At

> Just because someone has been offering the same treatment for many years doesn't mean they're up to date with the latest advances. Just saying...

EUDELO, all our doctors and nurses attend several congresses and conferences each year to keep up to date with the latest developments – and that's absolutely crucial.

As with looking for any aesthetic service on the internet, you need to be vigilant and mindful of unethical marketing gimmicks. Just because a clinic ranks highly on a search engine or has a super-slick website, doesn't mean it's the best or safest place to go. Look beyond glossy marketing and do your research thoroughly into the qualifications and experience of the practitioners you're considering visiting.

CLEANLINESS IS CRUCIAL

When aesthetic interventions are performed in a safe, clean environment, risks are minimised. I admit I'm obsessed with clean working, so I'm ultra-particular. These are some clean practise points to look for.

• **Has your practitioner thoroughly disinfected your entire skin?** A half-hearted rub with a teensy alcohol wipe isn't enough for treatments such as facial contouring. CliniSept® is my personal favourite for aesthetic treatments.

• **Did they disinfect your skin, then mark it up** with a non-sterile pen without disinfecting again? Best practice is to disinfect skin before *and* after mark-up, as well as during the course of the treatment, where needed.

• **Are they using a 'sterile field'** when doing more involved procedures such as facial contouring? Using a sterile dressing pack on the treatment trolley is best practise in my opinion.

- **Do they wear gloves** when treating? For more involving treatments, they might wear surgical masks, too.
- **Do they touch unsterile things** – a computer keyboard, light switch, cupboard handle or your hair, say – with their gloved hand, then continue to treat without changing gloves or disinfecting their gloved hands? I like to have a galley pot filled with CliniSept® on my treatment trolley that I not only use on the patient's skin before, during and after treatment, but also my hands, intermittently.
- **Do they wipe the (sterile) needle** on the back of their gloved hands or on gauze to remove a drop of product? This habit increases the risk of infection – better to gently shake the drop off rather than wiping it.
- **If they have long hair,** do they tie it back securely when injecting?
- **Do they have very long fingernails?** You won't believe how much bacteria can accumulate underneath them!
- **Does your practitioner wear a tie** when treating? Ties have been banned in NHS hospitals now, as they are notoriously unclean and can dangle into the treatment field.
- **What else is your practitioner wearing?** The most appropriate code is 'bare below the elbow', or tight sleeves that can be pushed up securely during treatment. At EUDELO, practitioners wear fresh surgical scrubs every day.

> • **Do they wear bulky jewellery?** Rings under gloves may be fine, but dangling bracelets and necklaces may increase the risk of infection.

Take a good look at your practitioner

Hygiene apart, how do they actually look? Do they look well? Does their skin look healthy and radiant? Aspirational, even? It goes without saying that they don't have to look perfect, or 10 years younger than their age. However, as a patient, I would want to see that my practitioner is looking after their skin, too. Most importantly, do they look overdone? Chances are if they don't look natural themselves, they're not going to give you a natural look either.

Research has identified the main criteria for beauty are a *natural* look, self-confidence and attractive skin (Ehlinger-Martin et al. 2016). I can tell you that *all* practitioners will tell you that natural results are important to them, and theirs will be too, but often, that's pure lip service. Way too many practitioners – and their patients – look terribly overdone. Just join me at an aesthetic conference and you'll know what I mean. Or take a look at 'before and after' images on social media after lip filler, say. I'm continually shocked to see colleagues showcase their 'natural results' online, only to find that in reality, these results don't look natural at all. Makes you wonder….

> *Every* clinic seems to promote natural results. But looking at some patients – and even practitioners themselves – tells a different story. That's why we decided to introduce a '100% natural result' guarantee at EUDELO.

It's a good idea to ask your practitioner what they've had done – and remember this shouldn't be obvious. Go on, don't be shy – it's totally fine to ask. If they haven't had anything done themselves, then why not? Don't they trust their own treatments or, if they are younger, don't they believe in prevention? Personally, I only offer treatments in my clinic that I would happily have myself – and in many cases, have.

Time is of the essence

It's important that a clinic gives you the time and care you deserve. If they rush you, that's not right. Here's your time-sensitive checklist:

• **How thorough was the assessment and consultation?** If you don't have anything to compare to, check out ours, described earlier, as an example of a good assessment routine.

• **Are you asked to apply numbing cream at home or in clinic yourself?** Or do they expect you to wait in the main waiting area while it takes effect?

• **How thoroughly are treatments performed?** Are you rushed in and out?

• **Is your face marked up before treatment?** Marking is not a sign of an insecure practitioner, but a methodical one!

• **Do they give you time after treatment** to settle and ask questions, or bundle you out of the door? On this note – did you get written post-treatment information and an emergency number to call in case of problems?

• **Do they offer post-procedure make-up** before you leave the clinic?

• **If you call back with a problem,** are your concerns addressed properly? Are you invited back to clinic for the practitioner to look at the issue?

All these important questions can make the difference between a good and bad experience.

THE AESTHETIC 10 COMMANDMENTS

I 'stole' and adjusted these from a great article in Brides Magazine. It summarises my aesthetic ethos perfectly.

1: **Thou shalt be discerning**. Avoid hairdressers, nail bars, hotel rooms, tiny back rooms and 'botox parties'. Make sure you're treated in a suitable clinic and check your practitioners' medical qualifications and experience. Don't be swayed by cheap deals that reputable practitioners are unlikely to offer. This is your face and your health you're playing with!

2: **Thou shalt plan ahead**. Never try out a new treatment a few days prior to an important event. Leave enough time to try it at least once before to see how you like it. Also budget for side effects like bruising and swelling to settle prior to the event (which might take up to three weeks). Just because you didn't bruise last time doesn't mean you won't again. Lastly, remember that certain treatments like peels may be seasonal and for some you may need a course.

3: **Thou shalt keep a history**. Note your past treatments, so that when a new practitioner asks you about them, you have a full record including timings and products used. Also, give

---

your practitioner a written list of your current
medication. "I take heart tablets, but can't
remember their name" is the last thing they want
to hear (nor is "I am allergic to an antibiotic, but I
can't remember which one"...).

4: **Thou shalt be true to thyself.** Don't try to look
like someone else. Bringing old photos of yourself
is helpful, so the practitioner sees the youthful
you and plans treatment accordingly. Don't bring
photos of celebrities or ask your practitioner to
copy a certain look.

5: **Thou shalt practise patience.** Don't expect
everything to be fixed in a single session. If you
want a subtle makeover and natural results,
repeated tweakments over time are the best way
forward. Looking after your skin isn't a one-off
event but an ongoing journey.

6: **Thou shalt listen up.** Heed your practitioner's
advice if they say no to certain requests. What you
want may not be what you need. So if they tell you
that a treatment is not for you, be happy to have
found someone you can trust and who doesn't say
yes to everything.

7: **Thou shalt neither stick nor twist.** Cosmetic
doctors are a little like husbands and wives – once
you've found 'the one', stay faithful so that they
can look after you. Continuous shopping around
for the next best thing will lead to long-term
frustration and disappointment.

8: **Thou shalt keep it real.** Cosmetic procedures can be very effective, but there's a limit to what even the most skilled practitioners can do. Be reasonable. We're medics, not magicians! Also remember that everyone is different and just because your best friend had a certain result, it might not be the same for you. There's no magic bullet.

9: **Thou shalt play the detective.** Ask questions about your planned treatment until you totally understand the benefits as well as the risks. Don't be pressured into having a treatment on the first day. Take time to consider your options.

10: **Thou shalt consider the bigger picture.** Respect the new wave of aesthetic concepts outlined in this book. Don't obsess about tiny details such as individual lines, but embrace the full-face approach and take into account all three key areas of facial ageing.

RIDE THE WAVE

After decades of minor advances, we're finally observing a genuine paradigm shift in aesthetic medicine. I'll leave you with a summary of its ground-breaking concepts as embodied by the EUDELO principles.

1:
THE EUDELO
3-KEY PRINCIPLE

Chasing isolated lines and wrinkles is out. If you want a truly balanced, natural looking facial rejuvenation, then full-face analysis and treatment is mandatory. The full-face approach takes into consideration all three key areas of facial appearance and ageing. These are:

- Facial volume & contour
- Skin quality & skin health
- Lines, wrinkles & furrows

2:

THE EUDELO
FOUNDATION PRINCIPLE

Segregated corrective procedures are out. If you want to enjoy the best possible skin long term, building a strong foundation with ongoing *regenerative* treatments is key. You're in this for the long haul, so skipping from one random one-off corrective treatment to another is missing an essential point. With regular bio-stimulation, you're investing in your skin's future. Time to join the skin gym!

3:

THE EUDELO
STAIRCASE PRINCIPLE

Looking after your skin as best you can follows a clear, step-wise approach. Corrective procedures aren't for everyone, which is fine – you decide how far your commitment takes you up the staircase. But skipping a step is not allowed! These are the EUDELO staircase steps from lowest to highest commitment.

- *FuturApproved*® skin-friendly lifestyle
- Evidence-based cosmeceutical skincare
- Dermatology grade facials
- Minimal-invasive regenerative treatments
- Corrective procedures

With its healthy living stepping stone at the very base, the *EUDELO Staircase Principle* demonstrates that anti-ageing today isn't only about how you look on the outside, but how youthful you are on the inside, too. It's a holistic approach that keeps you healthy and fresh both inside and out.

These three principles above are linked by a strong prevention and early intervention (P&E) ethic. P&E should be at the centre of whatever you do. The earlier you start your skin journey, the better and more natural-looking the outcome long term. It's an ongoing *journey*.

> If you want to see what the EUDELO system can achieve for real-life patients, have a look at www.Eudelo.com/Results.

Right – that's me done. Thank you so much for listening. As an aesthetic dermatologist, I thoroughly enjoyed writing this book – we're living in exciting times. Take good care of yourself and your skin. And remember – good skin never goes out of fashion!

> Don't forget to connect on social media, it's:
>
> Twitter: @EudeloClinic and @DrStefanieW
> Facebook: @Eudelo
> Instagram: @Eudelo and @DrStefanieW

APPENDIX

ABOUT THE AUTHOR AND EUDELO

Online: www.Eudelo.com and www.EudeloBoutique.com
Twitter: @EudeloClinic and @DrStefanieW
Facebook: @Eudelo
Instagram: @Eudelo and @DrStefanieW

Dr Stefanie Williams is a medical doctor, German-board certified Dermatologist and founder of *EUDELO Dermatology & Skin Wellbeing*.

Dr Stefanie graduated in Medicine in Germany. After many years of post-graduate specialist training and success in the rigorous German specialization exam, she was awarded the title of Specialist Dermatologist by the Hamburg Medical Council.

Dr Stefanie is an international key opinion leader in cosmetic dermatology and aesthetic medicine and has lectured at international conferences all over the world. Dr Stefanie lectures in Cosmetic Science at the University of the Arts, London. As a medical doctor, a dermatologist and a cosmetic scientist, Dr Stefanie is in a unique position to combine her in-depth knowledge of skin biology with her expertise in anti-ageing medicine, prevention and skincare.

Dr Stefanie is the author and co-author of more than 130 scientific articles, book chapters and abstracts and her cutting-edge skin research has led her to receive a number of prestigious awards. She was also part of the Aesthetic Medicine Expert Group (AMEG) that has written an important consensus white paper on preventing complications from aesthetic injectable treatments. Dr Stefanie is a reviewer for leading dermatology journals and the author of Amazon-No-1 Bestseller *Future Proof Your Skin. Slow down your biological clock by changing the way you eat.*

Dr Stefanie is regularly featured in glossy magazines and newspapers as an expert, including Vogue, Cosmopolitan, Tatler, Women's Health, Hello magazine, Grazia, Telegraph, The Times, Daily Mail and the Evening Standard to name but a few. Dr Stefanie has been named as one of Britain's best aesthetic doctors three years in a row in Tatler magazine and has appeared on radio and TV including BBC Radio 4 and ITV.

Based in Central London, *EUDELO Dermatology & Skin Wellbeing* is a multi-award winning private skin clinic. EUDELO is one of the UK's very few fusion clinics of medical and cosmetic dermatology. This means that EUDELO not only looks after the entire spectrum of skin diseases and troubled skin, but also offers a wide range of non-surgical cosmetic treatments, ensuring the highest quality and safety standards.

EUDELO's international reputation and impeccable standards have earned it a dedicated following with patients including actors, super models, high-flying business CEOs, diplomats and international royalty travelling from all over the world to see them. But perhaps there is no better testimony to EUDELO than the fact they count many fellow doctors and industry peers among their patients. EUDELO is by many considered as one of the world's benchmark clinics for cosmetic dermatology and aesthetic medicine.

ACKNOWLEDGEMENTS

I thank my husband Jay for the never-ending support he has given me throughout the (seriously) long journey of writing this book.

I thank my children Elias, Cyrus and Kaia for being patient with me and allowing me to write on so many occasions.

I thank Vicci Bentley and Vicky Eldridge for editorial help, Gemma Rowlands for proofreading, Natasha Chauhan for logistics and Couper Street Type Co. for layout and typesetting this book.

I thank Juliet Percival for the illustrations.

I thank my graphic designer team at *The House* and Rodrigo Hernández-Artiach for the book cover.

REFERENCES &

FURTHER READING

Abdel-Daim M, Funasaka Y, Kamo T, Ooe M, Matsunaka H, Yanagita E, Itoh T, Nishigori C. Effect of chemical peeling on photocarcinogenesis. J Dermatol. 2010;37(10):864-72. (a)

Abdel-Daim M, Funasaka Y, Kamo T, Ooe M, Matsunaka H, Yanagita E, Itoh T, Nishigori C. Preventive effect of chemical peeling on ultraviolet induced skin tumor formation. J Dermatol Sci. 2010;60(1):21-8. (b)

Abuaf OK, Yildiz H, Baloglu H, Bilgili ME, Simsek HA, Dogan B. Histologic Evidence of New Collagen Formulation Using Platelet Rich Plasma in Skin Rejuvenation: A Prospective Controlled Clinical Study. Ann Dermatol. 2016 Dec; (6):718-724.

Alam M, Barrett KC, Hodapp RM, Arndt KA. Botulinum toxin and the facial feedback hypothesis: can looking better make you feel happier? J Am Acad Dermatol. 2008;58(6):1061-72.

Alam M, Han S, Pongprutthipan M, Disphanurat W, Kakar R, Nodzenski M, Pace N, Kim N, Yoo S, Veledar E, Poon E, West DP. Efficacy of a needling device for the treatment of acne scars: a randomized clinical trial. JAMA Dermatol. 2014;150(8):844-9.

Aldag C, Nogueira Teixeira D, Leventhal PS. Skin rejuvenation using cosmetic products containing growth factors, cytokines, and matrikines: a review of the literature. Clin Cosmet Investig Dermatol. 2016;9:411-419.

Allah KC, Yéo S, Kossoko H, Assi Djè Bi Djè V, Richard Kadio M. [Keloid scars on black skin: myth or reality]. Ann Chir Plast Esthet. 2013;58(2):115-22.

Allergan Medical Institute: Facial Consumer Market Sizing in EU5, Rosetta June 2013. Percentages are based on a total screened population of 192.3 million consumers, ages 20 to 65years.

Anand C. Facial Contouring With Fillers, Neuromodulators, and Lipolysis to Achieve a Natural Look in Patients With Facial Fullness. J Drugs Dermatol. 2016;15(12):1536-1542.

Anson G, Kane MA, Lambros V. Sleep Wrinkles: Facial Aging and Facial Distortion During Sleep. Aesthet Surg J. 2016;36(8):931-40.

Arif T. Salicylic acid as a peeling agent: a comprehensive review. Clin Cosmet Investig Dermatol. 2015;8:455-61.

Armstrong AW, Harskamp CT, Dhillon JS, Armstrong EJ. Psoriasis and smoking: a systematic review and meta-analysis. Br J Dermatol. 2014;170(2):304-14.

Asserin J, Lati E, Shioya T, Prawitt J. The effect of oral collagen peptide supplementation on skin moisture and the dermal collagen network: evidence from an ex vivo model and randomized, placebo-controlled clinical trials. J Cosmet Dermatol. 2015;14(4):291-301.

Azevedo FR, Ikeoka D, Caramelli B. Effects of intermittent fasting on metabolism in men. Rev Assoc Med Bras (1992). 2013 Mar-Apr;59(2):167-73.

Babcock M, Mehta RC, Makino ET. A randomized, double-blind, split-face study comparing the efficacy and tolerability of three retinol-based products vs. three tretinoin-based products in subjects with moderate to severe facial photodamage. J Drugs Dermatol. 2015;14(1):24-30.

Bae JM, Lee DW. Three-dimensional remodeling of young Asian women's faces using 20-mg/ml smooth, highly cohesive, viscous hyaluronic acid fillers: a retrospective study of 320 patients. Dermatol Surg. 2013;39(9):1370-5.

Ballin AC, Brandt FS, Cazzaniga A. Dermal fillers: an update. Am J Clin Dermatol. 2015;16(4):271-83.

Barolet D, Christiaens F, Hamblin MR. Infrared and skin: Friend or foe. J Photochem Photobiol B. 2016;155:78-85.

Bass LS, Smith S, Busso M, McClaren M. Calcium hydroxylapatite (Radiesse) for treatment of nasolabial folds: long-term safety and efficacy results. Aesthet Surg J. 2010;30(2):235-8.

Bastiaens M1, Hoefnagel J, Westendorp R, Vermeer BJ, Bouwes Bavinck JN. Solar lentigines are strongly related to sun exposure in contrast to ephelides. Pigment Cell Res. 2004;17(3):225-9.

Baumann L, Narins RS, Beer K, Swift A, Butterwick KJ, Few J, Drinkwater A, Murphy DK. Volumizing Hyaluronic Acid Filler for Midface Volume Deficit: Results After Repeat Treatment. Dermatol Surg. 2015;41 Suppl 1:S284-92.

Beasley KL, Weiss RA. Radiofrequency in cosmetic dermatology. Dermatol Clin. 2014;32(1):79-90.

Beer K, Glogau RG, Dover JS, Shamban A, Handiwala L, Olin JT, Bulley B. A randomized, evaluator-blinded, controlled study of effectiveness and safety of small particle hyaluronic acid plus lidocaine for lip augmentation and perioral rhytides. Dermatol Surg. 2015;41 Suppl 1:S127-36.

Beri K, Milgraum SS. Neocollagenesis in Deep and Superficial Dermis by Combining Fractionated Q-Switched ND:YAG 1,064-nm With Topical Plant Stem Cell Extract and N-Acetyl Glucosamine: Open Case Series. J Drugs Dermatol. 2015;14(11):1342-6.

Bernstein EF, Lee J, Brown DB, Yu R, Van Scott E. Glycolic acid treatment increases type I collagen mRNA and hyaluronic acid content of human skin. Dermatol Surg. 2001;27(5):429-33.

Bernstein EF, Brown DB, Schwartz MD, Kaidbey K, Ksenzenko SM. The polyhydroxy acid gluconolactone protects against ultraviolet radiation in an in vitro model of cutaneous photoaging. Dermatol Surg. 2004;30(2 Pt 1):189-95.

Bodekaer M, Faurschou A, Philipsen PA, Wulf HC. Sun protection factor persistence during a day with physical activity and bathing. Photodermatol Photoimmunol Photomed. 2008;24(6):296-300.

Boehm JK, Williams DR, Rimm EB, Ryff C, Kubzansky LD. Association between optimism and serum antioxidants in the midlife in the United States study. Psychosom Med. 2013;75(1):2-10.

Borges J, Manela-Azulay M, Cuzzi T. Photoaging and the clinical utility of fractional laser. Clin Cosmet Investig Dermatol. 2016;9:107-14.

Borumand M, Sibilla S. Daily consumption of the collagen supplement Pure Gold Collagen® reduces visible signs of aging. Clin Interv Aging. 2014;9:1747-58.

Boukamp P. Skin aging: a role for telomerase and telomere dynamics? Curr Mol Med. 2005;5(2):171-7.

Boule LA, Kovacs EJ. Alcohol, aging, and innate immunity. J Leukoc Biol. 2017;102(1):41-55.

Bouloc A, Vergnanini AL, Issa MC. A double-blind randomized study comparing the association of Retinol and LR2412 with tretinoin 0.025% in photoaged skin. J Cosmet Dermatol. 2015;14(1):40-6.

Brand S, Holsboer-Trachsler E, Naranjo JR, Schmidt S. Influence of mindfulness practice on cortisol and sleep in long-term and short-term meditators. Neuropsychobiology. 2012;65(3):109-18.

Braz A, Humphrey S, Weinkle S, Yee GJ, Remington BK, Lorenc ZP, Yoelin S, Waldorf HA, Azizzadeh B, Butterwick KJ, de Maio M, Sadick N, Trevidic P, Criollo-Lamilla G, Garcia P. Lower Face: Clinical Anatomy and Regional Approaches with Injectable Fillers. Plast Reconstr Surg. 2015;136(5 Suppl):235S-257S.

Breithaupt A, Fitzgerald R. Collagen Stimulators: Poly-L-Lactic Acid and Calcium Hydroxyl Apatite. Facial Plast Surg Clin North Am. 2015;23(4):459-69.

Buckingham EM, Klingelhutz AJ. The role of telomeres in the ageing of human skin. Exp Dermatol. 2011;20(4):297-302.

Budamakuntla L, Loganathan E, Suresh DH, Shanmugam S, Suryanarayan S, Dongare A, Venkataramiah LD, Prabhu N. A Randomised, Open-label, Comparative Study of Tranexamic Acid Microinjections and Tranexamic Acid with Microneedling in Patients with Melasma. J Cutan Aesthet Surg. 2013;6(3):139-43.

Carney DR, Cuddy AJ, Yap AJ. Power posing: brief nonverbal displays affect neuroendocrine levels and risk tolerance. Psychol Sci. 2010;21(10):1363-8.

Correia AW, Pope CA 3rd, Dockery DW, Wang Y, Ezzati M, Dominici F. Effect of air pollution control on life expectancy in the United States: an analysis of 545 U.S. counties for the period from 2000 to 2007. Epidemiology. 2013;24(1):23-31.

Carruthers A, Kane MA, Flynn TC, Huang P, Kim SD, Solish N, Kaeuper G. The convergence of medicine and neurotoxins: a focus on botulinum toxin type A and its application in aesthetic medicine--a global, evidence-based botulinum toxin consensus education initiative: part I: botulinum toxin in clinical and cosmetic practice. Dermatol Surg. 2013;39(3 Pt 2):493-509.

Charles Finn J, Cox SE, Earl ML. Social implications of hyperfunctional facial lines. Dermatol Surg. 2003;29(5):450-5.

Cheng CW, Adams GB, Perin L, Wei M, Zhou X, Lam BS, Da Sacco S, Mirisola M, Quinn DI, Dorff TB, Kopchick JJ, Longo VD. Prolonged fasting reduces IGF-1/PKA to promote hematopoietic-stem-cell-based regeneration and reverse immunosuppression. Cell Stem Cell. 2014;14(6):810-23.

Cho JM, Lee YH, Baek RM, Lee SW. Effect of platelet-rich plasma on ultraviolet b-induced skin wrinkles in nude mice. J Plast Reconstr Aesthet Surg. 2011;64(2):e31-9.

Cohen BE, Elbuluk N. Microneedling in skin of color: A review of uses and efficacy. J Am Acad Dermatol. 2016;74(2):348-55.

Crisan M, Taulescu M, Crisan D, Cosgarea R, Parvu A, Cătoi C, Drugan T. Expression of advanced glycation end-products on sun-exposed and non-exposed cutaneous sites during the ageing process in humans. PLoS One. 2013 7;8(10):e75003.

Darlenski R, Surber C, Fluhr JW. Topical retinoids in the management of photodamaged skin: from theory to evidence-based practical approach. Br J Dermatol. 2010;163(6):1157-65.

Dayan SH, Arkins JP, Gal TJ. Blinded evaluation of the effects of hyaluronic acid filler injections on first impressions. Dermatol Surg. 2010 ;36 Suppl 3:1866-73.

Dayan SH, Arkins JP. The subliminal difference: treating from an evolutionary perspective. Plast Reconstr Surg. 2012;129(1):189e-190e.

Dayan SH, Humphrey S, Jones DH, Lizzul PF, Gross TM, Stauffer K, Beddingfield FC 3rd. Overview of ATX-101 (Deoxycholic Acid Injection): A Nonsurgical Approach for Reduction of Submental Fat. Dermatol Surg. 2016;42 Suppl 1:S263-S270.

de Almeida AR, Montagner S. Botulinum toxin for axillary hyperhidrosis. Dermatol Clin. 2014;32(4):495-504.

de Maio M. Ethnic and Gender Considerations in the Use of Facial Injectables: Male Patients. Plast Reconstr Surg. 2015;136(5 Suppl):40S-43S.

de Souza RJ, Mente A, Maroleanu A, Cozma AI, Ha V, Kishibe T, Uleryk E, Budylowski P, Schünemann H, Beyene J, Anand SS. Intake of saturated and trans unsaturated fatty acids and risk of all cause mortality, cardiovascular disease, and type 2 diabetes: systematic review and meta-analysis of observational studies. BMJ. 2015;351:h3978.

Díaz-Ley B, Cuevast J, Alonso-Castro L, Calvo MI, Ríos-Buceta L, Orive G, Anitua E, Jaén P. Benefits of plasma rich in growth factors (PRGF) in skin photodamage: clinical response and histological assessment. Dermatol Ther. 2015;28(4):258-63.

DiBernardo BE, Pozner JN. Intense Pulsed Light Therapy for Skin Rejuvenation. Clin Plast Surg. 2016;43(3):535-40.

Dimberg U, Thunberg M. Empathy, emotional contagion, and rapid facial reactions to angry and happy facial expressions. Psych J. 2012;1(2):118-27.

Ditre CM, Griffin TD, Murphy GF, Sueki H, Telegan B, Johnson WC, Yu RJ, Van Scott EJ. Effects of alpha-hydroxy acids on photoaged skin: a pilot clinical, histologic, and ultrastructural study. J Am Acad Dermatol. 1996;34(2 Pt 1):187-95.

Dorizas A, Krueger N, Sadick NS. Aesthetic uses of the botulinum toxin. Dermatol Clin. 2014;32(1):23-36.

Draelos ZD, Yatskayer M, Bhushan P, Pillai S, Oresajo C. Evaluation of a kojic acid, emblica extract, and glycolic acid formulation compared with hydroquinone 4% for skin lightening. Cutis. 2010;86(3):153-8.

Dréno B, Tan J, Kang S, Rueda MJ, Torres Lozada V, Bettoli V, Layton AM. How People with Facial Acne Scars are Perceived in Society: an Online Survey. Dermatol Ther (Heidelb). 2016;6(2):207-18.

Driskell RR1, Jahoda CA, Chuong CM, Watt FM, Horsley V. Defining dermal adipose tissue. Exp Dermatol. 2014;23(9):629-31.

Dziubanek G, Spychała A, Marchwińska-Wyrwał E, Rusin M, Hajok I, Ćwieląg-Drabek M, Piekut A. Long-term exposure to urban air pollution and the relationship with life expectancy in cohort of 3.5 million people in Silesia. Sci Total Environ. 2017;580:1-8.

Edison BL, Green BA, Wildnauer RH, Sigler ML. A polyhydroxy acid skin care regimen provides antiaging effects comparable to an alpha-hydroxyacid regimen. Cutis. 2004;73(2 Suppl):14-7.

Ehlinger-Martin A, Cohen-Letessier A, Taïeb M, Azoulay E, du Crest D. Women's attitudes to beauty, aging, and the place of cosmetic procedures: insights from the QUEST Observatory. J Cosmet Dermatol. 2016;15(1):89-94.

El-Domyati M, Barakat M, Awad S, Medhat W, El-Fakahany H, Farag H. Multiple microneedling sessions for minimally invasive facial rejuvenation: an objective assessment. Int J Dermatol. 2015;54(12):1361-9.

Elsaie ML, Kammer JN. Evaluation of plasma skin regeneration technology for cutaneous remodeling. J Cosmet Dermatol. 2008;7(4):309-11.

Emer J, Sundaram H. Aesthetic applications of calcium hydroxylapatite volumizing filler: an evidence-based review and discussion of current concepts: (part 1 of 2). J Drugs Dermatol. 2013;12(12):1345-54.

Epel ES, Lin J, Wilhelm FH, Wolkowitz OM, Cawthon R, Adler NE, Dolbier C, Mendes WB, Blackburn EH. Cell aging in relation to stress arousal and cardiovascular disease risk factors. Psycho-neuroendocrinology. 2006;31(3):277-87.

Epel ES, Lithgow GJ. Stress biology and aging mechanisms: toward understanding the deep connection between adaptation to stress and longevity. J Gerontol A Biol Sci Med Sci. 2014;69 Suppl 1:S10-6.

Fabbrocini G, De Padova MP, Tosti A. Chemical peels: what's new and what isn't new but still works well. Facial Plast Surg. 2009;25(5):329-36.

Fabbrocini G, De Vita V, Di Costanzo L, Pastore F, Mauriello MC, Ambra M, Annunziata MC, di Santolo MG, Cameli N, Monfrecola G. Skin needling in the treatment of the aging neck. Skinmed. 2011;9(6):347-51.

Fabbrocini G, De Vita V, Monfrecola A, De Padova MP, Brazzini B, Teixeira F, Chu A. Percutaneous collagen induction: an effective and safe treatment for post-acne scarring in different skin phototypes. J Dermatolog Treat. 2014;25(2):147-52.

Fabi SG, Massaki A, Eimpunth S, Pogoda J, Goldman MP. Evaluation of microfocused ultrasound with visualization for lifting, tightening, and wrinkle reduction of the décolletage. J Am Acad Dermatol. 2013;69(6):965-71.

Fabi SG, Goldman MP. Retrospective evaluation of micro-focused ultrasound for lifting and tightening the face and neck. Dermatol Surg. 2014;40(5):569-75.

Fabi SG. Noninvasive skin tightening: focus on new ultrasound techniques. Clin Cosmet Investig Dermatol. 2015;8:47-52.

Fan Y, Tang YY, Posner MI. Cortisol level modulated by integrative meditation in a dose-dependent fashion. Stress Health. 2014;30(1):65-70.

Faraut B, Boudjeltia KZ, Vanhamme L, Kerkhofs M. Immune, inflammatory and cardiovascular consequences of sleep restriction and recovery. Sleep Med Rev. 2012;16(2):137-49.

Farris PK. Topical vitamin C: a useful agent for treating photoaging and other dermatologic conditions. Dermatol Surg. 2005;31(7 Pt 2):814-7.

Farris P, Yatskayer M, Chen N, Krol Y, Oresajo C. Evaluation of efficacy and tolerance of a nighttime topical antioxidant containing resveratrol, baicalin, and vitamin e for treatment of mild to moderately photodamaged skin. J Drugs Dermatol. 2014;13(12):1467-72.

Few J, Cox SE, Paradkar-Mitragotri D, Murphy DK. A Multicenter, Single-Blind Randomized, Controlled Study of a Volumizing Hyaluronic Acid Filler for Midface Volume Deficit: Patient-Reported Outcomes at 2 Years. Aesthet Surg J. 2015;35(5):589-99.

Fink B, Matts PJ, D'Emiliano D, Bunse L, Weege B, Röder S. Colour homogeneity and visual perception of age, health and attractiveness of male facial skin. J Eur Acad Dermatol Venereol. 2012;26(12):1486-92. (a)

Fink B, Bunse L, Matts PJ, D'Emiliano D. Visible skin colouration predicts perception of male facial age, health and attractiveness. Int J Cosmet Sci. 2012;34(4):307-10. (b)

Fink B, Butovskaya M, Sorokowski P, Sorokowska A, Matts P. Visual Perception of British Women's Skin Color Distribution in Two Non-industrialized Societies, the Maasai and the Tsimane'. Evol Psychol. 2017;15(3):1474704917718957.

Finzi E, Rosenthal NE2. Treatment of depression with onabotulinumtoxinA: a randomized, double-blind, placebo controlled trial. J Psychiatr Res. 2014;52:1-6.

Fisher GJ, Datta SC, Talwar HS, Wang ZQ, Varani J, Kang S, Voorhees JJ. Molecular basis of sun-induced premature skin ageing and retinoid antagonism. Nature. 1996;379(6563):335-9.

Fischer T, Sattler G, Gauglitz G. [Lidocaine-containing hyaluronic acid filler on a CPM basis for lip augmentation : Experience from clinical practice]. Hautarzt. 2016;67(6):472-8.

Fitzpatrick RE, Rostan EF. Double-blind, half-face study comparing topical vitamin C and vehicle for rejuvenation of photodamage. Dermatol Surg. 2002;28(3):231-6.

Fluhr JW, Vienne MP, Lauze C, Dupuy P, Gehring W, Gloor M. Tolerance profile of retinol, retinaldehyde and retinoic acid under maximized and long-term clinical conditions. Dermatology. 1999;199 Suppl 1:57-60.

Fortes C, Mastroeni S, Melchi F, Pilla MA, Antonelli G, Camaioni D, Alotto M, Pasquini P. A protective effect of the Mediterranean diet for cutaneous melanoma. Int J Epidemiol. 2008;37(5):1018-29.

Fossel M, Blackburn G, Woynarowky D. The Immortality Edge. John Wiley & Sons Inc.; 2011.

Freedman BM. Hydradermabrasion: an innovative modality for nonablative facial rejuvenation. J Cosmet Dermatol. 2008;7(4):275-80.

Freedman BM Topical antioxidant application enhances the effects of facial microdermabrasion. J Dermatolog Treat. 2009;20(2): 82-7.

García-Martínez O, Reyes-Botella C, Díaz-Rodríguez L, De Luna-Bertos E, Ramos-Torrecillas J, Vallecillo-Capilla MF, Ruiz C. Effect of platelet-rich plasma on growth and antigenic profile of human osteoblasts and its clinical impact. J Oral Maxillofac Surg. 2012;70(7):1558-64.

Gold MH, Sensing W, Biron J. Fractional Q-switched 1,064-nm laser for the treatment of photoaged-photodamaged skin. J Cosmet Laser Ther. 2014;16(2):69-76.

Green BA, Yu RJ, Van Scott EJ. Clinical and cosmeceutical uses of hydroxyacids. Clin Dermatol. 2009;27(5):495-501.

Griffiths CE, Kang S, Ellis CN, Kim KJ, Finkel LJ, Ortiz-Ferrer LC, White GM, Hamilton TA, Voorhees JJ. Two concentrations of topical tretinoin (retinoic acid) cause similar improvement of photoaging but different degrees of irritation. A double-blind, vehicle-controlled comparison of 0.1% and 0.025% tretinoin creams. Arch Dermatol. 1995;131(9):1037-44.

Grimes PE, Green BA, Wildnauer RH, Edison BL. The use of polyhydroxy acids (PHAs) in photoaged skin. Cutis. 2004;73(2 Suppl):3-13.

Grove GL, Grove MJ, Leyden JJ, Lufrano L, Schwab B, Perry BH, Thorne EG. Skin replica analysis of photodamaged skin after therapy with tretinoin emollient cream. J Am Acad Dermatol. 1991;25(2 Pt 1):231-7.

Gümüştekín K, Seven B, Karabulut N, Aktaş O, Gürsan N, Aslan S, Keleş M, Varoglu E, Dane S. Effects of sleep deprivation, nicotine, and selenium on wound healing in rats. Int J Neurosci. 2004; 114(11):1433-42.

Gunn DA, de Craen AJ, Dick JL, Tomlin CC, van Heemst D, Catt SD, Griffiths T, Ogden S, Maier AB, Murray PG, Griffiths CE, Slagboom PE, Westendorp RG. Facial appearance reflects human familial longevity and cardiovascular disease risk in healthy individuals. J Gerontol A Biol Sci Med Sci. 2013;68(2):145-52.

Gupta A, Dai T, Hamblin MR. Effect of red and near-infrared wavelengths on low-level laser (light) therapy-induced healing of partial-thickness dermal abrasion in mice. Lasers Med Sci. 2014;29(1):257-65.

Gutowski KA. Hyaluronic Acid Fillers: Science and Clinical Uses. Clin Plast Surg. 2016;43(3):489-96.

Guzman-Alonso M, Cortazar T. Water content at different skin depths and the influence of moisturizing formulations. Household and Personal Care Today 2016;11(1):35-40.

Hamley S. The effect of replacing saturated fat with mostly n-6 polyunsaturated fat on coronary heart disease: a meta-analysis of randomised controlled trials. Nutr J. 2017;16(1):30.

Handel AC, Miot LD, Miot HA. Melasma: a clinical and epidemiological review. An Bras Dermatol. 2014;89(5):771-82.

Harris MO, Sundaram HA. Safety of Microfocused Ultrasound With Visualization in Patients With Fitzpatrick Skin Phototypes III to VI. JAMA Facial Plast Surg. 2015;17(5):355-7.

Heckmann M, Teichmann B, Schröder U, Sprengelmeyer R, Ceballos-Baumann AO. Pharmacologic denervation of frown muscles enhances baseline expression of happiness and decreases baseline expression of anger, sadness, and fear. J Am Acad Dermatol. 2003;49(2):213-6.

Hennenlotter A, Dresel C, Castrop F, Ceballos-Baumann AO, Wohlschläger AM, Haslinger B. The link between facial feedback and neural activity within central circuitries of emotion--new insights from botulinum toxin-induced denervation of frown muscles. Cereb Cortex. 2009;19(3):537-42.

Herane MI, Orlandi C, Zegpi E, Valdés P, Ancić X. Clinical efficacy of adapalene (differin) 0.3% gel in Chilean women with cutaneous photoaging. J Dermatolog Treat. 2012;23(1):57-64.

Hersant B, Calmon A, Meningaud JP. [The use of deoxycholic acid (ATX-101) in aesthetic medicine: A promising treatment]. Rev Stomatol Chir Maxillofac Chir Orale. 2015;116(6):350-2.

Hill RH 3rd, Czyz CN, Kandapalli S, Zhang-Nunes SX, Cahill KV, Wulc AE, Foster JA. Evolving Minimally Invasive Techniques for Tear Trough Enhancement. Ophthal Plast Reconstr Surg. 2015;31(4):306-9.

Hitchcock TM, Dobke MK. Review of the safety profile for microfocused ultrasound with visualization. J Cosmet Dermatol. 2014;13(4):329-35.

Ho ET, Trookman NS, Sperber BR, Rizer RL, Spindler R, Sonti S, Gotz V, Mehta R. A randomized, double-blind, controlled comparative trial of the anti-aging properties of non-prescription tri-retinol 1.1% vs. prescription tretinoin 0.025%. J Drugs Dermatol. 2012;11(1):64-9.

Hoge EA, Chen MM, Orr E, Metcalf CA, Fischer LE, Pollack MH, De Vivo I, Simon NM. Loving-Kindness Meditation practice associated with longer telomeres in women. Brain Behav Immun. 2013;32:159-63.

Hou A, Cohen B, Haimovic A, Elbuluk N. Microneedling: A Comprehensive Review. Dermatol Surg. 2017;43(3):321-339.

Huang TL, Charyton C. A comprehensive review of the psychological effects of brainwave entrainment. Altern Ther Health Med. 2008;14(5):38-50.

Huang YC, Cheng YC. Isotretinoin treatment for acne and risk of depression: A systematic review and meta-analysis. J Am Acad Dermatol. 2017;76(6):1068-1076.

Huber-Vorländer J, Kürten M. Correction of tear trough deformity with a cohesive polydensified matrix hyaluronic acid: a case series. Clin Cosmet Investig Dermatol. 2015;8:307-12.

Humbert PG, Haftek M, Creidi P, Lapière C, Nusgens B, Richard A, Schmitt D, Rougier A, Zahouani H. Topical ascorbic acid on photoaged skin. Clinical, topographical and ultrastructural evaluation: double-blind study vs. placebo. Exp Dermatol. 2003;12(3):237-44.

Humphrey CD, Arkins JP, Dayan SH. Soft tissue fillers in the nose. Aesthet Surg J. 2009;29(6):477-84.

Ingargiola MJ, Motakef S, Chung MT, Vasconez HC, Sasaki GH. Cryolipolysis for fat reduction and body contouring: safety and efficacy of current treatment paradigms. Plast Reconstr Surg. 2015;135(6):1581-90.

Li D, Lin SB, Cheng B. Intense Pulsed Light: From the Past to the Future. Photomed Laser Surg. 2016;34(10):435-447.

Lin FH, Lin JY, Gupta RD, Tournas JA, Burch JA, Selim MA, Monteiro-Riviere NA, Grichnik JM, Zielinski J, Pinnell SR. Ferulic acid stabilizes a solution of vitamins C and E and doubles its photoprotection of skin. J Invest Dermatol. 2005;125(4):826-32.

Linder J. Chemical peels and combination therapies. Plast Surg Nurs. 2013;33(2):88-91.

Jakubietz RG, Kloss DF, Gruenert JG, Jakubietz MG. The ageing hand. A study to evaluate the chronological ageing process of the hand. J Plast Reconstr Aesthet Surg. 2008;61(6):681-6.

Jones DH, Carruthers J, Joseph JH, Callender VD, Walker P, Lee DR, Subramanian M, Lizzul PF, Gross TM, Beddingfield FC 3rd. REFINE-1, a Multicenter, Randomized, Double-Blind, Placebo-Controlled, Phase 3 Trial With ATX-101, an Injectable Drug for Submental Fat Reduction. Dermatol Surg. 2016;42(1):38-49.

Kahan V, Andersen ML, Tomimori J, Tufik S. Can poor sleep affect skin integrity? Med Hypotheses. 2010;75(6):535-7.

Kamihiro S, Stergiadis S, Leifert C, Eyre MD, Butler G. Meat quality and health implications of organic and conventional beef production. Meat Sci. 2015;100:306-18.

Kaminaka C, Uede M, Matsunaka H, Furukawa F, Yamomoto Y. Clinical evaluation of glycolic acid chemical peeling in patients with acne vulgaris: a randomized, double-blind, placebo-controlled, split-face comparative study. Dermatol Surg. 2014;40(3):314-22.

Kelly JR, Iannone NE, McCarty MK. Emotional contagion of anger is automatic: An evolutionary explanation. Br J Soc Psychol. 2016;55(1):182-91.

Kerscher M, Bayrhammer J, Reuther T. Rejuvenating influence of a stabilized hyaluronic acid-based gel of nonanimal origin on facial skin aging. Dermatol Surg. 2008;34(5):720-6.

Kestemont P, Cartier H, Trevidic P, Rzany B, Sattler G, Kerrouche N, Dhuin JC. Sustained efficacy and high patient satisfaction after cheek enhancement with a new hyaluronic acid dermal filler. J Drugs Dermatol. 2012;11(1 Suppl):s9-16.

Khavkin J, Ellis DA. Aging skin: histology, physiology, and pathology. Facial Plast Surg Clin North Am. 2011;19(2):229-34.

Kilmer S, Semchyshyn N, Shah G, Fitzpatrick R. A pilot study on the use of a plasma skin regeneration device (Portrait PSR3) in full facial rejuvenation procedures. Lasers Med Sci. 2007;22(2):101-9.

Kim H, Kim M, Quan Y, Moon T, Mun J, Cho H, Park N, Moon W, Lee K, Kim H, Lee J, Ryoo H, Jung H. Novel anti-wrinkle effect of cosmeceutical product with new retinyl retinoate microsphere using biodegradable polymer. Skin Res Technol. 2012;18(1):70-6.

Kim KE, Cho D, Park HJ. Air pollution and skin diseases: Adverse effects of airborne particulate matter on various skin diseases. Life Sci. 2016;152:126-34.

Kircik LH. Histologic improvement in photodamage after 12 months of treatment with tretinoin emollient cream (0.02%). J Drugs Dermatol. 2012;11(9):1036-40.

Kircik LH. Evaluating tretinoin formulations in the treatment of acne. J Drugs Dermatol. 2014;13(4):466-70.

Kligman AM, Willis I. A new formula for depigmenting human skin. Arch Dermatol. 1975;111(1):40-8.

Kligman AM, Dogadkina D, Lavker RM. Effects of topical tretinoin on non-sun-exposed protected skin of the elderly. J Am Acad Dermatol. 1993;29(1):25-33.

Kong R, Cui Y, Fisher GJ, Wang X, Chen Y, Schneider LM, Majmudar G. A comparative study of the effects of retinol and retinoic acid on histological, molecular, and clinical properties of human skin. J Cosmet Dermatol. 2016;15(1):49-57.

Krueger N, Sadick NS. New-generation radiofrequency technology. Cutis. 2013;91(1):39-46.

Krueger N, Mai SV, Luebberding S, Sadick NS. Cryolipolysis for noninvasive body contouring: clinical efficacy and patient satisfaction. Clin Cosmet Investig Dermatol. 2014;7:201-5.

Krutmann J, Bouloc A, Sore G, Bernard BA, Passeron T. The skin aging exposome. J Dermatol Sci. 2017;85(3):152-161.

Ledon JA, Savas JA, Yang S, Franca K, Camacho I, Nouri K. Inflammatory nodules following soft tissue filler use: a review of causative agents, pathology and treatment options. Am J Clin Dermatol. 2013;14(5):401-11.

Lee T, Friedman A. Skin Barrier Health: Regulation and Repair of the Stratum Corneum and the Role of Over-the-Counter Skin Care. J Drugs Dermatol. 2016 1;15(9):1047-51.

Liebla H, Kloth LC. Skin Cell Proliferation Stimulated by Microneedles. J Am Coll Clin Wound Spec. 2012; 4(1): 2–6.

Liew S, Scamp T, de Maio M, Halstead M, Johnston N, Silberberg M, Rogers JD. Efficacy and Safety of a Hyaluronic Acid Filler to Correct Aesthetically Detracting or Deficient Features of the Asian Nose: A Prospective, Open-Label, Long-Term Study. Aesthet Surg J. 2016;36(7):760-72.

Louis J, Schaal K, Bieuzen F, Le Meur Y, Filliard JR, Volondat M, Brisswalter J, Hausswirth C. Head Exposure to Cold during Whole-Body Cryostimulation: Influence on Thermal Response and Autonomic Modulation. PLoS One. 2015 27;10(4):e0124776.

Lubkowska A, Szygula Z, Klimek AJ, Torii M. Do sessions of cryostimulation have influence on white blood cell count, level of IL6 and total oxidative and antioxidative status in healthy men? Eur J Appl Physiol. 2010;109(1):67-72.

Luebberding S, Alexiades-Armenakas MR. Fractional, nonablative Q-switched 1,064-nm neodymium YAG laser to rejuvenate photoaged skin: a pilot case series. J Drugs Dermatol. 2012;11(11):1300-4.

Luebberding S, Krueger N, Kerscher M. Mechanical properties of human skin in vivo: a comparative evaluation in 300 men and women. Skin Res Technol. 2014;20(2):127-35.

MacGregor JL, Tanzi EL. Microfocused ultrasound for skin tightening. Semin Cutan Med Surg. 2013;32(1):18-25.

Magid M, Reichenberg JS, Poth PE, Robertson HT, LaViolette AK, Kruger TH, Wollmer MA. Treatment of major depressive disorder using botulinum toxin A: a 24-week randomized, double-blind, placebo-controlled study. J Clin Psychiatry. 2014;75(8):837-44.

Magnani ND, Muresan XM, Belmonte G, Cervellati F, Sticozzi C, Pecorelli A, Miracco C, Marchini T, Evelson P, Valacchi G. Skin Damage Mechanisms Related to Airborne Particulate Matter Exposure. Toxicol Sci. 2016;149(1):227-36.

Maguire M, Maguire G. The role of microbiota, and probiotics and prebiotics in skin health. Arch Dermatol Res. 2017;309(6):411-421.

Makrantonaki E, Vogel M, Scharffetter-Kochanek K, Zouboulis CC. [Skin aging: Molecular understanding of extrinsic and intrinsic processes]. Hautarzt. 2015 Oct;66(10):730-7.

Malerich S, Berson D. Next generation cosmeceuticals: the latest in peptides, growth factors, cytokines, and stem cells. Dermatol Clin. 2014;32(1):13-21.

Marcon F, Siniscalchi E, Crebelli R, Saieva C, Sera F, Fortini P, Simonelli V, Palli D. Diet-related telomere shortening and chromosome stability. Mutagenesis. 2012;27(1):49-57.

Marinelli E, Montanari Vergallo G, Reale G, di Luca A, Catarinozzi I, Napoletano S, Zaami S. The role of fillers in aesthetic medicine: medico-legal aspects. Eur Rev Med Pharmacol Sci. 2016;20(22):4628-4634.

Masaki H. Role of antioxidants in the skin: anti-aging effects. J Dermatol Sci. 2010;58(2):85-90.

Matts PJ, Fink B, Grammer K, Burquest M. Color homogeneity and visual perception of age, health, and attractiveness of female facial skin. J Am Acad Dermatol. 2007;57(6):977-84.

Mattson MP, Longo VD, Harvie M. Impact of intermittent fasting on health and disease processes. Ageing Res Rev. 2016:S1568-1637(16)30251-3.

Mayes AE, Murray PG, Gunn DA, Tomlin CC, Catt SD, Wen YB, Zhou LP, Wang HQ, Catt M, Granger SP. Environmental and lifestyle factors associated with perceived facial age in Chinese women. PLoS One. 2010;5(12):e15270.

McLafferty E, Hendry C, Alistair F. The integumentary system: anatomy, physiology and function of skin. Nurs Stand. 2012;27(3):35-42.

Mehta-Ambalal SR. Neocollagenesis and Neoelastinogenesis: From the Laboratory to the Clinic. J Cutan Aesthet Surg. 2016; 9(3): 145–151.

Michaud T, Gassia V, Belhaouari L. Facial dynamics and emotional expressions in facial aging treatments. J Cosmet Dermatol. 2015;14(1):9-21.

Mitani H, Koshiishi I, Sumita T, Imanari T. Prevention of the photodamage in the hairless mouse dorsal skin by kojic acid as an iron chelator. Eur J Pharmacol. 2001;411(1-2):169-174.

Moradi A, Watson J. Current Concepts in Filler Injection. Facial Plast Surg Clin North Am. 2015;23(4):489-94.

Moruś M, Baran M, Rost-Roszkowska M, Skotnicka-Graca U. Plant stem cells as innovation in cosmetics. Acta Pol Pharm. 2014;71(5):701-7.

Nagata C, Nakamura K, Wada K, Oba S, Hayashi M, Takeda N, Yasuda K. Association of dietary fat, vegetables and antioxidant micronutrients with skin ageing in Japanese women. Br J Nutr. 2010;103(10):1493-8.

Nedeltcheva AV, Scheer FA. Metabolic effects of sleep disruption, links to obesity and diabetes. Curr Opin Endocrinol Diabetes Obes. 2014;21(4):293-8.

Nguyen HP, Katta R. Sugar Sag: Glycation and the Role of Diet in Aging Skin. Skin Therapy Lett. 2015;20(6):1-5.

Nielsen F, Mikkelsen BB, Nielsen JB, Andersen HR, Grandjean P. Plasma malondialdehyde as biomarker for oxidative stress: reference interval and effects of life-style factors. Clin Chem. 1997;43(7):1209-14.

Nikolakis G, Makrantonaki E, Zouboulis CC. Skin mirrors human aging. Horm Mol Biol Clin Investig. 2013;16(1):13-28.

Nofal E, Helmy A, Nofal A, Alakad R, Nasr M. Platelet-rich plasma versus CROSS technique with 100% trichloroacetic acid versus combined skin needling and platelet rich plasma in the treatment of atrophic acne scars: a comparative study. Dermatol Surg. 2014;40(8):864-73.

Noordam R, Gunn DA, Tomlin CC, Maier AB, Mooijaart SP, Slagboom PE, Westendorp RG, de Craen AJ, van Heemst D; Leiden Longevity Study Group. High serum glucose levels are associated with a higher perceived age. Age (Dordr).2013;35(1):189-95.

Ohshima H, Oyobikawa M, Tada A, Maeda T, Takiwaki H, Itoh M, Kanto H. Melanin and facial skin fluorescence as markers of yellowish discoloration with aging. Skin Res Technol. 2009;15(4):496-502.

Okano Y, Abe Y, Masaki H, Santhanam U, Ichihashi M, Funasaka Y. Biological effects of glycolic acid on dermal matrix metabolism mediated by dermal fibroblasts and epidermal keratinocytes. Exp Dermatol. 2003;12 Suppl 2:57-63.

Omi T, Sato S, Numano K, Kawana S. Ultrastructural observations of chemical peeling for skin rejuvenation (ultrastructural changes of the skin due to chemical peeling). J Cosmet Laser Ther. 2010;12(1):21-4.

Oresajo C, Stephens T, Hino PD, Law RM, Yatskayer M, Foltis P, Pillai S, Pinnell SR. Protective effects of a topical antioxidant mixture containing vitamin C, ferulic acid, and phloretin against ultraviolet-induced photodamage in human skin. J Cosmet Dermatol. 2008;7(4):290-7.

Oyetakin-White P, Suggs A, Koo B, Matsui MS, Yarosh D, Cooper KD, Baron ED. Does poor sleep quality affect skin ageing? Clin Exp Dermatol. 2015;40(1):17-22.

Pageon H, Zucchi H, Rousset F, Monnier VM, Asselineau D. Skin aging by glycation: lessons from the reconstructed skin model. Clin Chem Lab Med. 2014 1;52(1):169-74.

Paolo F, Nefer F, Paola P, Nicolò S. Periorbital area rejuvenation using carbon dioxide therapy. J Cosmet Dermatol. 2012;11(3):223-8.

Park HY, Kim JH, Jung M, Chung CH, Hasham R, Park CS, Choi EH. A long-standing hyperglycaemic condition impairs skin barrier by accelerating skin ageing process. Exp Dermatol. 2011;20(12):969-74.

Pavicic T, Gauglitz GG, Lersch P, Schwach-Abdellaoui K, Malle B, Korting HC, Farwick M. Efficacy of cream-based novel formulations of hyaluronic acid of different molecular weights in anti-wrinkle treatment. J Drugs Dermatol. 2011;10(9):990-1000.

Pawling R, Kirkham AJ, Hayes AE, Tipper SP. Incidental retrieval of prior emotion mimicry. Exp Brain Res. 2017;235(4):1173-1184.

Pellegrino R, Sunaga DY, Guindalini C, Martins RC, Mazzotti DR, Wei Z, Daye ZJ, Andersen ML, Tufik S. Whole blood genome-wide gene expression profile in males after prolonged wakefulness and sleep recovery. Physiol Genomics. 2012;44(21):1003-12.

Penna V, Stark GB, Voigt M, Mehlhorn A, Iblher N. Classification of the Aging Lips: A Foundation for an Integrated Approach to Perioral Rejuvenation. Aesthetic Plast Surg. 2015;39(1):1-7.

Perper M, Eber AE, Fayne R, Verne SH, Magno RJ, Cervantes J, ALharbi M, ALOmair I, Alfuraih A, Nouri K. Tranexamic Acid in the Treatment of Melasma: A Review of the Literature. Am J Clin Dermatol. 2017;18(3):373-381.

Pessoa RS, Oliveira SR, Menezes HH, de Magalhaes D. Effects of platelet-rich plasma on healing of alveolar socket: split-mouth histological and histometric evaluation in Cebus apella monkeys. Indian J Dent Res. 2009;20(4):442-7.

Pianez F, Nefer F, Paola P, Nicolò S. Periorbital area rejuvenation using carbon dioxide therapy. J Cosmet Dermatol. 2012;11(3):223-8.

Pianez LR, Custódio FS, Guidi RM, de Freitas JN, Sant'Ana E. Effectiveness of carboxytherapy in the treatment of cellulite in healthy women: a pilot study. Clin Cosmet Investig Dermatol. 2016;9:183-90.

Pinheiro NM, Crema VO, Millan BM, Carvalho FA, Mendonça AC. Comparison of the effects of carboxytherapy and radiofrequency on skin rejuvenation. J Cosmet Laser Ther. 2015;17(3):156-61.

Pinnell SR, Yang H, Omar M, Monteiro-Riviere N, DeBuys HV, Walker LC, Wang Y, Levine M. Topical L-ascorbic acid: percutaneous absorption studies. Dermatol Surg. 2001;27(2):137-42.

Potter MJ, Harrison R, Ramsden A, Bryan B, Andrews P, Gault D. Facial acne and fine lines: transforming patient outcomes with plasma skin regeneration. Ann Plast Surg. 2007;58(6):608-13.

Pozner JN, DiBernardo BE. Laser Resurfacing: Full Field and Fractional. Clin Plast Surg. 2016;43(3):515-25.

Prager W, Wissmüller E, Kollhorst B, Williams S, Zschocke I. Comparison of two botulinum toxin type A preparations for treating crow's feet: a split-face, double-blind, proof-of-concept study. Dermatol Surg. 2010;36 Suppl 4:2155-60.

Prochazkova E, Kret ME. Connecting minds and sharing emotions through mimicry: A neurocognitive model of emotional contagion. Neurosci Biobehav Rev. 2017;80:99-114.

Proksch E, Segger D, Degwert J, Schunck M, Zague V, Oesser S. Oral supplementation of specific collagen peptides has beneficial effects on human skin physiology: a double-blind, placebo-controlled study. Skin Pharmacol Physiol. 2014;27(1):47-55 (a)

Proksch E, Schunck M, Zague V, Segger D, Degwert J, Oesser S. Oral intake of specific bioactive collagen peptides reduces skin wrinkles and increases dermal matrix synthesis. Skin Pharmacol Physiol. 2014;27(3):113-9. (b)

Puri P, Nandar SK, Kathuria S, Ramesh V. Effects of air pollution on the skin: A review. Indian J Dermatol Venereol Leprol. 2017;83(4):415-423.

Rabello-Fonseca RM, Azulay DR, Luiz RR, Mandarim-de-Lacerda CA, Cuzzi T,Manela-Azulay M. Oral isotretinoin in photoaging: clinical and histopathological evidence of efficacy of an off-label indication. J Eur Acad Dermatol Venereol. 2009;23(2):115-23.

Rafal ES, Griffiths CE, Ditre CM, Finkel LJ, Hamilton TA, Ellis CN, Voorhees JJ. Topical tretinoin (retinoic acid) treatment for liver spots associated with photodamage. N Engl J Med. 1992 6;326(6):368-74.

Ramanadham SR, Rohrich RJ. Newer Understanding of Specific Anatomic Targets in the Aging Face as Applied to Injectables: Superficial and Deep Facial Fat Compartments--An Evolving Target for Site-Specific Facial Augmentation. Plast Reconstr Surg. 2015;136(5 Suppl):49S-55S.

Ramaut L, Hoeksema H, Pirayesh A, Stillaert F, Monstrey S. Microneedling: Where do we stand now? A systematic review of the literature. J Plast Reconstr Aesthet Surg. 2017. pii: S1748-6815(17)30250-4.

Randhawa M, Rossetti D, Leyden JJ, Fantasia J, Zeichner J, Cula GO, Southall M, Tucker-Samaras S. One-year topical stabilized retinol treatment improves photodamaged skin in a double-blind, vehicle-controlled trial. J Drugs Dermatol. 2015;14(3):271-80. (a)

Randhawa M, Seo I, Liebel F, Southall MD, Kollias N, Ruvolo E. Visible Light Induces Melanogenesis in Human Skin through a Photoadaptive Response. PLoS One. 2015;10(6):e0130949. (b)

Rasmussen HN, Scheier MF, Greenhouse JB. Optimism and physical health: a meta-analytic review. Ann Behav Med. 2009;37(3):239-56.

Rau AS, Reinikovaite V, Schmidt EP, Taraseviciene-Stewart L, Deleyiannis FW. Electronic Cigarettes Are as Toxic to Skin Flap Survival as Tobacco Cigarettes. Ann Plast Surg. 2017;79(1):86-91.

Reid G, Abrahamsson T, Bailey M, Bindels LB, Bubnov R, Ganguli K, Martoni C, O'Neill C, Savignac HM, Stanton C, Ship N, Surette M, Tuohy K, van Hemert S. How do probiotics and prebiotics function at distant sites? Benef Microbes. 2017;20:1-14.

Renata S, Tomasz D, Andrzej K, Sławomir T. Impact of 10 sessions of whole body cryostimulation on cutaneous microcirculation measured by laser Doppler flowmetry. J Hum Kinet. 2011;30:75-83.

Reuther T, Bayrhammer J, Kerscher M. Effects of a three-session skin rejuvenation treatment using stabilized hyaluronic acid-based gel of non-animal origin on skin elasticity: a pilot study. Arch Dermatol Res. 2010;302(1):37-45.

Rinnerthaler M, Bischof J, Streubel MK, Trost A, Richter K. Oxidative stress in aging human skin. Biomolecules. 2015 21;5(2):545-89.

Rittié L, Fisher GJ. Natural and sun-induced aging of human skin. Cold Spring Harb Perspect Med. 2015 5;5(1):a015370.

Rizvi S, Raza ST, Mahdi F. Telomere length variations in aging and age-related diseases. Curr Aging Sci. 2014;7(3):161-7.

Robinson LR, Fitzgerald NC, Doughty DG, Dawes NC, Berge CA, Bissett DL. Topical palmitoyl pentapeptide provides improvement in photoaged human facial skin. Int J Cosmet Sci. 2005;27(3):155-60.

Rohrich RJ, Pessa JE. The fat compartments of the face: anatomy and clinical implications for cosmetic surgery. Plast Reconstr Surg. 2007;119(7):2219-27.

Rohrich RJ, Pessa JE, Ristow B. The youthful cheek and the deep medial fat compartment. Plast Reconstr Surg. 2008;121(6):2107-12.

Romana-Souza B, Santos Lima-Cezar G, Monte-Alto-Costa A. Psychological stress-induced catecholamines accelerates cutaneous aging in mice. Mech Ageing Dev. 2015;152:63-73.

Rozing MP, Westendorp RG, de Craen AJ, Frölich M, de Goeij MC, Heijmans BT, Beekman M, Wijsman CA, Mooijaart SP, Blauw GJ, Slagboom PE, van Heemst D; Leiden Longevity Study Group. Favorable glucose tolerance and lower prevalence of metabolic syndrome in offspring without diabetes mellitus of nonagenarian siblings: the Leiden longevity study. J Am Geriatr Soc. 2010;58(3):564-9

Rzany B, Cartier H, Kestermont P, Trevidic P, Sattler G, Kerrouche N, Dhuin JC. Correction of tear troughs and periorbital lines with a range of customized hyaluronic acid fillers. J Drugs Dermatol. 2012;11(1 Suppl):s27-34.

Samson N, Fink B, Matts PJ. Visible skin condition and perception of human facial appearance. Int J Cosmet Sci. 2010;32(3):167-84.

Samson N, Fink B, Matts P. Interaction of skin color distribution and skin surface topography cues in the perception of female facial age and health. J Cosmet Dermatol. 2011;10(1):78-84.

Sarkar R, Arora P, Garg KV. Cosmeceuticals for Hyperpigmentation: What is Available? J Cutan Aesthet Surg. 2013; 6(1): 4–11.

Sasaki GH. Micro-Needling Depth Penetration, Presence of Pigment Particles, and Fluorescein-Stained Platelets: Clinical Usage for Aesthetic Concerns. Aesthet Surg J. 2017;37(1):71-83.

Sasson H, Carpenter CL. Achievement of peak bone mass in women is critically dependent on adolescent calcium intake. OA Sports Medicine. 2013;1(2):16.

Scarano A, Mortellaro C, Mavriqi L, Di Cerbo A. Evaluation Effectiveness of the Voltaic Arc Dermabrasion in Perioral Rhytides Eradication. J Craniofac Surg. 2016;27(5):1205-8.

Schalka S, Steiner D, Ravelli FN, Steiner T, Terena AC, Marçon CR, Ayres EL, Addor FA, Miot HA, Ponzio H, Duarte I, Neffá J, Cunha JA, Boza JC, Samorano Lde P, Corrêa Mde P, Maia M, Nasser N, Leite OM, Lopes OS, Oliveira PD, Meyer RL, Cestari T, Reis VM, Rego VR. Brazilian consensus on photoprotection. An Bras Dermatol. 2014;89(6 Suppl 1):1-74.

Schalkwijk CG, Stehouwer CD, van Hinsbergh VW. Fructosemediated non-enzymatic glycation: sweet coupling or bad modification. Diabetes Metab Res Rev. 2004;20(5):369-82.

Schroeder P, Lademann J, Darvin ME, Stege H, Marks C, Bruhnke S, Krutmann J. Infrared radiation-induced matrix metalloproteinase in human skin: implications for protection. J Invest Dermatol. 2008;128(10):2491-7.

Schulte BC, Wu W, Rosen T. Azelaic Acid: Evidence-based Update on Mechanism of Action and Clinical Application. J Drugs Dermatol. 2015;14(9):964-8.

Shammas MA. Telomeres, lifestyle, cancer, and aging. Curr Opin Clin Nutr Metab Care. 2011;14(1):28-34.

Shaw RB Jr, Katzel EB, Koltz PF, Kahn DM, Puzas EJ, Langstein HN. Facial bone density: effects of aging and impact on facial rejuvenation. Aesthet Surg J. 2012;32(8):937-42.

Shen J, Terry MB, Gurvich I, Liao Y, Senie RT, Santella RM. Short telomere length and breast cancer risk: a study in sister sets. Cancer Res. 2007;67(11):5538-44.

Sieron A, Cieúlar G, Stanek A, Jagodzinski L, Drzazga Z, Birkner E, Bilska-Urban A, Mostowy A, Kubacka M, Wiúniowska B, Romuk E, Skrzep-Poloczek B, Mrowiec J, Cholewka A, Adamek M, Puszer M. Cryotherapy. Theoretical bases, biological effects, clinical applications. by α-medica press 2010

Silverberg JI, Hanifin JM. Adult eczema prevalence and associations with asthma and other health and demographic factors: a US population-based study. J Allergy Clin Immunol. 2013;132(5):1132-8.

Siri-Tarino PW, Sun Q, Hu FB, Krauss RM. Meta-analysis of prospective cohort studies evaluating the association of saturated fat with cardiovascular disease. Am J Clin Nutr. 2010;91(3):535-46.

Small R. Botulinum toxin injection for facial wrinkles. Am Fam Physician. 2014;90(3):168-75.

Smith KC. Reversible vs. nonreversible fillers in facial aesthetics: concerns and considerations. Dermatol Online J. 2008;14(8):3.

Solish N, Swift A. An open-label, pilot study to assess the effectiveness and safety of hyaluronic acid gel in the restoration of soft tissue fullness of the lips. J Drugs Dermatol. 2011;10(2):145-9.

Sorg O, Saurat JH. Topical retinoids in skin ageing: a focused update with reference to sun-induced epidermal vitamin A deficiency. Dermatology. 2014;228(4):314-25.

Steventon K. Expert opinion and review article: The timing of comedone extraction in the treatment of premenstrual acne--a proposed therapeutic approach. Int J Cosmet Sci. 2011;33(2):99-104.

Stewart N, Lim AC, Lowe PM, Goodman G. Lasers and laser-like devices: part one. Australas J Dermatol. 2013;54(3):173-83.

Streker M, Reuther T, Krueger N, Kerscher M. Stabilized hyaluronic acid-based gel of non-animal origin for skin rejuvenation: face, hand, and décolletage. J Drugs Dermatol. 2013;12(9):990-4.

Sundram K, Karupaiah T, Hayes KC. Stearic acid-rich interesterified fat and trans-rich fat raise the LDL/HDL ratio and plasma glucose relative to palm olein in humans. Nutr Metab (Lond). 2007;15;4:3.

Sundaram H, Signorini M, Liew S, Trindade de Almeida AR, Wu Y, Vieira Braz A, Fagien S, Goodman GJ, Monheit G, Raspaldo H. Global Aesthetics Consensus: Botulinum Toxin Type A-- Evidence-Based Review, Emerging Concepts, and Consensus Recommendations for Aesthetic Use, Including Updates on Complications. Plast Reconstr Surg. 2016;137(3):518e-529e.

Suryadevara AC. Update on perioral cosmetic enhancement. Curr Opin Otolaryngol Head Neck Surg. 2008;16(4):347-51.

Tiainen AM, Männistö S, Blomstedt PA, Moltchanova E, Perälä MM, Kaartinen NE, Kajantie E, Kananen L, Hovatta I, Eriksson JG. Leukocyte telomere length and its relation to food and nutrient intake in an elderly population. Eur J Clin Nutr. 2012;66(12):1290-4.

Tobin DJ. Introduction to skin aging. J Tissue Viability. 2017;26(1):37-46.

Torok HM. A comprehensive review of the long-term and short-term treatment of melasma with a triple combination cream. Am J Clin Dermatol. 2006;7(4):223-30.

Turlier V, Delalleau A, Casas C, Rouquier A, Bianchi P, Alvarez S, Josse G, Briant A, Dahan S, Saint-Martory C, Theunis J, Bensafi-Benaouda A, Degouy A, Schmitt AM, Redoulès D. Association between collagen production and mechanical stretching in dermal extracellular matrix: in vivo effect of cross-linked hyaluronic acid filler. A randomised, placebo-controlled study. J Dermatol Sci. 2013;69(3):187-94.

Valtin H. "Drink at least eight glasses of water a day." Really? Is there scientific evidence for "8 x 8"? Am J Physiol Regul Integr Comp Physiol. 2002;283(5):R993-1004.

van Drielen K, Gunn DA, Noordam R, Griffiths CE, Westendorp RG, de Craen AJ, van Heemst D. Disentangling the effects of circulating IGF-1, glucose, and cortisol on features of perceived age. Age (Dordr). 2015;37(3):9771.

Veale D, Gledhill LJ, Christodoulou P, Hodsoll J. Body dysmorphic disorder in different settings: A systematic review and estimated weighted prevalence. Body Image. 2016;18:168-86.

Vellai T. Autophagy genes and ageing. Cell Death Differ. 2009;16(1):94-102.

Vierkötter A, Schikowski T, Ranft U, Sugiri D, Matsui M, Krämer U, Krutmann J. Airborne particle exposure and extrinsic skin aging. J Invest Dermatol. 2010;130(12):2719-26.

Vleggaar D, Fitzgerald R, Lorenc ZP, Andrews JT, Butterwick K, Comstock J, Hanke CW, O'Daniel TG, Palm MD, Roberts WE, Sadick N, Teller CF. Consensus recommendations on the use of injectable poly-L-lactic acid for facial and nonfacial volumization. J Drugs Dermatol. 2014;13(4 Suppl):s44-51.

Wang F, Garza LA, Kang S, Varani J, Orringer JS, Fisher GJ, Voorhees JJ. In vivo stimulation of de novo collagen production caused by cross-linked hyaluronic acid dermal filler injections in photodamaged human skin. Arch Dermatol. 2007;143(2):155-63.

Weiss JS, Ellis CN, Headington JT, Tincoff T, Hamilton TA, Voorhees JJ. Topical tretinoin improves photoaged skin. A double-blind vehicle-controlled study. JAMA. 1988 Jan 22-29;259(4):527-32.

Wentzensen IM, Mirabello L, Pfeiffer RM, Savage SA. The association of telomere length and cancer: a meta-analysis. Cancer Epidemiol Biomarkers Prev. 2011;20(6):1238-50.

Wijsman CA, Rozing MP, Streefland TC, le Cessie S, Mooijaart SP, Slagboom PE, Westendorp RG, Pijl H, van Heemst D; Leiden Longevity Study group. Familial longevity is marked by enhanced insulin sensitivity. Aging Cell. 2011;10(1):114-21.

Williams S, Krueger N, Davids M, Kraus D, Kerscher M. Effect of fluid intake on skin physiology: distinct differences between drinking mineral water and tap water. Int J Cosmet Sci. 2007;29(2):131-8.

Williams S, Tamburic S, Stensvik H, Weber M. Changes in skin physiology and clinical appearance after microdroplet placement of hyaluronic acid in aging hands. J Cosmet Dermatol. 2009;8(3):216-25. (a)

Williams S, Tamburic S, Lally C. Eating chocolate can significantly protect the skin from UV light. J Cosmet Dermatol. 2009;8(3):169-73. (b)

Wong CH, Mendelson B. Newer Understanding of Specific Anatomic Targets in the Aging Face as Applied to Injectables: Aging Changes in the Craniofacial Skeleton and Facial Ligaments. Plast Reconstr Surg. 2015;136(5 Suppl):44S-48S.

Wu DC, Fitzpatrick RE, Goldman MP. Confetti-like Sparing - A Diagnostic Clinical Feature of Melasma. J Clin Aesthet Dermatol. 2016; 9(2): 48–57.

Wulf HC, Stender IM, Lock-Andersen J. Sunscreens used at the beach do not protect against erythema: A new definition of SPF is proposed. Photodermatol Photoimmunol Photomed. 1997;13: 129-132.

Xu Q, Parks CG, DeRoo LA, Cawthon RM, Sandler DP, Chen H. Multivitamin use and telomere length in women. Am J Clin Nutr. 2009;89(6):1857-63.

Yamamoto Y, Uede K, Yonei N, Kishioka A, Ohtani T, Furukawa F. Effects of alpha-hydroxy acids on the human skin of Japanese subjects: the rationale for chemical peeling. J Dermatol. 2006;33(1):16-22.

Yoon HS, Kim YK, Matsui M, Chung JH. Possible role of infrared or heat in sun-induced changes of dermis of human skin in vivo. J Dermatol Sci. 2012;66(1):76-8.

Yue B, Yang Q, Xu J, Lu Z. Efficacy and safety of fractional Q-switched 1064-nm neodymium-doped yttrium aluminum garnet laser in the treatment of melasma in Chinese patients. Lasers Med Sci. 2016;31(8):1657-1663.

Zeitter S, Sikora Z, Jahn S, Stahl F, Strauß S, Lazaridis A, Reimers K, Vogt PM, Aust MC. Microneedling: matching the results of medical needling and repetitive treatments to maximize potential for skin regeneration. Burns. 2014;40(5):966-73.

Zhu W, Gao J. The use of botanical extracts as topical skin-lightening agents for the improvement of skin pigmentation disorders. J Investig Dermatol Symp Proc. 2008;13(1):20-4.

Zhuang Y, Lyga J. Inflammaging in skin and other tissues - the roles of complement system and macrophage. Inflamm Allergy Drug Targets. 2014;13(3):153-61.

Zouboulis CC, Adjaye J, Akamatsu H, Moe-Behrens G, Niemann C. Human skin stem cells and the ageing process. Exp Gerontol. 2008;43(11):986-97.

Zouboulis CC, Makrantonaki E. Hormonal therapy of intrinsic aging. Rejuvenation Res. 2012;15(3):302-12.